HISTORY IN THE MAKING...

"When I think of the beaches of Normandy choked with the flower of American and British youth, and when, in my mind's eye, I see the tides running red with their blood, I have my doubts . . . I have my doubts."

—CHURCHILL TO EISENHOWER, early in 1944

"There were bodies and blood all over. How was I supposed to run? I had a horror of stepping on corpses. But then [Colonel George] Taylor did an amazing thing. He stood up and shouted, 'Two kinds of people are staying on this beach, the dead and those who are going to die. Now let's get the hell out of here.' And he led us off."

—SAMUEL FULLER, a thirty-one-year-old corporal

"Even now it brings pain to recall what happened there on June 6, 1944. I have returned many times to honor the valiant men who died on that beach. They should never be forgotten. Nor should those who lived to carry the day by the slimmest of margins. Every man who set foot on Omaha Beach that day was a hero."

—GENERAL OMAR BRADLEY

"Bonsoir, *padre. You have just been liberated.*"

—AMERICAN PARATROOPER to a village priest, after landing at Saint-Germain-de-Varreville

America at D-Day

A Book of Remembrance

RICHARD GOLDSTEIN

A DELTA BOOK

Published by
Dell Publishing
a division of
Bantam Doubleday Dell Publishing Group, Inc.
1540 Broadway
New York, New York 10036

Library of Congress Cataloging in Publication Data

Goldstein, Richard.
America at D-Day : a book of remembrance / Richard Goldstein.
p. cm.
Includes bibliographical references and index.
ISBN 0-385-31283-0
1. World War, 1939–1945—Campaigns—France—Normandy. I. Title.
D756.5N.N6G66 1994
940.54'2142—dc20 93-37889
CIP

Interior design by Jeremiah B. Lighter

Manufactured in the United States of America

Published simultaneously in Canada

June 1994

10 9 8 7 6 5 4 3 2 1
RRH

FOR NANCY

Contents

	Acknowledgments	ix
	Preface by General Matthew B. Ridgway	xi
CHAPTER ONE	"You Will Enter the Continent of Europe"	1
CHAPTER TWO	"A Coiled Spring"	11
CHAPTER THREE	"The Light of Battle Was in Their Eyes"	28
CHAPTER FOUR	"I Dropped like an Overripe Pear"	50
CHAPTER FIVE	"All the World's Ships Were Coming Our Way"	75
CHAPTER SIX	"We Were Very Eager to Go In"	93
CHAPTER SEVEN	"In the Gray Light of a Summer Dawn"	104
CHAPTER EIGHT	"I Am in Ste.-Mère-Église"	116
CHAPTER NINE	"Grandfather Puffed a Bit"	127
CHAPTER TEN	"Mission Accomplished . . . Many Casualties"	155
CHAPTER ELEVEN	"The Thin Wet Line of Khaki"	174
CHAPTER TWELVE	"Now Let's Get the Hell Out of Here"	203
CHAPTER THIRTEEN	"Let Our Hearts Be Stout"	231
CHAPTER FOURTEEN	"These Are the Boys of Pointe du Hoc"	263
	Sources	289
	Index	293

Acknowledgments

I'm grateful to the men of D-Day who shared their memories with me and provided accounts from their personal journals. Five decades later, the images of June 6, 1944, remain vivid. And the bonds among the veterans are strong. A talk with one man would invariably lead to a request that I contact a wartime buddy.

For generously providing me with materials from his files, a special word of appreciation to Major General Albert H. Smith, Jr., who went ashore at Omaha Beach as a captain with the 1st Division and later served as its acting commander in Vietnam.

General Matthew B. Ridgway was most gracious in providing his reflections a half century after leading the 82nd Airborne Division into Normandy.

For help in obtaining photographs and other materials, a thank-you to the research staffs at the National Archives' Still Picture Branch, the Library of Congress, the United States Military Academy, the Dwight D. Eisenhower, Ronald Reagan, and Franklin D. Roosevelt libraries, and the Don F. Pratt Memorial Museum at Fort Campbell, Kentucky.

Richard Merrill, Robert Murphy, Gus Nathan, Colonel George Pappas, Edward Regan, and Dr. John Duvall, the director of the 82nd Airborne Museum at Fort Bragg, North Carolina, were especially kind in helping me locate D-Day veterans.

I appreciate the efforts and support of Shawn Coyne at Dell and Mitch Horowitz.

Stuart Krichevsky of Sterling Lord Literistic very ably represented me.

My wife, Nancy, was there as always with her love and encouragement.

Reflections on a Day for Valiant and Courageous Men: D-Day 1944

by MATTHEW B. RIDGWAY, *General, U.S. Army (Retired)*

As I reflect on the multitudes of soldiers, sailors, and airmen who braved the potential for sudden death on that perilous morning, June 6, 1944, I ponder the legacy of these Allied fighting men who gave so much to restore freedom to the world. No doubt, considerable planning, air and sea force, and an aggressive and timely offensive impressed the German defenders, who slowly inched back toward their beloved homeland only to surrender their conquest the following year. A blind reverence to Clausewitzian principles failed to consider the fighting spirit of Allied Forces who dropped from the skies, penetrating so-called impregnable defenses on the ground, and flew or glidered in for the ultimate defeat of the last standing true "Army" of the Third Reich. Under the spirited leadership of General Eisenhower, we fought heavily fortified defenses, maneuvering our troopers, who worked their way in behind the massive defenses to ensure victory. Despite galelike conditions over four thousand ships and eleven thousand American, Canadian, and British planes made up our invasion. We had met Stalin's demand for a "second front" with utmost offensive spirit leading to the ultimate rout of German invaders. The Allies were beginning "Overlord" with a vengeance for the German occupation of France and the heavy losses then endured by the British and innocent civilians. Our valiant paratroopers of both the 82nd and 101st, and the British "Pegasus," met stiff opposition in securing lines of passage, bridgeheads, and critical road junctions. Many individual and small groups of courageous troopers died alone those first few precious hours from direct fire and drowning in the canals and flooded marshes. These troopers "Led the Way" for the thousands of soldiers and their overwhelming airpower and armored vehicles to ultimately free the once wonderful Normandy city of Cherbourg.

I think of these events as intense and masterful displays of the dedication and offensive spirit of the Allies, who, thousands of miles from home, relentlessly fought to make the land once again free for human habitation. Today, as I read about the tyranny of Iraqi forces in Kuwait and the Serbs in once peaceful Yugoslavia, I cherish the knowledge that American forces stand ready as they did some five decades ago to fight for freedom and human dignity.

★

General Ridgway died on July 26, 1993, shortly after composing this tribute to the Allied Forces of D-Day.

★

CHAPTER ONE

"You Will Enter the Continent of Europe"

THEY GATHERED on a blazingly hot afternoon at the battlefield where eight decades earlier Abraham Lincoln had envisioned "a new birth of freedom" for America.

From thirty-six states—from the old Union and the old Confederacy—the nation's governors assembled to pay tribute to the ideals of democracy that Lincoln had proclaimed and that a new generation of young men was fighting and dying for.

Gettysburg. Memorial Day, 1944.

Governor J. Melville Broughton of North Carolina, representing the old South, took the speaker's stand, and a band accompanied his remarks with a quiet rendition of "Dixie."

"North and South stand united today," he said. "Our bond of friendship and loyalty is sealed by the blood of our sons, who side by side are fighting at this moment on far-flung battlefields to preserve an America worthy of Washington and Jefferson, Lincoln and Lee."

Lincoln's Gettysburg Address was read once more. And then taps was sounded, paying honor to the men of Gettysburg, of Antietam, of Shiloh, and to those who had given their lives at places most Americans had not even heard of just a few springtimes before—Corregidor, Anzio, Guadalcanal.

By the time another week had passed, there would be a new place-name resonant of Americans in battle: A seven-thousand-yard crescent-shaped stretch of France's Normandy coastline would be known for generations to come as Omaha Beach.

On this thirtieth day of May '44, the soldiers of a unit with its roots in the Civil War were making final preparations for the long-awaited assault on the northern coast of France.

These were the troops of the Stonewall Brigade, the military descendants of the men once commanded by General Thomas J. Jackson, Confederate States of America.

In July 1861, Stonewall Jackson's brigade of Virginians had tasted battle for the first time, holding off the Union Army at Manassas, Virginia—not too far from Gettysburg—in the first Battle of Bull Run.

The Stonewall Brigade eventually became a part of the 29th Infantry Division, its ranks filled by National Guardsmen from Virginia, Maryland, and Pennsylvania. Then, as the nation mobilized for World War II, draftees flooded the division from beyond the region as well. Still, the echoes of the Civil War were reflected on the shoulder patch: the emblem was a Korean monad—a symbol of eternal life—that was one half blue, the other half gray.

While the governors were assembling in Gettysburg, the Stonewall Brigade was about to break camp at Dorset in the south of England. For many months—discomfited by weather that seemed perpetually damp and cold—the troops had been put through invasion exercises on the nearby beaches of Devonshire. They had been loaded, time after time, onto a converted luxury liner renamed the USS *Thomas Jefferson*, then had scrambled onto landing craft that rocked in the English Channel, finally dropping their ramps to spill the soldiers onto the sands.

Now the men would be taken by truck to the ports of Poole and Portland.

Their military forebears had been heroes of the Confederacy in the first major land battle of the Civil War. The men of the Stonewall Brigade would cross the Channel in the first wave of assault troops launching the most massive amphibious invasion in history.

They would arrive on the shores of France at 6:30 A.M. on June the sixth: H-Hour of D-Day.

Back in October 1940, speaking over the BBC to the French people four months after the fall of France, Churchill had said:

"Good night then. . . . Strength for the morning. For the morning will come. Brightly will it shine on the brave and true, kindly on all who suffer for the cause. *Vive la France*."

Now the promised morning had arrived.

By nightfall of June 6, some 155,000 Allied troops—carrying out an enormously complex operation but gaining a foothold through numerous acts of individual courage—would breach Hitler's Atlantic Wall. It was the beginning of the end for Nazi Germany.

The return to France would come virtually four years to the day after another fleet had made its way across the Channel—in the opposite direction. On June 4, 1940, frantically summoned fishing boats and pleasure craft had completed the evacuation of 338,000 British and French soldiers trapped by the Germans at Dunkirk. Eighteen days later France capitulated, and Hitler did his infamous victory jig.

Then the Luftwaffe turned to England, its bombing raids a prelude to invasion. But the Battle of Britain would be won by the Royal Air Force. Hitler would turn toward the East—the invasion of Russia in June '41.

Three springtimes later the decisive battle in the West was still awaited, but the Germans were on the defensive.

In November '42 the British Eighth Army, led by General Bernard L. Montgomery, had smashed Field Marshal Erwin Rommel's Afrika Corps at El Alamein, and American soldiers, joined by British forces, invaded at Algiers, Oran, and Casablanca. By May '43 the Nazis had been routed in North Africa.

Then the Allies went on the attack in the Mediterranean. Sicily was taken during the summer of '43. By September, Mussolini's government had collapsed and the Italian campaign was under way.

The Germans had been stopped on their drive to the Caucasus in the winter of '43. Stalin—who had long been pleading with America and Britain for a Second Front—had begun to orchestrate a Russian counteroffensive by springtime '44. And the German heartland had been pounded by American and British bombers, Berlin hit again and again.

On the evening of June 5, 1944, Franklin D. Roosevelt went on the air to announce the capture of Rome, the first of the Axis capitals to fall. The President offered no hint of the events unfolding in France. But as he spoke, it was the middle of the night, June the sixth, in Normandy. American paratroopers had been fighting on French soil for more than two hours.

The first thrust on the road toward invasion had come two years earlier. On August 19, 1942, a raid was carried out against the Normandy port of Dieppe by a largely Canadian force along with British troops and some fifty American Rangers, backed by naval and air support. The raiders penetrated a few miles inland, then retreated, as planned, after nine hours. But the costs were huge: of the 6,100 troops who embarked, 3,100 were killed or taken prisoner. Yet the action had shown that an amphibious attack could indeed be made on fortified positions along the northern coast of France.

Planning for the great invasion began in March 1943, under the direction of Lieutenant General Frederick Morgan, the commander of Britain's I Corps. His target date: May 1, 1944. The planning unit was given a rather undramatic name. It was known as COSSAC, which was actually Morgan's title. He was chief of staff to the supreme allied commander. Who that would be, nobody knew yet.

And where would the invasion come?

An obvious crossing point was the Pas de Calais, the narrowest stretch of the English Channel. Only twenty miles separated the cliffs of Dover from the French port of Calais. But the Germans saw this as a likely choice as well and had brought up big guns and heavy troop concentrations.

The other alternative would be the Normandy coast.

A fleet crossing the notoriously choppy Channel to invade on a broad front in Normandy would have a hundred-mile trip. But the Normandy beaches were less exposed to winds than was the coast at Calais, and the German fortifications were not as strong as the defenses opposite Dover.

Normandy it would be.

The plan drawn up in COSSAC's early months was relatively modest. It called for two British divisions and one American division to land on a thirty-mile stretch, supported by British paratroopers to be dropped near Caen. There would be no assault on the Cherbourg Peninsula.

But by early '44 a much more ambitious invasion scheme had been drawn up. Five infantry divisions would go ashore—two American, two British, and one Canadian. Two American airborne divisions would be dropped in addition to the British parachutists. The invasion front would stretch for sixty miles, and it would include landings on the Cherbourg Peninsula, followed by a drive on the port of Cherbourg.

A fleet of more than five thousand vessels—ships along with landing craft on their decks—would cross the Channel, and an array of warships would bombard the French coast: Operation Neptune.

The overall campaign would get its code name from Churchill. It would be known as Overlord.

It looked like this:

In the far western sector the United States 4th Infantry Division would assault a stretch of beach code-named Utah running on the eastern shore of the Cherbourg Peninsula. The troops would be landed some five hours after the dropping of two American airborne divisions. The "Screaming Eagles" of the 101st Airborne were to seize the exits from the beach while the "All-American" 82nd Airborne would capture key crossings over the Douve and Merderet rivers and take the village of Ste.-Mère-Église, which stood astride a key road and German communications network.

To the east of Utah Beach the United States 1st and 29th Divisions would land on Omaha Beach, a stretch running roughly from the village of Vierville-sur-Mer on the west to Colleville-sur-Mer on the east.

American Rangers would climb an almost sheer cliff known as Pointe du Hoc to take out a battery of six 155mm guns that could cut down troops on both Utah and Omaha beaches and hit the fleet as well.

The British and Canadians—along with a scattering of Free French troops and soldiers from other occupied nations—would land on three beaches east of Omaha: Gold Beach, assigned to Britain's 50th Division; Juno Beach, to be assaulted by Canada's 3rd Division; and Sword Beach, where the British 3rd Division would land, supported by Britain's 6th Airborne.

If all went well, there would be a quick linkup of the American, British, and Canadian forces, and then a breakout where opportunities were the greatest.

This would hardly be the first time in the tide of European history that the Normandy coast had witnessed the massing of armies.

In 1066 William of Normandy had assembled 696 ships and 13,000 men along with 200 horses at the mouth of the Dives River—just east of what would be Operation Neptune's left flank—then sailed across the Channel to conquer Harold and England.

In the Hundred Years' War two English kings had crossed the Channel to invade France. Edward III had landed at St.-Vaast-la Hougue on the Cherbourg Peninsula in 1346 and captured Caen that year. And Henry V, his forces vastly outnumbered, smashed the French army at Agincourt in 1415.

Now, nine centuries after the Battle of Hastings, a descendant of one of William the Conqueror's soldiers, William Moion, would sail across the English Channel, but toward the French shore. He was Rear Admiral Don Pardee Moon, and he would command American naval forces off Utah Beach from the bridge of the flagship *Bayfield*.

As 1943 neared an end, it came time to select a supreme commander for the invasion forces. Although the initial planning had been carried out mostly by British officers, Washington was providing much of the manpower and munitions. So the overall command would go to an American.

General George C. Marshall, the Army chief of staff, was the dominant figure in the American war effort, and he coveted the supreme commander's post. But Roosevelt thought him indispensable in Washington, so Marshall would stay at the Pentagon.

The burdens would fall instead upon a West Pointer who had missed out on combat in World War I, had spent two decades in obscurity in a peacetime Army, and had never directly commanded troops in battle. But he was a man whose star had risen quickly.

Dwight David Eisenhower, only a colonel in the months before Pearl Harbor, was named on December 6, 1943, as the man to carry responsibility for the invasion.

His roots suggested nothing of this. Descended from German Mennonites, he was born in Denison, Texas, on October 14, 1890, two years after his parents had moved from Kansas when the family store went bankrupt. After two years in Texas, the Eisenhowers returned to Kansas, settling in Abilene, where the father, David, took a job as a foreman in a creamery. Dwight, the third of six sons, attended the Abilene public schools and then applied for West Point.

He would graduate in 1915, in "the class that stars fell on"—thirty cadets would become generals in World War II.

But Eisenhower spent World War I at home, assigned as a training officer. Then came various staff positions, mainly in armor. In the 1930s he served as an aide to Douglas MacArthur, first in the unwelcome task of putting down the veterans' bonus march on Washington, then as a technical assistant in the Philippines.

As America prepared for war, Eisenhower's career flourished. He caught Marshall's eye as a commander in the massive Louisiana training exercises, then moved to Washington as a war planner. He was later sent to London as commander of the Army's European Theater of Operations, and in the fall of 1942 was given command of the Allied invasion of North Africa.

He was decidedly not the sort to carry ivory-handled revolvers, to make

1 *The D-Day beaches and the plan of attack.* (Franklin D. Roosevelt Library)

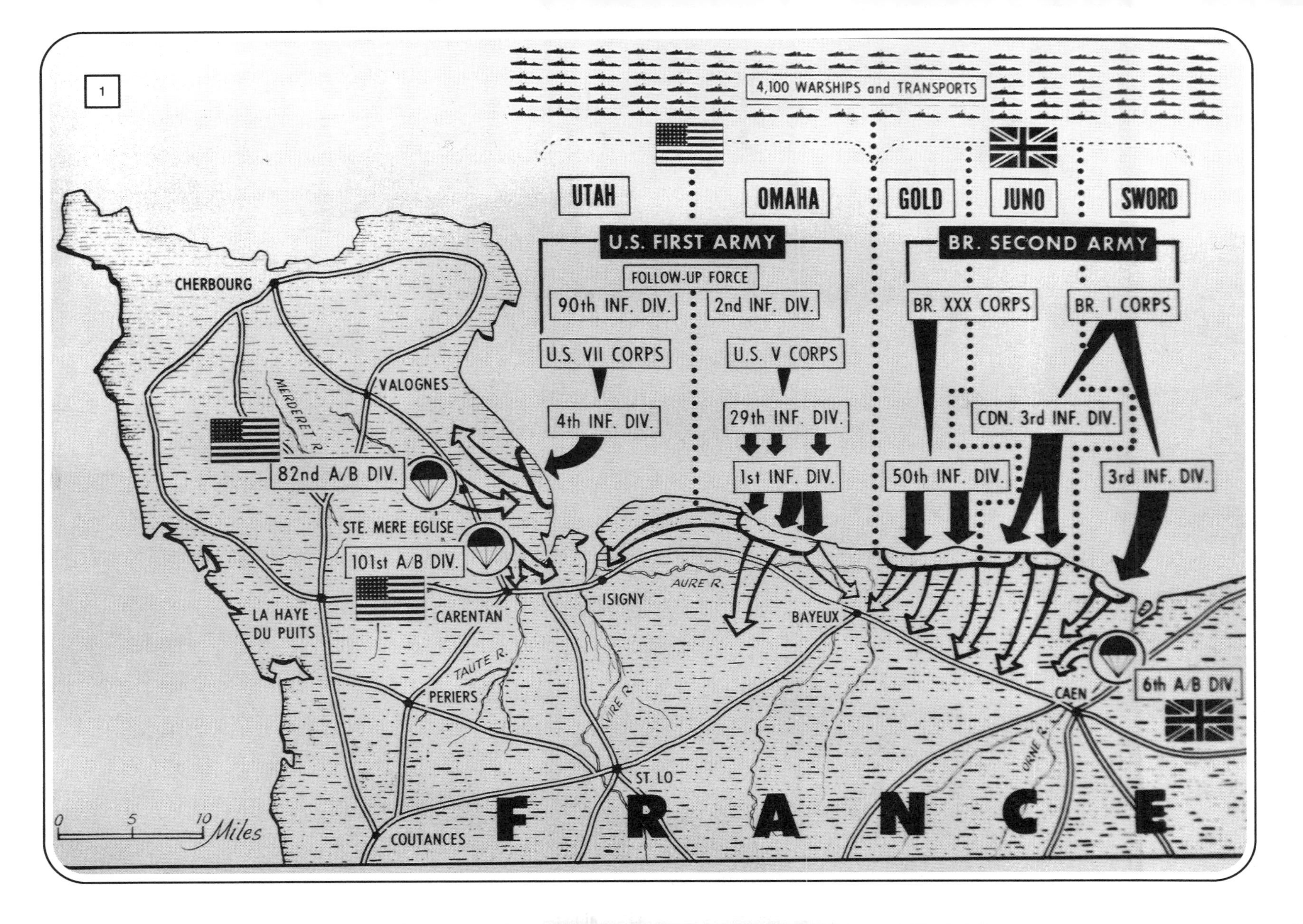
1
4,100 WARSHIPS and TRANSPORTS
UTAH
OMAHA
GOLD
JUNO
SWORD
U.S. FIRST ARMY
FOLLOW-UP FORCE
90th INF. DIV.
2nd INF. DIV.
U.S. VII CORPS
U.S. V CORPS
4th INF. DIV.
29th INF. DIV.
1st INF. DIV.
BR. SECOND ARMY
BR. XXX CORPS
BR. I CORPS
CDN. 3rd INF. DIV.
50th INF. DIV.
3rd INF. DIV.
82nd A/B DIV.
101st A/B DIV.
6th A/B DIV.
CHERBOURG
VALOGNES
MERDERET R.
STE. MERE EGLISE
CARENTAN
LA HAYE
DU PUITS
ISIGNY
AURE R.
BAYEUX
TAUTE R.
PERIERS
VIRE R.
ST. LO
COUTANCES
CAEN
ORNE R.
FRANCE
0
5
10
Miles

blood-and-guts speeches. But he seemed to be the man who could manage the egos of those who did, who could navigate the minefield of political and military differences arising between the Americans and the British.

As *Time* magazine put it in June '44:

"The master of this titanic effort is a generally affable, obviously brainy, fifty-three-year-old Midwestern American. As a professional soldier he is distinctly the command-and-staff rather than the warrior type.

"Ike Eisenhower never took a platoon or a company into battle.

"He has no specific battle experience remotely comparable to that of Britain's Generals Montgomery and Alexander, or such U.S. generals as Bradley and Patton.

"What he has got is the proved ability to work generals—along with airmen, Navy men, and lesser soldiers by the millions—in effective harmony in carrying out large-scale operations."

The charismatic Montgomery would oversee command of the invasion's ground operations as head of the 21st Army Group. Once again he would meet an army under the command of Erwin Rommel.

The American land forces would be directly led by a man who resembled Eisenhower in many ways.

Omar Nelson Bradley was also a native of the Middle West, born in the hamlet of Clark, Missouri, the son of a poor schoolteacher. Like Eisenhower he graduated from West Point in the Class of '15, and he, too, would never see a World War I trench.

Between the wars Bradley held a succession of teaching and training positions, and as late as 1940 he was only a lieutenant colonel, riding a bus to his job at the old Munitions Building in Washington.

But Bradley, like Eisenhower, would rise quickly. Sent to Fort Benning, Georgia, in 1941 to organize a huge officer training operation, he impressed George Marshall, and when American troops went into action, he was given key command roles. He took over the II Corps in North Africa and led it in the Sicilian campaign.

2 *Troops of the 29th Infantry Division—destined to be in the first wave at Omaha Beach—are reviewed by General Dwight D. Eisenhower at Plymouth, England, in February 1944. The division commander, Major General Charles Gerhardt, is directly behind Eisenhower. The assistant division commander, Brigadier General Norman Cota, is at far left. Air Chief Marshal Sir Arthur Tedder, Ike's British deputy, is behind Cota.*

(Dwight D. Eisenhower Library)

2

Then Marshall sent Bradley to England for the biggest job he had ever faced: he was to organize the United States First Army, the command unit for American forces in the Normandy invasion.

Known as "the GI's general" because of his concern for the ordinary foot soldier, Bradley fit the image of the infantryman. He was anything but glamorous. A lanky, bony-faced man, he would wear an old trench coat in the field, his trousers stuffed into paratrooper boots.

A. J. Liebling, who covered Bradley's campaigns, described him as "the least dressed-up commander of an American army in the field since Zachary Taylor, who wore a straw hat."

Contrasting Bradley to Patton, who preceded him as commander of the II Corps, Liebling wrote: "After the Green Hornet, with his ruddy, truculent face and his beefy leather-sheathed calves, the new general, lanky and diffidently amiable, seemed a man of milk."

Time's Christian Wertenbaker would describe Bradley as a man "as unruffled as an Ozark lake on a dead-calm day."

But he had proved to be a tough fighter.

On the fog-shrouded night of January 15, 1944, a private military train pulled into the Addison Road Station in West London after a trip through the countryside from Scotland's Prestwick Airport. A WAC waiting in a Packard staff car saluted the man who emerged from a coach codenamed "Bayonet"—on the final leg of his trip from Washington. The auto headed to Hayes's Lodge off Berkeley Square. Its passenger, Dwight D. Eisenhower.

Ike would now take up his duties as supreme commander, Allied Expeditionary Force. He would do so with a directive from the combined chiefs of staff of the United States and Britain:

> You will enter the Continent of Europe and, in conjunction with the other United Nations, undertake operations aimed at the heart of Germany and the destruction of her armed forces.

"A Coiled Spring"

THEY CALLED IT "Bolero"—a rare aesthetic flourish on the part of military men—but the code name for the massive buildup of troops and equipment in England was apt. For just as Maurice Ravel's orchestral *Bolero* ascended to a grand climax, so, too, would the Allied forces' Bolero achieve a staggering presence as the winter of '44 turned toward spring.

While Eisenhower and his staff refined invasion plans at Widewing, their camouflaged headquarters in Bushey Park outside London, an officer who provided a sharp contrast to Ike was overseeing a phenomenal supporting operation. Major General John C. H. Lee had seen combat in World War I, winning the Silver Star. More revelant for his fortunes of the moment, he was close friends with General Brehon Somervell, who, back in Washington, was overseeing the American supply efforts for the entire war. Somervell put Lee in charge of seeing that Eisenhower got what he needed to stage the invasion and the buildup in France that would follow.

If Ike was a diplomat and seemingly self-effacing, Lee was anything but. He had an ego to match his mission, inspiring the men in his command to suggest that J.C.H. stood for "Jesus Christ Himself." Lee loved to hobnob with English royalty and used a former press agent for Samuel Goldwyn to publicize his undertakings.

But even the most creative PR mind would have no need to exaggerate when it came to trumpeting the Allied supply operation. An oft-repeated quip had it that only the barrage balloons being stored in England—devices to keep enemy planes from swooping low over ships—were keeping Britain from sinking under the enormous weight of supplies.

At Army posts, in storage dumps along roadways, at air bases, in warehouses, the equipment was stacked row after interminable row: tanks with canvas "bloomers" designed to swim through the Channel, then emerge firing on a beachhead; Hawkins mines capable of blowing the tread off an enemy tank; bangalore torpedoes to cut through barbed wire; Gammon grenades, smoke grenades, fragmentation grenades; flamethrowers; gas masks; huge concrete blocks to be towed by tugs and sunk to create artificial harbors; Browning automatic rifles; M-1 rifles and even the similar German standard-issue rifle—the Mauser Karabiner-98K—fired by GIs in training so they'd know how to use one in a pinch if they took it off a German soldier.

For the 8,000 military doctors and medics awaiting the invasion, there were 800,000 pints of plasma, 600,000 doses of penicillin, 100,000 pounds of sulfa.

The Engineer topographical units printed more than 125 million maps in 1944 alone, the fruits of aerial reconnaissance on the French shore. Some 867 tons of maps were shipped to England monthly as D-Day approached.

And the Quartermaster corps waged a war on waste: it salvaged well-worn GI boots, supervised their repair in English shoe factories, then returned them to the soldiers virtually good as new.

By June '44, 129 airfields had been carved out of the British countryside for the bombers and fighters of the Eighth and Ninth Air Forces, and another 19 fields were built for the C-47's (the military version of the Douglas DC-3) and the canvas gliders to carry the airborne troops and their equipment.

The French transport system had been devastated by Allied bombing, and so a replacement rail network was created in England. It would be taken across the Channel and then assembled in France to move the men and equipment pouring ashore. Some 1,000 locomotives and 20,000 railroad cars had been shipped from the United States by D-Day, and 270 miles of railroad track were constructed in Britain.

The supplies ranged from the most unglamorous items ("bags, vomit" for the inevitable seasickness of a Channel crossing) to the prosaic (cigarettes, toothbrushes) to the intellectual (phrase books, so a GI could approach a Norman farmhouse and tell the occupants in presumably impeccable French, "The invasion has begun").

Even the most mundane items could not escape the military bureaucracy.

The Hollywood director Garson Kanin was a captain attached to

Eisenhower's headquarters during the spring of '44. He would work with the director Carol Reed, then in the British Army, to put together the award-winning documentary *The True Glory*, an account of combat from D-Day to victory in Europe.

Among Kanin's prewar films was *They Knew What They Wanted*. He would recall years later how a particular quartermaster corporal knew exactly what he wanted to distribute.

"The preparation for D-Day was almost as exciting as D-Day itself. Things had been planned down to the last button.

"We had one whole department of sixty men working on nothing but toilet paper.

"Once in the British sector, Carol Reed and I had to go relieve ourselves. The facility was a slit trench about fourteen inches wide. Sitting at one end of it was a lance corporal, at a table. He had little stacks of toilet paper in front of him. As you came up to him, he'd wet the tip of his finger and count off the little squares, one, two, three. Reed, tall, elegant, asked, 'May I have another, please?' The corporal said, 'I beg your pardon, sir?' Reed said, 'I'm making this film for General Eisenhower. May I have an extra sheet of toilet paper?'

" 'Oh, no sir, I can't do that, I have orders.' "

Feeding and transporting the troops required a formidable force. Some 4,500 new cooks were trained in the first months of '44 and more than 3,800 trucks and drivers were needed to transport supplies to the embarkation points from camps all over England.

By the beginning of June, 1.1 million American soldiers, 427,000 airmen, and 124,000 sailors were massed in Britain or offshore in the fleet. In all, 2.87 million Allied troops, in 39 divisions plus air and support units, were poised for the invasion.

As D-Day drew near, the images of World War I trench warfare were haunting, particularly for the British, who had lost a generation of young men. Churchill had long been wary of a massive cross-Channel invasion, had instead looked toward a war against Germany waged from the underbelly of Europe—Italy and the Balkans.

Early in '44 Churchill had told Eisenhower: "When I think of the beaches of Normandy choked with the flower of American and British youth, and when, in my mind's eye, I see the tides running red with their blood, I have my doubts . . . I have my doubts."

If casualties were to be kept to acceptable levels—and indeed if the invasion were to succeed—military intelligence would have to score victories of its own. The task was twofold: espionage and deception.

The invasion planners went to extraordinary lengths to learn every detail about the Normandy beaches, the lands behind them, and the German troop concentrations. There would be one great lapse—the failure to identify the Germans' 352nd Division, which had moved up behind Omaha Beach. Beyond that there were enormous successes.

The key to intelligence activities was the breaking of the German code early in the war by British cipher experts. The Allies were listening in on communications among German units with a code-breaking device known as Ultra.

Months before the invasion, British frogmen sneaked onto the Normandy beaches to take soil samples. Some 10 million snapshots supplied by ordinary British citizens from their prewar French vacation albums and reconnaissance photos from aircraft supplied additional information.

And Allied double agents—"Garbo" and "Brutus" were the sobriquets of two of the more successful ones—were feeding false information to the Nazis.

It would be crucial to keep the Germans guessing as to where the invasion would be staged.

The Allied goal: to convince the Nazis that the main thrust would come in Norway or, more likely, at Calais, thereby keeping German divisions uselessly on guard far from Normandy.

3 *Amphibious jeeps at an English storage depot.* (Franklin D. Roosevelt Library)

4 *Preparation for D-Day casualties: in the shock ward of an English evacuation hospital, a demonstration of oxygen therapy apparatus.* (Franklin D. Roosevelt Library)

5 *An ordnance depot in England stockpiling 40mm antiaircraft guns.* (Franklin D. Roosevelt Library)

6 *A GI tries to take command of a telephone cable drum manufactured by the United States Rubber Company. The cable and piles of telephone poles stacked alongside are to be used in rebuilding the French phone system following the invasion.* (Franklin D. Roosevelt Library)

7 *When jeeps can't do the job, perhaps bicycles will be able to negotiate rough terrain. Coast Guardsmen load them onto ship for transport to France.* (National Archives)

3
USA 709736-S
USA 704706-S

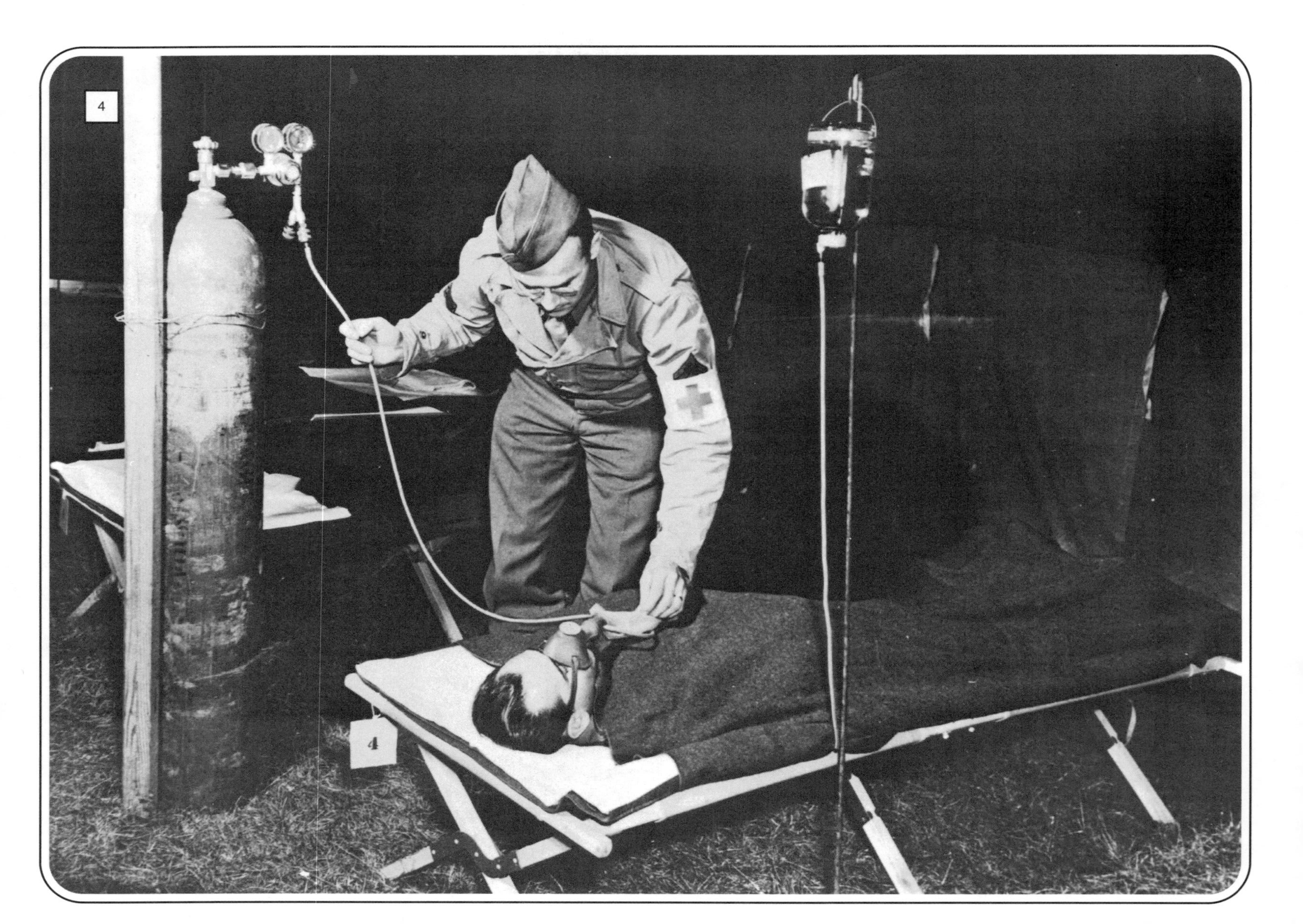
4
4

5

7

Under a scheme called Fortitude North, a fictitious British Fourth Army was simulated in Scotland, supposedly poised to invade Norway.

A more complicated and ambitious ruse was Fortitude South, which spawned FUSAG—the 1st United States Army Group. This was a phantom force of 250,000 men under the command of Lieutenant General George S. Patton, Jr., who had earned a formidable reputation in North Africa and Sicily. Patton was indeed in England, but the troops he would eventually command in France were nowhere near. They were training in the continental United States and Hawaii.

FUSAG was actually a handful of radio trucks driving back and forth along the roads of Kent and East Anglia—across the Channel from Calais—sending out wireless communications mimicking what might be produced by a huge force. While the meaningless radio traffic was being monitored by the Germans, mowers killed off grass in open fields to simulate tank tracks for the photos to be taken by German reconnaissance flights. And some 250 dummy landing craft dotted ports in Dover and nearby piers. Even fanciful unit insignias were designed.

As an added flourish, agents were dispatched to Geneva to openly buy up every available map and guide for Calais. German spies would soon be tipped off and would draw the appropriate—but wrong—conclusions.

The massive bombing of French railroads and bridges, in an effort to block German reinforcements once the invasion began, was also carried out with an eye to deception. The bombings would not be concentrated behind the Normandy beaches in order to avoid signaling where the invasion would strike.

Combat correspondents were enlisted as well in the games being played with German intelligence.

During the first week of May, reporters who were to accompany the airborne or first waves of ground troops were told to proceed with their equipment to a London rendezvous. John MacVane of the National Broadcasting Company kissed his wife, Lucy, good-bye, and "set off for what I thought was the invasion at last."

The twenty newsmen, American and British, were loaded into autos and driven to either the Euston or King's Cross railroad stations—which Allied intelligence knew were being watched by German spies—then sent off not southward across the Channel but north to Troon, Scotland, to observe commando training.

"The authorities wanted to have us stop writing and broadcasting for a few days," MacVane would recall, "so that when the real time came and we did do just that, the Germans would not automatically assume it indicated the imminence of the invasion."

British civilians in the south were ordered to undertake especially onerous sacrifices in the interests of secrecy. A strip of coastline ten miles deep was declared a security zone, and many of the people living in troop-marshaling areas were required to relocate.

But amid the most devilish schemes the intelligence people could conjure and amid all the precautions, security gaffes arose that seemed straight out of Hollywood B movies.

—In late March a United States Army sergeant, dispatching a package of Overlord documents from England to the Pentagon, got them mixed up with a clothes parcel he sent to his sister in the Midwest. The loosely wrapped material—containing information on troop strength, equipment, and a tentative invasion date—came undone and was viewed by postmen in Chicago. Intelligence officers who were brought in were made particularly nervous by the fact that the sergeant was of German extraction and his sister lived in a German-American area. The soldier was questioned and confined to quarters until after D-Day, but he was cleared of espionage suspicions.

—United States Army staff officers prepared a document satirizing naval objections to giving the Army major authority over the invasion beaches. The inscription on the cover, instead of the customary "American SECRET—British MOST SECRET" was "American STUPID—British MOST STUPID." That seemed harmless enough, but the document's title was perilously close to the real thing. It was called "Operation Overboard." A copy of the spoof reached the homefront and was almost printed in the United States Military Academy magazine *The Pointer*.

—At an April '44 cocktail party in London's Claridge Hotel, Major General Henry J. Miller, commander of the Ninth Air Force Service Command, was overheard saying, "On my honor, the invasion will come before June fifteenth." Miller had been a West Point classmate of both Eisenhower and Bradley, but when Eisenhower was told of the indiscretion, he ordered Miller returned to his permanent rank of colonel and sent back to the United States.

Intelligence authorities experienced a huge scare from a seemingly innocuous source: the crossword puzzles of *The Daily Telegraph*, one of Britain's eight national papers.

On May 2 a British staffer at Eisenhower's headquarters scanning that day's puzzle spotted a most unsettling clue for "17 across." It read: "One of the U.S." The answer: "Utah."

Three weeks later, another puzzle clue offered "Red Indian on the Missouri." The answer: "Omaha."

The author of the puzzle, a physics teacher from suburban London named Leonard Sidney Dawe, was placed under surveillance.

On May 27, yet another clue: "But some big-wig like this has stolen some of it at times." The answer: "Overlord."

On June 2, "15 down" read: "Britannia and he hold to the same thing." The answer: "Neptune."

The counterintelligence agents had seen more than enough. They picked up Dawe and his associate, Melville Jones, for interrogation.

The Britishers insisted there was no special significance to the clues, and the authorities could not reveal fears that German spies had succeeded in learning top-secret code names and were sending them back to Berlin via the puzzles. Finally, the intelligence officials decided the whole thing was a bizarre coincidence.

Not so. In May 1984, a British real estate manager named Ronald French, who had been a pupil of Dawe, broke an oath of secrecy. In an interview with *The Daily Telegraph*, French told of having heard American and Canadian troops use several code names. French, then fourteen years old, submitted these names to Dawe as part of an exercise in which the students helped him compile his puzzles. French would remember how, shortly after D-Day, Dawe found the code words in the boy's notebooks and "he was horrified. He said the books must be burned at once. He confiscated them . . . and made me swear on the Bible that I would tell no one."

"I have kept to that oath until now," said French.

Another security scare arose in the aftermath of a disastrous training exercise, the story hushed up by censorship and unraveled only after the war had ended.

In the predawn hours of April 28, 1944, a group of German E boats (the *E* simply stood for enemy) operating out of Cherbourg approached the English coastline off Devon. The boats, carrying twin twenty-one-inch torpedo tubes, specialized in hit-and-run nighttime raids. They would attack and then flee, capable of making forty knots. On this night they had received wireless intelligence reports indicating unusual activity off England's southwest coast.

The reports were accurate. The German crews spotted a group of ships in Lyme Bay, off a beach area called Slapton Sands, where the terrain resembled the east coast of the Cherbourg Peninsula. They had come upon convoy T-4 of Exercise Tiger, a large-scale operation training for the assault at Utah Beach. Troops of the United States 4th Division and the 1st Amphibious Engineer Brigade were about to offload armor from their LSTs (landing ship, tanks). The tanks and other vehicles—filled with gasoline and carrying explosives—were jammed bumper-to-bumper aboard the ships.

The American convoy was to have been protected by two British vessels—HMS *Azalea*, a corvette, and HMS *Scimitar*, an aging destroyer. But a chain of mistakes was about to unfold. The troops would have no protection at all.

A British destroyer, HMS *Onslow*, detected the E boats approaching on its radar, and it reported the sighting. But the *Azalea* took no action and never even relayed the message to the American LSTs, assuming they had received the warning as well. The LSTs, however, would be victimized by a typographical error: they were supplied with an incorrect frequency number for communicating with the *Azalea* and shore headquarters. Because their radios were tuned to the wrong frequency, they heard nothing.

HMS *Scimitar*, meanwhile, was nowhere in sight because of another snafu. The destroyer had suffered minor damage the night before in a collision with a landing craft and was ordered to stay in port. Her captain had asked that he be allowed to carry out his protective mission for the LSTs because his ship was in no danger of sinking. But his request for permission was routed to the wrong headquarters and temporarily lost.

Shortly before 2:00 A.M. an E boat attacked *LST 507*—carrying a few hundred American troops and numerous vehicles—firing a torpedo that crashed through its hull and exploded near the engine room. Flames erupted throughout the ship. Burning gasoline poured over the deck and set leaking fuel oil ablaze. Soon the Channel waters as well as the LST were ablaze.

Now, another foul-up: The soldiers aboard *LST 507* had never been put through abandon-ship drills, had not even been taught how to affix their inflatable life belts. The life preservers were supposed to be attached under the armpits. Instead, as the troops leapt overboard, many of them put the belts around their waists. The low center of gravity would send the soldiers, weak and suffering from shock, facedown into the cold yet fiery waters.

At 2:17 A.M. a German torpedo struck another ship—*LST 217*—on her starboard side, and a second torpedo crashed into the ship minutes later. The LST exploded, a giant ball of orange fire rising into the night sky as her troops jumped into the water. Less than ten minutes after being hit, the ship went to the bottom. Of the 496 men aboard, 424 would be lost.

Soon afterward *LST 289* was struck by a torpedo, but this one was defective—a malfunctioning depth control kept it on the surface. The torpedo struck the stern, but the ship managed to stay afloat with only a few casualties.

Compounding the string of errors, HMS *Azalea* never moved to pick up survivors.

The next day an official report gave the casualty count as 638 killed and 89 wounded. A few months later a United States Army historian revised the figure to 749 dead. In the 1980s a former Royal Navy officer named Harry Unsworth, undertaking an independent investigation, estimated that at least 800 troops may have lost their lives. The casualties would far outstrip those in the D-Day landing to come at Utah Beach.

In the hours after the attack Allied intelligence feared a consequence beyond the casualties: the secrets of D-Day might have fallen into German hands.

Ten officers involved in the training exercise were on the "Bigot" list—the code name for those entrusted with Overlord's most sensitive secrets. Some of these officers might have known the date and place for the invasion. Could a couple of them have been captured and spirited away by the E boats?

Intelligence officers checked the list of the dead and the survivors and accounted for all of the Bigot personnel. But there may have been other officers in Exercise Tiger privy to important classified information. So now came a grisly task: divers were sent into the Channel to account for every man who had gone to the bottom.

The divers cut open the wreckage of the two sunken ships, even entered the tanks that had gone down with them, and removed the dog tags from all the bodies they could find. Intelligence officials would check the names against the unit rosters. To their great relief just about everyone was accounted for. (It was determined after the war that no survivors had, in fact, been captured.)

Now came an attempt by the Allies to cover up the disaster.

German communiqués revealed little. They reported that three ships in a convoy had been sunk (actually two had gone down, another one damaged but remaining afloat) but made no mention of casualties. The American and British authorities said nothing.

The survivors, and the troops who had witnessed the attack from nearby ships, were ordered to remain silent. And the medical personnel who were about to treat the wounded and the men suffering from immersion and shock were given some definite instructions as well.

The afternoon following the attack forty doctors and eight nurses of the 228th Station Hospital—a Quonset-hut facility in Sherborne, Dorset—were ordered to report immediately to their recreation room. Colonel James Kendall, the Army doctor commanding the unit, addressed them.

Dr. Ralph Greene, one of the Army physicians in the 228th, would recall years later what Kendall had said:

"We're in the war at last. In less than an hour we'll receive hundreds of emergency cases of shock due to immersion, compounded by explosion wounds. SHAEF [Supreme Headquarters, Allied Expeditionary Force] demands that we treat these soldiers as though we're veterinarians; you will ask no questions and take no histories. There will be no discussion. Follow standard procedures. Anyone who talks about these casualties, regardless of their severity, will be subject to court-martial."

As the doctors and nurses filed out of the room, counterintelligence troops with bayonet-affixed rifles surrounded the complex.

A half hour later, Greene saw a stream of ambulances arrive with "wet, shivering, blue-skinned, blanketed, and bandaged young Army and Navy men."

The doctors treated their patients without saying anything to them, and the men themselves were silent.

There was one more problem in keeping the attack secret: What would be done with the bodies recovered from the water?

A mass grave was carved out by bulldozers in a meadow near Slapton Sands, and more than 300 bodies—stacked one on top of the other, still clad in soaking uniforms—were placed inside. At least 450 dead would remain below the waters of Lyme Bay.

An investigation undertaken by the British placed blame on an inadequate escort for the troops and a lack of initiative by the captain of HMS *Azalea*.

The final casualty involved an American flag officer—the overall commander of Exercise Tiger, Rear Admiral Don P. Moon.

Moon was severely reprimanded by his superior, Rear Admiral Arthur D. Struble, in the presence of Moon's officers. Six weeks later Moon would command the naval task force off Utah Beach. Following the invasion, his flagship, the *Bayfield*, moved on to Naples harbor for the invasion of southern France. On the morning of August 5, 1944, Moon was sitting in his cabin. He took out his .45 caliber revolver and put a bullet through his head.

Several high-ranking officers in Exercise Tiger speculated that the Slapton Sands disaster led to Moon's suicide. But he left no note. The death was officially attributed to combat fatigue.

As the soldiers destined for the first waves at Omaha and Utah hit the beaches of Slapton Sands again and again during the spring, the buildup of men and munitions was reaching enormous proportions.

American servicemen were everywhere in Britain. And the British people seemed happy to have them after their many months of standing alone. They provided homes away from home for the servicemen, romances blossomed, and the GIs endeared themselves to the children in little towns suddenly overwhelmed with Yanks.

Glen Brimblecombe of Ilsington village in Devon was one lucky youngster amid the deprivations of wartime. He would recall years later how "I wanted a bicycle for Christmas. Very selfish, I know now, for Mom could not afford it. Mac, an American sailor from Stover Camp, whom I can still remember, appeared on Christmas morning with a brand-new Elswick bicycle."

But there was a disquieting side to all this. As the saying went, the Americans were "overpaid, oversexed, and over here."

By springtime '44 the American ambassador to Britain, John Winant, had been besieged with complaints from the British. There were too many incidents of drunken behavior, reckless driving, even rape. Edward R. Murrow, having broadcast from London since the days of the blitz, had noticed it too. Some GIs, he observed, "model their attitude after that of the Germans in Italy."

Winant turned to Murrow's wife, Janet—also a CBS correspondent—for help in dealing with the uproar. He asked her to travel through England, hear out the complaints, and help him deal with them. She agreed to do what she could.

With D-Day obviously drawing near—and many a GI pondering whether his own days were numbered—things sometimes got out of control.

On a weekend in late May, United States paratroopers stationed at Tollerton, outside Nottingham, threw a huge barbecue. One guest was a nineteen-year-old British girl who had previously attended camp dances, finding them strictly chaperoned by Red Cross escorts and quite proper. This time it was different. Most of the soldiers were drunk and prostitutes were all over the place. She would remember how "the whole thing degenerated into a free-for-all with each man trying to get a girl, any girl, into his tent. The buses had been sent away by the troops and the whole camp had girls of a decent standard trying to stick together to get out. We were well into the country, several miles from town—while taxi-loads of tarts poured in. I literally fought my way out of that camp with a girlfriend. I remember lying in bed safe at home and shaking with terror."

By the time June arrived, the village of Grantham in Lincolnshire felt itself under siege. Local religious leaders and townsfolk sent a petition to Herbert Morrison, Britain's home secretary, asking him to do something about the "deplorable" state of affairs involving American servicemen.

The Reverend Jay O. Barrett, a Baptist minister in the town, had written in his church paper how it wasn't safe for a woman to be alone after dark in Grantham. But he noted that some of the girls were aggressive in their own right. And he looked at the furor through the perspective of wartime:

"Let us remember that many of these men from the United States will never return to their homes."

The folks of Grantham called a town meeting on June 3 to discuss their problems. But by then the American infantrymen, paratroopers, airmen, and sailors poised for the strike across the Channel had put the wild times, the tender times, behind them. They were waiting for the word to "go."

As Eisenhower would put it: "The mighty host was tense as a coiled spring, and indeed that is exactly what it was—a great human spring, coiled for the moment when its energy should be released and it would vault the English Channel in the greatest amphibious assault ever attempted."

CHAPTER THREE

"The Light of Battle Was in Their Eyes"

FOR AMERICANS at home, the signs of invasion were everywhere as May came to a close.

Mailboxes were suddenly empty all too many mornings. "Invasion Curbs Delay Our Mail," readers of *The New York Times* were told. It seemed that the censors were getting increasingly nervous, and so the letters from the boys in England were languishing in the Army post offices overseas.

If there was little news from the GIs, there was much to report out of Washington signaling that D-Day was near. For the Pentagon was assuring the homefront that no efforts would be spared in caring for the casualties.

Hospital ships and planes would be carrying the wounded to four debarkation ports, the Army reported. The evacuees would arrive at New York City, Boston, Charleston, South Carolina, or Hampton Roads, Virginia. Then the men would be transferred to hospitals that were near their hometowns or specially equipped for the care they would need.

The Army's transportation corps noted that the nation's railroads were ready for the burdens. Hospital trains would be carrying two hundred patients each, accompanied by doctors and nurses. And crews were being trained to lift litters through sleeper-car windows "with a minimum of jostling."

How many casualties did the Pentagon expect? It wouldn't say. But *Life* magazine provided an unnerving figure in its May 22 issue. A photo spread titled "American Invaders Mass in England" reported that "a responsible Army official has estimated that total casualties in the first month of the invasion, including prisoners and wounded, will come to 150,000."

8 *A backward glance will remind Don Brewer, a Coast Guard coxswain, of what he's fighting for as he writes a final letter home on the eve of D-Day.* (National Archives)

Churches were becoming more crowded as tensions rose. At the White House the anxiety was given voice by Eleanor Roosevelt—albeit privately. The Roosevelts had four sons in the service, and one of the President's longtime advisers, Harry Hopkins, had lost a son in the Marshall Islands campaign during February '44. Mrs. Roosevelt might have been speaking for all mothers and fathers in a letter to the columnist Doris Fleeson.

"I feel as though a sword were hanging over my head, dreading its fall, and yet know it must fall to end the war," she wrote. "I pray that Germany will give up now that the Russians are approaching and our drive in Italy has begun. However, I have seen no encouraging signs."

After a service at the Tomb of the Unknown Soldier at Arlington National Cemetery, Mrs. Roosevelt wrote to journalist Joseph Lash: "I dread the invasion so much that it is getting on my nerves. . . ."

But life went on, and people found ways to put their worries aside for a couple of hours.

On the afternoon of Saturday, June 3, a crowd of 34,000 gathered in New York for the Belmont Stakes, the final leg of thoroughbred racing's Triple Crown. At the Polo Grounds a more modest turnout watched the New York Giants play the Pittsburgh Pirates. On Broadway the Lyceum Theater offered *The Doughgirls*, a war-theme comedy. On radio's Blue Network there was a respite from war news: Horace Heidt and his Hollywood orchestra held the air.

Then, at 4:39 P.M. Eastern time, the bells began to ring on the Associated Press teletype machines in newsrooms around the nation, alerting editors to a major dispatch. Seconds later the news agency signaled the biggest story of the war:

FLASH
EISENHOWER'S HEADQUARTERS ANNOUNCE ALLIED LANDINGS FRANCE

The horses were coming into the homestretch at Belmont. But Ted Husing, calling the race on the Columbia Broadcasting System, was cut off just twenty seconds after the "flash" as CBS broke in to announce the invasion. The Blue Network silenced Horace Heidt's tunes, and the National Broadcasting Company interrupted *Doctors at War*.

The Giants and Pirates were tied at 6–6 and were about to enter the tenth inning when the "flash" was handed to the public-address announcer.

He told the crowd of the invasion. There was a brief roar, and then the 9,171 fans stood to join the players—their caps over their hearts—in a moment of silent prayer.

At the Lyceum Theater on West Forty-fifth Street the cast of *The Doughgirls* was taking curtain calls. Maurice Burke, who had spoofed the presidential press secretary, Stephen Early, stepped to the front of the stage and announced the news. The audience cheered lustily. And then Pat Liddy, the box-office manager, dashed across the street to the Palace Bar and Grill to spread the word. Harry Kaplan, the bartender, found himself besieged by calls for drinks.

The AP "flash" had been followed by a somewhat garbled communiqué on Russian-front fighting. And then, as Americans waited for details from Ike's headquarters, the communiqué broke off. At 4:41 P.M.—just two minutes after the "flash"—the wires turned frantic.

Panic unfolded on the Associated Press internal teletype in New York, from where the reports out of London were relayed to newspapers and radio stations around the nation.

> 12235 SOVIET MONITOR RUSSIAN COMMUNIQUE "DURING JUNE 3 NORTHWEST AND NORTH OF 1AS1 OUR ROOPS SUCCESSFULLY BEAT OFF AT
>
> BUST TT FLASH PSE BUST TT FLASH PSE
>
> PSE ACK THAT BUSTING OF THAT FLASH QUICKLY PSE BUST THAT FLASH ACK QUICKLY PSE ACK THAT BUSTING OF THAT FLASH QUICKLY VPSE BUST THAT FLASH ACK QUICKLY

The AP operator in New York immediately sent out a "bust" on the wires. At 4:48 P.M. the newsroom teletypes clattered again: "Kill the flash and bulletin from London announcing Allied landings in France." Then, at 4:49: "A kill is mandatory. Make certain the story is not published."

A twenty-two-year-old British teletype operator named Joan Ellis, hired by the AP five months before, had punched out the "flash" earlier while practicing her skills on a disconnected machine. She thought she had subsequently thrown away the tape on which the "flash" was printed. She had not.

Before transmitting the first take of the Russian communiqué, she had unknowingly run the practice tape containing the "flash" through the very live circuit.

Seconds after the "flash" was transmitted from London to New York—and then to newsrooms throughout the United States and Latin America—the AP's London office supervisor, Irene Henshall, spotted the printout on her wire machine. She screamed. Henshall summoned another teletype operator, George Angus, and they sprang into action with repeated messages to "bust" the flash. Too late.

The "flash" never made it into an American newspaper, but millions must have heard the radio bulletins, and network switchboards were deluged with phone calls. The homefront anxiety had been turned up a considerable notch.

It was late Saturday night in the south of England. For Eisenhower the tension had been unrelenting. He had been complaining of constant ringing in his ears, a symptom of alarming high blood pressure. The doctors had detected hypertension, but decided not to inform him. They did, however, prescribe medication, supplementing remedies for his chronic cold.

And he was chain-smoking and drinking fifteen cups of coffee a day. At meals he developed a habit of tapping his fingers on the table. He complained of a sore left eye. Doctors decided it came from overwork, and they applied hot packs. He was losing weight and had trouble sleeping. Some nights Eisenhower's orderly, Sergeant Mickey McKeogh, would notice him sitting in bed with the lights off, staring out the window.

Now, the invasion was at hand.

The May 1 target date had been pushed back to provide more time for training and the assembling of landing craft. On May 8 Eisenhower had chosen the time: D-Day would be Monday, June 5. If conditions were not right, the invasion could be launched on either the sixth or the seventh.

The Allies needed a low tide shortly after dawn—when the infantrymen would begin hitting the beaches—so the engineers could spot mine-laden beach obstacles and blow them up. The paratroopers required moonlight for their drop hours earlier so they could find each other in the Normandy fields.

The right combination of conditions would be present during June in only two periods—the early and middle portions of the month.

As Eisenhower prepared for bed late Saturday night, he faced just a few hours' rest, if he could sleep at all. For by dawn he had to decide whether to put the invasion into motion in the early hours of Monday.

Now, with all in readiness, he was bedeviled by a force he could not control—the weather.

Earlier Saturday evening Eisenhower had been driven to Southwick House, a three-story mansion north of Portsmouth—the headquarters of Admiral Bertram Ramsay, the British chief of the invasion's naval forces—for a crucial briefing session with his commanders. There was bad news, delivered by the chief meteorologist, Group Captain J. M. Stagg, a Scotsman. The weather had been perfect during May, but a high-pressure system was moving out and a low front was coming in. Monday promised to be stormy with a cloud base for the bombers of no more than five hundred feet.

Eisenhower had decided after that briefing to let the ships carrying troops to Omaha and Utah—the two beaches farthest from the English shore—start out across the Channel, subject to their being recalled.

After sleeping fitfully he returned to Southwick House for another briefing at 4:30 A.M. Sunday. The weatherman kept to his gloomy forecast. Turbulent seas on Monday would imperil the landing craft and hamper naval fire. Overcast skies would prohibit aerial bombardment.

Montgomery wanted to go ahead anyway, but Eisenhower would not risk it. He called off the invasion for twenty-four hours. The ships en route to France were brought back.

The Allied commanders convened again at Southwick House at 9:30 Sunday night, gathering behind blackout curtains in the blue-carpeted library, its walls lined with mostly empty dark oak bookshelves. Ike's deputies were served coffee in easy chairs, and then the meeting began around a table covered with green baize. Captain Stagg was called in for another weather report.

The window frames were rattling under high winds and heavy rain—exactly what Stagg had predicted—but now he offered hope: the rain would cease in a couple of hours, followed by at least thirty-six hours of generally clear weather with moderating winds.

But the cloud cover would still be hanging over Normandy on Tuesday to frustrate Allied aircraft, and Britain's Trafford Leigh-Mallory, the overall air commander, worried that heavy bombers would not be able to drop their loads on target.

Eisenhower looked to his chief of staff, General Walter Bedell Smith.

"It's a helluva gamble but it's the best gamble possible," said Smith.

Then Eisenhower turned to Montgomery.

"Do you see any reason for not going Tuesday?"

Monty: "I would say—Go!"

Now the burden was Eisenhower's. He sat silently for a few moments, and then he decided.

"I'm quite positive we must give the order. I don't see how we can possibly do anything else."

Admiral Ramsay rushed out to dispatch the fleet—but the decision was not yet irrevocable.

There would be another meeting at 4:30 A.M. Monday.

Eisenhower returned to his trailer complex, slept poorly, then awakened at 3:30, the rain still lashing in horizontal streaks. He was driven back to Southwick House through a mile of mud-caked roads for the decisive meeting.

The commanders were assembled in their battle dress except for Montgomery, who wore his customary light brown corduroys, a pullover sweater, and a black beret. Steaming coffee was served and then the chief weatherman was called in once more.

Stagg promised clear skies within a few hours—and even then the rain was beginning to stop.

The meteorologist left, and now the final decision would be made.

The anxiety over bombing conditions endured, but the commanders agreed that the risks must be faced.

Eisenhower was silent for a moment. Then: "Okay, let's go."

Now, it was out of his hands. The generals, the admirals, had done their work, but the paratroopers, the infantrymen, the Coast Guard coxswains on the assault craft, the sailors, would determine whether the invasion would succeed or fail.

And what of the Germans? Could the most sensitive plans of such a monumental undertaking have been kept a secret? Had Nazi intelligence learned where the Allies would strike, perhaps even the tentative hour and the day? The fears had hung over Eisenhower's headquarters as final preparations for battle were made.

An estimate issued by German intelligence on Saturday had indeed warned that "invasion could be considered possible within the next fortnight."

And the chief of the German intelligence service, Admiral Wilhelm Canaris, had learned of a key coded message to be broadcast to the French underground from Britain. It was to be taken from the sonnet *"Chanson d'Automne"* ("Song of Autumn") by the nineteenth-century French poet Paul Verlaine. The underground would be alerted for sabotage by the first line—"The long sobs of the violins of autumn." It was to expect invasion within forty-eight hours with the broadcast of the second line—"Wound my heart with a monotonous languor."

On the previous Thursday, June 1, German monitors had picked up transmission of the first line. The Fifteenth Army along the Pas de Calais had been placed on alert. But the Seventh Army in Normandy had not been ordered to raise its readiness.

At 10:15 P.M. Monday—the moment when the paratroopers would begin to lift off the runways in England—the second half of the message would be intercepted. The Fifteenth Army would be put on even higher alert. But the Seventh Army inexplicably would not be informed. The intelligence officer at the headquarters of Field Marshal Gerd von Rundstedt—the German commander for France and the Low Countries—saw no grounds for alarm, deciding it would be ridiculous for the Allies to announce the invasion timetable over the BBC.

There was another piece of good fortune unfolding for the Allies. At 7:00 A.M. Sunday morning (8:00 A.M. British time), a black Horch convertible pulled out of the Norman village of La Roche-Guyon, the headquarters of Army Group B, the Germans' most powerful Western force. The automobile was headed on an eight-hour trip to Herrlingen, Germany, and it was carrying Field Marshal Erwin Rommel. He had been hoping for some home leave, and now, with the weather so poor, an invasion hardly seemed likely over the next few days. (There had been no German aerial reconnaissance over the Channel during the first days of June, and naval patrols scheduled for Monday night would be canceled. Admiral Theodor Krancke, the German naval commander, had decided the tides and weather were "not right" for an invasion.) Rommel was planning to meet with Hitler at Obersalzberg, but he had a more personal reason for the trip. He was taking a pair of women's gray shoes—a present—with him. His wife's birthday was June the sixth.

Elsewhere in Normandy, Rommel's senior commanders were leaving their headquarters—an important war-games exercise was scheduled for Tuesday at Rennes in Brittany.

Eisenhower spent Monday morning at the South Parade Pier in Portsmouth, seeing off British soldiers of the 3rd and 50th Divisions, then returned to his trailer.

A few hours later he was playing a parlor game—Hounds and Fox—with his naval aide, Captain Harry Butcher. Afterward they found another diversion in an obviously futile effort to ease the tension.

"We played a game of cracker-box checkers, and just as I had him cornered with my two kings and his one remaining king, damned if he didn't jump one of my kings and get a draw," Butcher would note in his diary.

After lunch Eisenhower called four "pool" reporters—Merrill Mueller of NBC, Edward Roberts of United Press, Stanley Burch of Reuters, and Robert Barr of the BBC—to a tent at his headquarters.

Army carpenters had spruced up the otherwise Spartan enclosure by lining the inner wall with slats from packing cases stained to imitate fine paneling. A few rugs had been spread on the concrete floor. There was a single map on a wall.

Eisenhower sat behind a large desk, atop it a green telephone, a lamp, an inkwell, a package of cigarettes. He told the newsmen the invasion was on, and for an hour and a half he briefed them on the final preparations.

At one point he jumped from his chair, looked outside, and remarked, "Good heavens, there's some sunshine."

When the session was over, he took a stroll, accompanied only by Mueller.

The NBC man asked Eisenhower about his nerves.

Stopping for a moment, he replied: "I'm so goldurn nervous, I boil over."

Eisenhower had been smoking throughout the briefing, but Mueller saw only a few signs of tension. "I caught him only twice, wringing his hands or jiggling his English change."

Eisenhower had prepared a message to the troops and a broadcast to the people of occupied Europe. When all the reporters were gone, he sat at a portable table and scrawled yet a third statement on a pad. But this one he hoped would never be released.

> Our landings in the Cherbourg-Havre area have failed to gain a satisfactory foothold and I have withdrawn the troops. My decision to attack at this time and place was based upon the best information available. The troops, the air and the Navy did all that Bravery and devotion to duty could do. If any blame or fault attaches to the attempt it is mine alone.

He placed the statement in his wallet and went to dinner.

Throughout the south of England and on the 5,300 ships and landing craft in the Channel, the soldiers and sailors were making their own final preparations.

In August 1941, Roosevelt and Churchill had met aboard the United States cruiser *Augusta* in Newfoundland's Argentia Bay to draft the Atlantic Charter. Now the ship would serve as the headquarters in the Channel for General Bradley and Rear Admiral Alan G. Kirk, commander of all American naval forces in the invasion.

On Sunday morning, church services had been held in the *Augusta*'s steamy forward mess hall. The young chaplain, Lieutenant Junior Grade R. G. Gordon, led the hymn-singing: "For Those in Peril on the Sea," "Onward, Christian Soldiers," "O God, Our Help in Ages Past."

In a typed leaflet given to each man and titled "Our Purpose," Chaplain Gordon had excerpted one of the articles of the Atlantic Charter:

> To destroy Nazi tyranny and establish a peace which will afford to all nations the means of dwelling in safety within their own boundaries, and which will afford insurance that all the men in all the lands may live out their lives in freedom from fear and want.

That evening thirty sailors and marines gathered around a piano in the mess hall, and they were singing: "Praise the Lord and Pass the Ammunition," "When Irish Eyes Are Smiling," "For Me and My Gal," "Deep in the Heart of Texas," "Auld Lang Syne."

One of the marines turned to John Mason Brown, drama critic of the *New York Post* and *New York World-Telegram* before the war, now a lieutenant on Admiral Kirk's staff.

"Christ! Mr. Brown," he said. "A night like this makes you think of the folks back home, don't it?"

Later that evening Brown's spirits were buoyed by a vision in the sky.

9

"We saw it when our hearts were at their heaviest with wondering and impatience, and when the slight rain had ceased for a moment. It was then that, rising off our stern from the wet green-checkered fields of England to arch in the gray skies above us straight across the Channel to France, there had appeared the most luminous rainbow any of us had ever seen. For ten minutes it had shone, tropical in its colors. Those of us who had seen it smiled as we looked upon it, our hearts lifting."

Aboard the transport ships, ground troops were studying their maps one more time after spending their final days in England sealed off in oval-shaped assembly areas dubbed "sausages."

Because of security concerns there had been no formal good-byes from the troops to the British families that befriended them. But some GIs had conveyed their leave-taking wordlessly.

In the Sussex village of Singleton, soldiers from the 4th Cavalry Regiment had regularly visited a particular home, playing chess with the husband or taking snoozes on the sofa.

One morning in early June, parting her curtains, the woman of the house noticed packages on the windowsills. She would recall how the troops had left "wallets with mothers' and girls' pictures, asking me to take care of them until they could call again."

Bob Sheehan, a second lieutenant with the 60th Chemical Depot Company, was riding in a motorcade on Monday, heading toward the steamer that would take him across the Channel.

Late in the day the column stopped before a row of houses, and men, women, and children stood watching.

"They waved now and then," Sheehan would remember, "but truth to tell, they were waved out.

"Then from the house to our left emerged a mother-figure with bowls of strawberries and cream. She handed them to me and gave a gulpy kiss on my forehead. 'Good Luck,' she said. 'Come back safe.'

"The rest of the onlookers were then galvanized into action. Figures hurried down to waiting vehicles and crews were invited to come in for a hurried wash and, in some cases, shave. Yet others brought out tea or lemonade. There was a kind of togetherness that I had never seen before. A

9 *Edward Waters, a Catholic chaplain from Oswego, New York, conducts services at a pier in Weymouth, England.* (National Archives)

sharing of spirit. It was no longer them and us. We were family and danger was afoot."

Charles Collingwood of CBS, who would cross the Channel on D-Day with troops assaulting Utah Beach, observed a poignant parting gesture at the shore.

It came from the WRENS, women serving in the British Navy. A group of them lived in dormitories above one of the harbors, and the American sailors would playfully keep them under observation with their binoculars. When they discovered that the WRENS knew semaphore—the signaling code employing ships' lights—they would flash them, "How About a Date?"

The signaling was ordered halted on security grounds, but the night before the men sailed, a young woman emerged from one of the WREN houses and began to blink lights in semaphore. Then, knowing she was violating the rules, she ran back into the building. Her one-word message: "Courage."

In these final days the men of the 82nd and 101st Airborne were isolated in long rows of pyramid-style tents.

They wrote letters, heard one military band concert after another, sharpened their knives. As they studied aerial photos, maps, and three-dimensional scale models of Normandy, it seemed as if military intelligence had overlooked nothing: The 506th Regiment of the 101st was told how the German commandant at one of its objectives, the village of St.-Côme-du-Mont, owned a white horse and had as a girlfriend a French schoolteacher who lived on a side street just two buildings away from a German gun emplacement.

In a bizarre touch, troops wearing German uniforms and carrying enemy weapons roamed through the marshaling areas to familiarize the parachutists with what they would encounter.

Two battalions of the 501st Regiment, 101st Airborne, had moved to Merryfield Airport and another battalion was at a field outside Reading, one hundred miles away.

Father Francis L. Sampson, the regiment's Catholic chaplain, shuttled

9A *Colonel Howard R. (Jumpy) Johnson, commander of the 501st Parachute Regiment, during a February 1944 night training exercise in England.*
(U.S. Army photo, Don F. Pratt Memorial Museum)

9A

between the airfields to hear confessions. It took him more than two days to complete the task. On the eve of the paratroopers' departure he spent an hour distributing communion at two Masses.

"I could later write with certainty to the parents of men who did not return from Normandy that their sons had been well prepared for death," he would recall.

On Monday evening the airborne commanders summoned their men for final pep talks.

A fierce send-off was provided by Colonel Howard R. (Jumpy) Johnson, the 501st Regiment's commander, a Naval Academy graduate who had been commissioned in the infantry. He had gotten the nickname because he was one of the few men in the 101st to have made more than a hundred training jumps, and, as Father Sampson would remember, "he was a fighter, nothing else, and he pretended to be nothing else."

Johnson had a well-deserved reputation for flamboyance. Every day he practiced knife-throwing, using a six-foot plywood board for a target. On one side he had placed Hitler's life-sized picture, and on the other, a likeness of the Japanese warlord Hideki Tojo. "I hate those two bastards," he would yell.

When Johnson sent a knife through Hitler's throat, he'd give out with a scream. But twice his knife rebounded and cut him, one time nicking his arm, the other time scraping a leg. He wouldn't let medics look at the gashes.

As his men prepared to board their planes for the drop into Normandy, Johnson perched before them on the hood of a jeep for his farewell speech. At the emotional peak he reached for a trench knife strapped to his boot. He pulled and pulled. But it wouldn't come out of its sheath. Now he was getting red faced. Finally he grabbed a bowie knife from his waist belt and screamed: "I swear to you that before the dawn of another day this knife will be stuck in the foulest Nazi belly in France. Are you with me?"

"We're with you," the paratroopers roared. "We're with you."

"Then let's go get 'em! Good hunting."

Lieutenant Colonel Edward (Cannonball) Krause, commander of the 3rd Battalion, 505th Parachute Regiment, 82nd Airborne, was also atop a jeep, speaking to his troopers at their Midlands field.

9B *Lieutenant Colonel Robert Wolverton, commander of the 506th Parachute Regiment's 3rd Battalion, gets ready for the drop into Normandy.* (National Archives)

9B

Holding the Stars and Stripes above his head, Krause shouted: "We have here the flag that you raised over the city of Naples. I want it to be the first flag to fly over a liberated town in France. The mission is that we will put it up in Ste.-Mère-Église before dawn. You have only one order—to come and fight with me wherever you land. When you get to Ste.-Mère-Église, I will be there."

The men responded with cheers.

In the final moments before takeoff, Krause's troops put on a show of their own. Their faces blackened to ward off glare, they treated themselves to a minstrel show, singing Al Jolson's "Mammy," waving their hands and blinking their white-fringed eyes.

But there were quiet men as well in the airborne, and one of them called his soldiers together in an orchard near Ramsbury, seventy miles west of London.

The 750 men of the 506th Parachute Regiment's 3rd Battalion leaned against trees as their commanding officer, Lieutenant Colonel Robert Wolverton of Elkins, West Virginia, provided last-minute instructions.

Then Wolverton put military tactics aside for a moment.

"Men, I am not a religious man, and I don't know your feelings in this matter, but I am going to ask you to pray with me for the success of the mission before us. And while we pray, let us get on our knees and not look down but up, with faces raised to the sky."

The men did so. Colonel Wolverton continued:

"God Almighty, in a few short hours we will be in battle with the enemy. We do not join battle afraid. We do not ask favors or indulgence, but ask that, if you will, use us as your instrument for the right and as an aid in returning peace to the world. We do not know or ask what our fate will be. We ask only this, that if die we must, that we die as men would die, without complaining, without pleading, and safe in the feeling that we have done our best for what we believed was right."

He concluded by calling for a reunion: "That's all, boys. We will meet in the Hotel Muehlebach in Kansas City the first anniversary after the war."

As the hour for takeoff drew near, Eisenhower went to Newbury for a personal farewell to the airborne.

10 *Paratroopers of the "Screaming Eagles"—the 101st Airborne—strike a suitably martial pose.* (National Archives)

10

Some of his most tension-filled moments had been spent deciding whether to go ahead with the paratrooper drop on the Cherbourg Peninsula behind Utah Beach.

At one of the key strategy sessions Britain's Trafford Leigh-Mallory, the Allied air chief, had told Bradley: "I cannot approve your plans. Your losses will be far more than what your gains are worth."

Leigh-Mallory was convinced that the relatively slow C-47's carrying the paratroopers would be easy targets for antiaircraft fire and fighter planes. And the countryside—dotted with hedgerows and mine-ladened poles—made glider landings extremely hazardous.

Bradley agreed there were great risks, but felt they had to be weighed against the need to capture the port of Cherbourg. To do that there would have to be infantry landings on Utah Beach. And without the airborne to secure the exits from the beach, the seaborne assault could well fail.

On May 30, Leigh-Mallory had called Eisenhower to register a final protest, saying he could expect seventy percent casualties among glider troops and fifty percent among the paratroopers carried in the C-47's. Eisenhower went to his tent, agonized for more than an hour, chain-smoking ten cigarettes, then phoned the British commander with his decision: The airborne drop was on.

Now, Eisenhower would be looking these men in the eye.

It was a ninety-minute trek to the 101st Airborne's encampment, Eisenhower's convoy moving slowly amid numerous checkpoints and trucks and troop carriers clogging the roads.

Among the units Eisenhower visited was the 502nd Parachute Regiment, which had been at a tented marshaling area at Greenham Common for the past week.

When the men heard that Eisenhower was en route, there was no great excitement. He had visited the division previously, and besides, the troops were preoccupied with checking and rechecking their gear and taking final glances at the sandbox mockups of their objectives.

Then, as Eisenhower's convoy approached about 8:30 P.M., the word spread: Ike had a lovely female driver with him.

The men began dashing off to take a look.

As the troops ran down the company street, Eisenhower's entourage came up the road. The groups converged. Suddenly, the paratroopers snapped to attention.

Eisenhower got out of his car, and as some of the troopers undoubtedly gawked at his driver, Kay Summersby, he immediately sought to put the men at ease.

They were a ferocious-looking lot. Their faces and hands were darkened with burnt cork, cooking oil, and cocoa so their features wouldn't reflect the moonlight as they stalked the Germans in the darkened fields. And many of the troops had smeared Apache-style warpaint on their faces, shaved their heads, and cropped what was left of their hair into "warpath" designs.

Eisenhower whispered to Major General Maxwell D. Taylor, the 101st's commander, "I don't know if your boys will scare the Germans, but they sure as hell scare me."

But now there would be few martial words. Eisenhower was not about to emulate Jumpy Johnson or Cannonball Krause.

As he talked to the paratroopers, photos were taken. One of them was destined to be reproduced time and again.

The caption, written by the Army Signal Corps, would read: "General Eisenhower gives the order of the day—'full victory, nothing else'—to paratroopers somewhere in England just before they board their airplanes to participate in the first assault in the Invasion of the Continent of Europe."

It wasn't like that at all. Eisenhower was simply trying to relax the men and, perhaps, put himself at ease in the process.

One of the paratroopers he chatted with was Lieutenant Wallace Strobel, a platoon commander in E Company of the 502nd Regiment who happened to be marking his twenty-second birthday.

Ike asked Strobel where he was from, and when he learned it was Michigan, he remarked: "Great, great fishing there. Been there several times, and I liked it."

He asked Strobel if he felt ready for his mission and was told by the lieutenant how the men had been well briefed and were all set for their drop.

Ike asked a paratrooper from Pennsylvania if he'd gotten his broad shoulders by working in the mines (he had), inquired of a onetime farmer from Dakota how much wheat he had coaxed per acre. A Texan promised the Supreme Commander a job after the war.

Then it came time for the men to board their planes. As they headed off, Eisenhower shouted, "Good luck," and he saluted time after time.

"The enthusiasm, toughness and obvious fitness of every single man were high and the light of battle was in their eyes," he would tell General Marshall in a cable to the Pentagon the next morning.

After shaking hands with Maxwell Taylor at the ramp of his C-47, Eisenhower was driven to the manor house that served as the headquarters building of the 101st. Midnight was approaching, but there was still some daylight left under Britain's Double Summer Time.

As Lieutenant Wallace Strobel's transport took off, he stood in the open doorway "and I could see a group of men watching and waving at the planes as they passed."

It was Ike and his staff. They had gone up to the roof to watch the C-47's depart at seven-second intervals, then circle overhead before aligning in formation.

NBC's Merrill Mueller glanced at Eisenhower just then. He saw tears in his eyes.

11 *Eisenhower with Lieutenant Wallace Strobel (wearing Number 23) and fellow troops of the 101st Airborne at Greenham Common field shortly before their departure for Normandy.* (National Archives)

CHAPTER FOUR

"I Dropped like an Overripe Pear"

THE SKIES OVER England were filled, the rumble of the planes unmistakable evidence that D-Day was at hand.

It began at 10:15 Monday night when the pathfinders—men who would set up signals to mark the drop zones for their fellow paratroopers—lifted off in the khaki-colored C-47's.

There were more than eight hundred American aircraft—converted DC-3's, the staple of prewar commercial aviation—and they flew in the "V of V's" alignment, forty-five planes to a formation. Each plane carried eighteen paratroopers in bucket seats and a crew of four. They crossed the Channel blacked out, only the tiny lavender bulbs on their wingtips visible.

The "Screaming Eagles" of the 101st Airborne were going into combat for the first time, and they were doing it without their founder, Major General Bill Lee. Known as "the father of the airborne," Lee had built the division at Fort Benning, Georgia, then brought his troops to southwestern England during the fall of 1943. But in February '44 he had suffered a major heart attack and was transferred back to the United States. Maxwell Taylor, the artillery commander of the 82nd Airborne, succeeded Lee, setting up his headquarters at Newbury, Berkshire, in mid-March. But the troops of the 101st would not forget the man who had molded them. When they jumped into Normandy, instead of shouting the traditional "Geronimo," they would yell, "Bill Lee."

The men of the "All-American" 82nd Airborne, commanded by Major General Matthew B. Ridgway, were combat veterans, having fought in the Mediterranean. They had been transferred to Northern Ireland in December '43, then moved to bases in the English Midlands—their headquarters at Leicester—the following February.

For the thirteen thousand paratroopers the first moments of D-Day were awkward ones: Just making it onto the plane was a daunting task even for a superbly conditioned soldier. The burdens were staggering.

Donald Burgett of the 506th Regiment could barely get aboard his C-47 at Honiton Airfield. This is what he took to France:

One suit of olive drab, worn under his jumpsuit; helmet, boots, gloves, main parachute, reserve chute, Mae West life preserver, rifle, .45 caliber automatic pistol, trench knife, jump knife, hunting knife, machete, one cartridge belt, two bandoliers, two cans containing 676 rounds of .30 caliber machine-gun ammunition, 66 rounds of .45 caliber ammo, one Hawkins mine capable of blowing the track off a tank, four blocks of TNT, one entrenching tool with two blasting caps taped on the outside, three first-aid kits, two morphine needles, one gas mask, a canteen of water, three days' supply of K rations, two days' supply of D rations (hard tropical chocolate bars), six fragmentation grenades, one Gammon grenade, one orange smoke grenade and one red smoke grenade, one orange panel (orange was the recognition color for fellow troops), one blanket, one raincoat, one change of socks and underwear, two cartons of cigarettes. And some odds and ends.

In addition to all this, some paratroopers carried mortars in canvas bags fastened to their legs by web straps and wires.

Dropped in separate bundles would be bangalore torpedoes, bazooka rockets, heavy explosives, extra ammunition, and medical and food supplies.

Burgett had to be lifted bodily into his plane, and then he pulled himself along the floor until, with the assistance of his crew chief, he got into his seat.

When everyone was aboard, his plane's loudspeaker was activated and a message from Eisenhower was read wishing the men luck.

"A canteen cup of whiskey would have been more appreciated," Burgett thought.

"We had so much equipment on and were so uncomfortable that the best way to ride was to kneel on the floor and rest the weight of the gear and the chutes on the seat itself," he would remember.

One correspondent "wrote that we were knelt in prayer. Actually, it was just a comfortable way to ride."

Nelson Bryant of D Company, 508th Regiment, was faring no better than Burgett as he entered his plane.

"The week before, my comrades and I had waited day after day at an airdrome in England for the launching of what General Eisenhower called the 'great crusade.' I was so ready for the effort that it was a relief when we were finally ordered to climb aboard our aircraft. And I was horrified when the harness of the parachute they handed me was so small, I couldn't buckle it on. Engines were warming up, and I imagined myself standing on the tarmac, all the planes and gliders gone. I was finally given a parachute that—with help, and by expelling most of the air from my lungs—I could don."

The generals would be with their men. In the fading light, Matthew Ridgway—he, too, weighed down by his gear—climbed aboard his C-47. He was a veteran of hard fighting with the 82nd Airborne but had never jumped in combat.

As the planes of the 52nd Troop Carrier Command revved their engines, Ridgway took a final look at the greenery of the Midlands before wrapping his seat belt tight. He felt his "soul was at peace."

There had been little time for soul-searching during the long days of training, and yet, as Ridgway would reflect years later, he had looked inside himself.

"In the darkness after you have gone to bed, when you are not the commander, with stars on your shoulders, but just one man, alone with your God in the dark, your thoughts inevitably turn inward, and out of whatever resources of the spirit you possess, you prepare yourself as best you may for whatever tests may lie ahead.

"I cannot speak for other men, but for me in such moments there has always been great comfort in the story of the anguish of Our Lord in the Garden of Gethsemane. And in all humbleness, without in any way seeking to compare His trials to mine, I have felt that if He could face with calmness of soul the great suffering He knew was to be His fate, then I surely could endure any lesser ordeal of the flesh or spirit that might be awaiting me. . . .

"Sometimes, at night, it was almost as if I could hear the assurance that

12 *Airborne troops prepare to board a C-47. The white stripes on the plane are an Allied recognition symbol for D-Day air operations.* (National Archives)

13 *Leaving English soil behind.* (National Archives)

12
P
315087
ETO-HQ-44-4711
377579

13

God the Father gave to another soldier, named Joshua: 'I will not fail thee nor forsake thee.' "

In his wallet Ridgway carried a stained and faded photograph of a Scottish soldier's monument in Edinburgh. The soldier was sitting with his head up, a rifle across his knees, seemingly in the lull of battle. Beneath him was an inscription carved in stone that had guided Ridgway as a soldier.

"If it be Life that waits, I shall live forever unconquered; if Death, I shall die at last, strong in my pride and free."

Maxwell Taylor struggled with an unwelcome burden as he departed at 11:00 P.M. aboard the lead C-47 in his 101st Airborne squadron.

Over the past weekend an old friend, Colonel Frank Reed, had come down from London, and Taylor suggested a game of squash on an Air Forces court at a nearby field. Soon, Taylor was taking a licking and so he pressed hard to keep up. Suddenly, he heard a pop: he had pulled a tendon. By Monday evening he could hardly walk.

Taylor did have a bit of unauthorized sustenance to see him through: a bottle of Irish whiskey stored in his leg bag.

The planes carrying the 101st Airborne departed first, and by 11:30 P.M. all of the 490 aircraft with the 6,638 "Screaming Eagles" were aloft. Close behind them were the 377 C-47's carrying the 6,418 "All-American" troops of the 82nd Airborne.

At least one of the paratroopers felt reasonably secure as the planes flew toward the French coast. Private Robert C. Hillman of the 502nd Regiment was certain that his parachute was going to open properly.

"I know my chute is okay because my mother checked it," Hillman told Wright Bryan of NBC, who was doing interviews aboard Hillman's C-47, then would return to England without jumping.

"My mother works for the Pioneer Parachute Company in our town, and her job is giving the final once-over to all the chutes they manufacture."

(Mr. and Mrs. Ronald Hillman, who had not heard from Robert since receiving a letter on April 10, would be the first parents in America to learn

14 *Matthew B. Ridgway (left), commander of the 82nd Airborne on D-Day, confers with James M. Gavin, who had been the assistant commander, early in 1945.* (National Archives)

14A *Maxwell D. Taylor, the 101st Airborne commander during the Normandy drop, in September '44.* (U.S. Army photo, Don F. Pratt Memorial Museum)

14

14A

that a son was definitely in the invasion. A worried Mrs. Hillman reported to her parachute-packing job in Manchester, Connecticut, as usual Tuesday morning after hearing her son's voice on the radio. "We know he was all right—early today, anyway," she told reporters. That night Mrs. Hillman appeared in a local radio broadcast urging war-bond purchases.)

The C-47's flew in a corridor skirting Guernsey and Jersey—in the German-occupied Channel Islands group—before heading across the Cherbourg Peninsula from the west to their drop zones.

All seemed well for the first portion of the trip. Then, without warning, the planes entered a dense cloud bank. The pilots began to separate, both horizontally and vertically, and minutes later, when the transports came out of the clouds, the V formations had fallen apart.

When Maxwell Taylor's formation passed alongside the Channel Islands, he could see "a great gray wall to the southeast where the Cherbourg Peninsula should be."

"The flank planes, fearing collisions, veered right and left and some increased altitude. Then the hookup signal quickly came."

Soon, the clouds broke, and as Taylor's formation passed over the Merderet River, broken patches of ground could be seen.

But the brief encounter with the cloud bank experienced by virtually all the aircraft had enormous consequences. Most of the planes would drop their troops either short of or beyond their assigned drop zones, leaving them scattered and isolated all over the Cherbourg Peninsula. The lucky ones would land in apple orchards, in fields where cattle grazed. Others would descend into the midst of German positions or plunge into marshes and streams and promptly drown, weighed down by their huge bundles.

In some planes the red lights in the cabins had already come on—signaling four minutes to the drop—and the men were standing, their fifteen-foot webbed static lines hooked to the cable running overhead, when the aircraft became lost in the clouds. As the pilots maneuvered to avoid collisions, the paratroopers were thrown off balance or even knocked down.

Amid the chaos, German antiaircraft guns were beginning to fire, and many planes were hit, the parachutists wounded in the cabins. A bundle of high explosives in the plane carrying the headquarters of E Company, 506th Regiment, was detonated by flak. The C-47 disintegrated, and the force of the blast knocked down the men in a nearby plane waiting to jump.

Finally, over the roar of the engines, the thousands of paratroopers heard the order to "check your equipment," and each trooper glanced at the connections of the man in front of him. They sounded off: "Sixteen okay, "Fifteen okay," "Fourteen okay." The jumpmasters crouched in the open doorway, looking for landmarks, and then the green jump lights came on and the "sticks" swooped out of the cabins within seconds.

As midnight struck, Colonel Joel Crouch guided his C-47 toward the village of St.-Germain-de-Varreville.

Standing at the door of the plane was Captain Frank Lillyman of Syracuse, New York, the leader of the pathfinders. Lillyman was in severe pain. Three days earlier he had suffered torn ligaments in a jump, but he concealed the injury for fear he'd be left in England.

Now, with his plane cruising at only 450 feet above the French countryside, the green cabin light flashed. Lillyman went out the door, a big black cigar in his mouth. It was 12:15 A.M.

Seconds later Lillyman dropped into a field shadowed by tall poplar trees—the first American soldier to arrive in France. As he got to his feet, he spotted figures moving near him, and he readied his tommy gun. He edged toward the shadowy group and clicked a noisemaker simulating the sound of a cricket—a recognition signal for the paratroopers. There was no chirping in response, and he was set to open fire. Then he heard a noise—the sound of mooing.

Moving past the cows with a feeling of great relief, Lillyman rounded up seven of his men and they made their way to a church, figuring the steeple would be a good place for their Eureka radio beacon marking a drop zone.

They banged on the door of the rectory, awakening a priest, who emerged holding a lantern.

One of Lillyman's fellow officers, Lieutenant Lavally, could speak French. He would be the spokesman for the heavily armed band.

"*Bonsoir*, padre," said Lavally. "You have just been liberated."

The pathfinders were a courageous bunch, but Private Robert Murphy of A Company, 505th Regiment, was as intrepid as any of them. On D-Day he was a month shy of his nineteenth birthday, but had already fought with the 82nd Airborne in Italy, having joined the Army back in October '42 at Fort Devens, Massachusetts, not long after his seventeenth birthday.

"My father and I—he was a World War I infantry sergeant—forged a birth certificate: twice. The first time it didn't work, it was a lousy job. I was a little over sixteen then."

15

The Boston native was "a pretty big and strong kid" with combat experience, but he shared a special anxiety with his fellow pathfinders as the time neared for their D-Day jump: they could expect to have only the members of their "stick" beside them when they descended ahead of the main body of parachutists.

"As pathfinders we knew that when we got there, there was not going to be anybody but us and the enemy. When you're on a pathfinder mission, there's eighteen fellas between you and the whole German army—eighteen against two million."

Murphy descended in the vicinity of Ste.-Mère-Église—right on target. His plane had flown lower than most, moving under the clouds, so his pilot had not been disoriented, and he was dropped from an altitude of only three hundred to four hundred feet. "I got the opening shock and jolt, and about a tenth of a second later I hit the ground."

His Eureka radio beacon had an antenna. He had to move it "because a fella was coming down right on top of it—he would have been stuck with the antenna. That's how good we got our men in."

Despite his stick's compact drop, the tension of the moment got the better of Murphy, and as a consequence he soon found himself with little ammunition. When he cut up his parachute so he could take pieces of it with him for warmth at night, he also snipped away his bandolier carrying three hundred rounds. "And off I went—out of all my ammunition for my tommy gun except the clip that I had in the gun."

Many of the approximately 120 pathfinders were not so fortunate as Murphy, having been dropped far from their assigned zones.

The plane carrying pathfinders right behind Frank Lillyman's stick was hit by antiaircraft fire, an engine set ablaze. It ditched in the English Channel, but the troops managed to scramble out. They bobbed in the water for thirty minutes, then were spotted by a British boat. They could hear someone yell, "Shoot the bastards! They're Jerries."

"We're American paratroopers," they shouted.

The men were picked up.

The pathfinders' woes only added to the confusion of the pilots, who were off course and trying to evade flak as it came time to drop the main group of paratroopers.

15 *En route to France* (National Archives)

Many men in the 501st Regiment were dropped too soon, and only a bizarre mishap brought its commander, Colonel Howard (Jumpy) Johnson, into the zone where he was supposed to be.

Just as Johnson and his stick headed for the doorway of their C-47, a bundle became jammed in the opening. It took thirty seconds of frantic shoving for the parcel to be dislodged so the men could begin their descent.

They figured they would overshoot their drop zone, but they came down right where they were supposed to be. The green-light signal had been given too early: the thirty-second delay saved them. Many paratroopers from the 501st who were dropped on cue were never seen again. Johnson would later assume they had come down in marshes near Carentan and drowned.

The descent could be both terrifying and fascinating.

"God Almighty, the machine-gun fire was just coming up there, you could hear it hitting your parachute," Captain Jack Dulaney of the 101st Airborne would recall. "I even slipped my chute, let most of the air out of it so I could drop as fast as I could to get out of the line of fire. I remember hitting the water, and I saw these other planes coming over and the machine guns were just following them and there were thousands of tracer bullets and I remember thinking, *I'm the only man alive in France; they're slaughtering us.*"

When Lieutenant Guy Remington heard his jumpmaster's command to "stand up and hook up," he realized to his amazement that he had dozed off during the two-hour flight. Now his plane was rocking as the pilot dodged flak. The troopers stood in line for twelve and a half minutes, waiting to jump, "a long and terrible time."

Then the green light flashed, the jumpmaster shouted, "Go!" and Remington was the second man out.

"The black Normandy pastures tilted and turned far beneath me. The first German flare came arching up, and instantly machine guns and forty-millimeter guns began firing from the corners of the fields, striping the night with yellow, green, blue, and red tracers: I pitched down through a wild Fourth of July.

"Fire licked through the sky and blazed around the transports heaving high overhead. I saw some of them go plunging down in flames. One of them came down with a trooper, whose parachute had become caught on the tailpiece, streaming out behind. I heard a loud gush of air as a man went hurtling past, only a few yards away, his parachute collapsed and burning. Other parachutes, with men whose legs had been shot off slumped in the harness, floated gently toward the earth."

After landing on a hedge Remington discovered four tracer holes through one of his pants legs, two through the other one. Another bullet had ripped away both his breast pockets. But he didn't have a scratch.

The 3rd Battalion of the 506th Regiment—Lieutenant Colonel Robert Wolverton and his men—came down above a meadow near Angoville-au-Plain. The Germans had figured this would be an ideal spot for any paratrooper landing and had surrounded the area with machine guns and mortars. Pathfinders arriving thirty minutes before the battalion's drop had knocked out a pair of machine guns with hand grenades, but as the main body of paratroopers approached overhead, the German troops set a barn ablaze, giving them perfect light to see the descending parachutes. Twenty men were shot dead in less than one minute as they floated down. Among them was Colonel Wolverton, who had led his troops in prayer at that orchard near Ramsbury a few hours before.

There were no reports of parachute malfunctions, but some troopers were dropped so low that they had no chance.

Donald Burgett descended from only 250 to 300 feet—some 400 feet below the prescribed altitude. He managed to come down safely near the village of Ravenoville, twelve miles north of his intended drop zone. As he lay on his back, working to undo the snaps on his harness, he witnessed something that would remain vivid for years to come.

"Another plane came in low and diagonally over the field. Streams of tracers from several machine guns flashed upward to converge on it. Then I saw vague, shadowy figures of troopers plunging downward. Their chutes were pulling out of the pack trays and just starting to unfurl when they hit the ground. Seventeen men hit the ground before their chutes had time to open.

"They made a sound like large ripe pumpkins being thrown down to burst against the ground."

Burgett swore to himself: "That dirty son of a bitch of a pilot. He's hedgehopping and killing a bunch of troopers just to save his own ass. I hope he gets shot down in the Channel and drowns real slow."

The paratroopers of the 507th Regiment, though dropped near their zone, fell into inundations along the Merderet River. Flooded areas along the Douve and Merderet were undetected on aerial photos and invisible from the planes. Although the water was often only two or three feet deep, many a heavily laden paratrooper would drown after being unable to rise following the prescribed sideways landing roll.

Even for paratroopers descending into fields, the impact of hitting the ground and the confusion of those first moments behind enemy lines brought mishaps. Private Ernest Blanchard, dropping into Ste.-Mère-Église, discovered after freeing himself from his harness that he had sliced off the top of his thumb.

After the main body of paratroopers had been dropped, gliders came in, carrying antitank guns, medical supplies, even jeeps, and additional troops. The gliders—attached to C-47's by three-hundred-yard nylon tow ropes, then released for their descent—arrived in a first wave at 4:00 A.M. with another group due that evening.

If most everything had seemed to go wrong for the parachutists, the glider troops would fare little better.

Fewer than half of the 82nd Airborne's fifty gliders touched down in their assigned zone, northwest of Ste.-Mère-Église. Many of the others crashed into hedgerows (dense mounds of earth and foliage), slammed into buildings, hit tall mine-laden poles dubbed "Rommel's asparagus," or sank in the streams and marshes around the Merderet River.

Eighteen pilots were killed, and Father Ignatius Maternowski, the Catholic chaplain of the 508th Regiment, was shot to death while trying to extricate glider troopers who had come under machine-gun fire upon crash-landing.

The main body of the 82nd Airborne—trying to hold bridges over the Douve and Merderet rivers and capture Ste.-Mère-Église—would have to make do without most of the heavy guns and vehicles it had expected to pick up from the gliders.

The 101st Airborne's fifty-two gliders—with some 375 troops and equipment—headed toward a landing zone at Hiesville.

Many of the glider pilots had made only a few training flights, and those were in daylight. But the 101st's lead glider—"The Fighting Falcon," a large No. 1 painted on its nose and huge "Screaming Eagle" insignias on the canvas sides—was piloted by an experienced flier. He was Colonel Mike Murphy, a former stunt pilot who had played a key role in training the glider pilots. His cockpit passenger was the 101st Airborne's assistant commander, Brigadier General Don F. Pratt.

Murphy made a perfect landing in a wet pasture marked out by pathfinder lights, but then the glider skidded. It careened out of control for more than seven hundred feet, finally crashing into poplar trees. Murphy suffered two broken legs. Upon impact, a jeep that had been chained inside the cabin broke free. General Pratt was crushed in the wreckage.

So only four hours after the landings began, the 101st Airborne had lost its number-two officer. The casualties among the glider troops were, however, not high. Most of the gliders came down on or close to their landing zone. While many were wrecked, their equipment was mostly intact.

For the thousands of paratroopers on French soil the first moments were harrowing.

Only two regiments—the 505th and 506th—had been dropped on target. The men of the 508th were widely scattered, one stick coming down forty miles from the nearest drop zone. Those troops would trek for twenty-one days—mounting a few small ambushes along the way—before reaching an outpost of the 90th Infantry Division.

The isolation experienced by many of the pathfinders would be felt as well by the paratroopers following them who had descended far from their zones.

"The most terrible thing is when you hit the ground and you don't see anybody and you don't hear anything and you're all alone," Sergeant Robert Miller of the 502nd Regiment told the GI newspaper *Yank*. "Being lonely like that is the worst feeling in the world."

Francis L. Sampson, the Catholic chaplain of the 501st Regiment, landed alone in a stream over his head after floating down with flak all around him. He grabbed his knife and cut away the bags containing his Mass kit and a doctor's field kit, but he could barely move to free himself, the burden of his equipment a seeming straitjacket. His chute remained open and then a strong wind blew him a hundred yards downstream—but

15A *Don F. Pratt, assistant commander of the 101st Airborne, in the doorway of his Waco glider, the Fighting Falcon.* (U.S. Army photo, Don F. Pratt Memorial Museum)

16 *The wreckage of a glider in an orchard on the Cherbourg Peninsula.* (National Archives)

15A

16

into shallow water. After lying exhausted for about ten minutes ("It seemed an hour, for, judging from the fire, I thought that we had landed in the middle of a target range") Sampson crawled to the edge of the stream and returned to the spot where he had landed. He began diving for his Mass equipment. After the fifth or sixth dive he retrieved it.

Time magazine's William Walton, having undergone parachute training in England, jumped with the airborne. But the correspondent didn't quite make it all the way down. He landed in the branches of a pear tree, dangling three feet above the ground.

"My chute harness slipped up around my neck in a stranglehold, covering the knife in my breast pocket," Walton would remember. "I was helpless, a perfect target for snipers, and I could hear some of them not far away.

"In a hoarse, frightened voice I kept whispering the password, hoping someone would hear and help. From a nearby bridge I heard voices. I hung still a moment, breathless.

"Then I heard them more clearly. Never has a Middle Western accent sounded better. I called a little louder. Quietly, Sergeant Auge, a fellow I knew, crept out of the hedge, tugged at the branches, and with his pigsticker cut my suspension cords. I dropped like an overripe pear."

Private First Class Stanley Kotlarz of the 505th Regiment also landed in a tree, and figured he was fifteen feet off the ground. He was not.

"Everything was blacked out," he recalls. "You couldn't see nothin'. I unbuckled my chest pack and cut the two leg straps and let myself down. I dropped about forty feet and I landed right in a corner where cows used to be. It was gooey and soupy. I landed in muck up to my knees. In that manure it's like being dropped in a vacuum—you had all that weight on you.

"But that saved me. I was crappy and dirty but at least it saved my legs from getting broken up."

Maxwell Taylor jumped from five hundred feet, encountering only occasional bursts of small-arms fire flying upward. But at the last moment a strong gust blew him away from his stick, and only by a mighty tug on his

17 *Francis L. Sampson of Sioux Falls, South Dakota, the Catholic chaplain of the 501st Regiment, gives absolution to fallen paratroopers of the 101st Airborne at Ste.-Marie-du-Mont.* (National Archives)

17

shroud lines did he escape becoming entangled in the top of a tall tree. As he hit the ground, he instinctively pulled up on the leg he'd injured in the weekend squash game and landed with all his weight on his other leg.

Taylor heard a German machine pistol being fired in an adjoining field. After wrestling with the numerous snaps of his parachute, he cut himself loose. Then, reluctantly abandoning his leg bag and its Irish whiskey, he set out in the wet morning grass with pistol in one hand and cricket noisemaker in the other, looking for his men.

As he crept to the edge of a field, he heard someone just around the corner of a hedgerow and he veered toward the sound, ready to open fire.

"But then there was the welcome sound of a cricket to which I quickly responded in kind and jumped around the corner. There in the dim moonlight was the first American soldier to greet me, a sight of martial beauty as he stood bareheaded, rifle in hand, bayonet fixed, and apparently ready for anything. We embraced in silence and took off together to round up others of our comrades who were beginning to appear."

Matthew Ridgway came down in an apple orchard, right where he was supposed to be. As he hit the ground, he grabbed for his .45 caliber automatic pistol, a handy weapon until he could free himself of his harness and get to his rifle. But in struggling to rid himself of the harness, he dropped the pistol. As he groped for it in the grass, he saw something out of the corner of his eye.

"As I knelt, still fumbling in the grass, I recognized in the dim moonlight the bulky outline of a cow," Ridgway would recall. "I could have kissed her."

The presence of cows meant that the field Ridgway had dropped into contained neither conventional mines nor an array of the mine-laced "Rommel's asparagus" stakes designed to impale gliders trying to land.

In addition to the cricket-simulating noisemakers, the paratroopers were given passwords. But their nervousness inspired them to improvise, just to be certain that the soldier concealed behind a hedge was really a fellow American.

"People wanted to make sure," Jack Dulaney recalled. "They'd say, 'Babe Ruth,' 'apple pie,' 'Joe DiMaggio,' 'Red Grange'—anything that came to mind."

O. B. Hill, a communications sergeant in the 508th Regiment, came down in a ditch, then heard what he figured was a group of maybe fifteen Germans marching by.

"I stayed down until I heard a voice which gave me the word for the night, which was 'Thunder.' I was supposed to answer, 'Welcome,' but with all the excitement I couldn't remember, and said, 'Oh, shit.' It was Bill Brown, one of my corporals."

(There were actually three passwords. A trooper would first call out, "Flash." The proper response was "Thunder." The counter password was "Welcome.")

The scattered paratroopers formed together in small bands through the predawn hours, linking up as best they could. Then they tried to find their objectives, no easy task considering that most of them were lost, their maps of little help. And communicating was a haphazard affair, most of the radio sets having been dropped separately from their operators in bundles nowhere in sight.

But the scattered drop brought some advantages. It confused the German commanders, whose outposts were reporting paratrooper sightings all over the Cherbourg Peninsula, the numbers highly exaggerated. Adding to the Germans' disarray, the Americans had also dropped dummy parachutists—three-foot-high figures packed with firecrackers igniting on impact.

The Germans had three divisions on the peninsula. Two of them, the 709th and 243rd, were "static formations," possessing little mechanical transport. And many of the troops in those divisions had been taken prisoner on the Eastern front, then had "volunteered" for military service as the best of their dismal alternatives. Their physical fitness and allegiance to the Third Reich were highly suspect. But a first-rate German unit—the 91st Air Landing Division—had recently arrived in the area. Its troops were well-trained and mobile. The division commander, General Wilhelm Falley, was, however, in for a surprise.

Not long after midnight Falley was being driven from his command post north of Picauville toward Rennes in Brittany for war games to which all commanders from the German Seventh Army in Normandy had been summoned. Upon hearing reports of paratroopers landing he ordered his driver to turn back. As Falley's Horch left a main road, it passed in front of Lieutenant Malcolm Brannen and four troopers from the 508th Regiment's

3rd Battalion. The Americans opened fire, shattering the auto's windshield. The driver was killed and Falley was hurled from the car. He shouted, "Don't kill, don't kill." But he edged toward his pistol. A shot rang out. Falley fell dead.

But it was usually the American paratroopers who were outnumbered as they groped for their objectives in those first hours. Some sought directions at farmhouses. It was, however, a chancy business since the Normans faced retribution if the invasion went badly and the Gestapo were to find out they had aided the enemy. Colonel Robert Sink, commander of the 506th Regiment, roused a farmer from his cottage near St.-Côme-du-Mont. But the man was shaking so with fright that he could hardly place his finger on Sink's map to show him where he was.

Jack Dulaney of the 101st Airborne would have a rueful remembrance of his first encounter with the Normans, coming right after he was wounded in the arm.

"The Frenchmen were hostile. It was language for one thing, but I think they figured the Germans were gonna kick our ass. They were waiting to see who won. Right after I'd gotten shot, it was just breaking daylight and all of a sudden an old man and a young boy, little fellow about nine years old, materialized, and I'm trying to ask him in my fractured French where the hell I was, and he drew back his cane and sputtered, and the little kid slugged me with a rock."

Some paratroopers had a long journey before a Frenchman was encountered. Frank Costa, a communications sergeant in the 3rd Battalion of the 507th Regiment, landed in a swamp far from his drop zone. Hacking away his harness to keep himself from drowning, he lost his rifle and his helmet. His only remaining weapon was a trench knife, and he was frightened and alone. He waded for thirty minutes in cold water up to his chest, finally found two other lost troopers, and they struggled through marches for two hours before reaching the little town of Graignes, fifteen miles south of Ste.-Mère-Église.

The three paratroopers approached a small home, knocked on the door, and shouted out to the people inside.

"They peeked out of a first-floor window and their eyes bulged out as

18 *A group of C-47's—planes that carried paratroopers and towed gliders—returning to England.* (National Archives)

18

though we were from another planet," Costa would recall. "Our faces were streaked with black; our jumpsuits were wet and wrinkled and torn, and our hair was matted and unruly. But when we convinced them that we were Americans, they got excited and opened the door.

"We told them: 'This is D-Day! American soldiers have landed in France.' "

CHAPTER FIVE

"All the World's Ships Were Coming Our Way"

FOR THE CREW OF *Lady Lightnin'* the night had brought nothing but frustration. The B-24 bomber had taken off from Sudbury airfield in England at 2:15 A.M. on one of the first missions mounted by the Eighth Air Force on D-Day, its target the railroad marshaling yard on the east side of Caen. But *Lady Lightnin'* could drop no bombs—the cloud cover was too thick.

As Second Lieutenant Ray Zuker of the 486th Bomb Group flew back to England, he broke through the clouds, descending toward a Royal Air Force base near Southampton to refuel before returning to his own field.

He looked down at the choppy English Channel. The scene was awesome.

"When we let down through the overcast, it was the break of dawn," he remembers. "We could see the battleships firing at the coast. And literally you could have walked, if you took big steps, from one side of the Channel to the other. There were that many ships out there."

Among the battlewagons was the USS *Texas*. And one of its crewmen, Seaman Marvin Kornegay, was soon to become a celebrity back home in Mount Olive, North Carolina. A *Saturday Evening Post* correspondent named Cecil Carnes was writing an article titled "Marvin Was There on D-Day," a look at the *Texas* through the eyes of this twenty-year-old sailor, who would help load its five-inch shells.

Marvin Kornegay had been raised on a farm, the youngest of thirteen children. He could hardly have imagined ever witnessing the sight that unfolded an hour or so before *Lady Lightnin'* made its pass overhead.

"That morning they sounded reveille and I went topside and I didn't see nothin'," Marvin of the *Texas* would remember almost a half century later. "Then I went back topside and all you could see was landing craft. And I was wondering—where in the world had so many landing craft come from in so short a period of time?"

It was the greatest armada in world history, and it stretched twenty miles from end to end—battleships, destroyers, cruisers, cutters, oil tankers, white hospital ships, Channel steamers, minesweepers, tugboats, midget submarines, and an array of assault boats to carry the infantrymen ashore.

In the Western Naval Task Force, 931 ships steamed toward the Bay of the Seine off Omaha and Utah beaches, and they carried 1,079 landing craft that would be lowered from decks for the run-in to the sands.

In the Eastern Naval Task Force—off the British and Canadian beaches of Gold, Juno, and Sword—1,796 ships and 1,527 landing craft headed to France.

From Portsmouth, from Plymouth, from Torquay, Portland, Dartmouth, Southampton, and more than a dozen other ports in the south of England; from the Bristol Channel, the Irish Sea, through St. George's Channel, they came—5,300 ships and boats sailing for what everyone called "the Far Shore."

They formed up into fifty-nine convoys, then rendezvoused at "Piccadilly Circus," thirteen miles southeast of the Isle of Wight. There the fleet was divided into five groups, one for each of the invasion beaches.

In the vanguard came the minesweepers, and they were already at work on the eve of D-Day, putting down buoys—pinpricks of red and green lights—to frame the lanes they were clearing. Early Monday evening one of the sweepers—the USS *Osprey*—hit a mine. The blast blew a large hole in her forward engine room. The boat was ablaze, and at 6:15 P.M. orders came to abandon her. She sank soon afterward, taking six men to the bottom. They were the first American casualties of D-Day.

The mightiest ships in the United States fleet were the pre–World War I battlewagons—the *Texas*, the *Arkansas*, and, in a magnificent turnabout, the *Nevada*, badly damaged by Japanese bombs at Pearl Harbor and now returning for action on the Western front.

Among the cruisers the *Augusta* carried General Bradley and Admiral

19 *The battleships* Nevada *(in foreground) and* Texas *off Belfast, Northern Ireland, in mid-May '44.* (National Archives)

19

Kirk. On the ship's afterdeck an Army war room had been constructed in a ten-by-twenty-foot shed. A terrain study of the assault beaches—divided into letter and color designations—was taped to a sheet-metal wall. "Between them," Bradley would recall, "a pinup girl lounged on a far more alluring beach."

And a host of destroyers would also be flying the American flag this day—the *Herndon*, the *McCook*, the *Corry*, the *Satterlee*—thirty in all.

For direct command of the American operations two flagships, their antennas bristling high above their decks, would anchor in the Channel—Rear Admiral Don Pardee Moon's *Bayfield* off Utah Beach, Rear Admiral John L. Hall's *Ancon* off Omaha.

Alongside the American ships, the British fleet steamed into the Channel: the battleships *Ramillies, Rodney*, and *Warspite*; the cruisers *Glasgow, Belfast*, and *Black Prince*; the destroyer *Vigilant*. And the flags of the conquered nations were flying as well. They fluttered over the French cruisers *Georges Leygues* and *Montcalm*; the Polish destroyer *Krakowiak*; the Norwegian destroyer *Svenner*; the Greek corvette *Tompazis*; the Dutch sloop *Soemba*.

In the shadow of the warships a naval alphabet soup of landing ships and landing craft fought the choppy seas. There were LSTs (landing ship, tank) and LCTs (landing craft, tank), LCIs (landing craft, infantry) and LCVPs (landing craft, vehicle-personnel), LCAs (landing craft, assault) and even LBKs (landing barge, kitchen).

Behind the battleships, the destroyers, and the cruisers moved the elements of a highly secret and enormously complex undertaking: Operation Mulberry.

"You can almost always force an invasion, but you can't always make it stick," Bradley had cautioned correspondents on the eve of D-Day.

In order to make this invasion "stick," the Allied planners had worked a piece of technological wizardry.

20 *LCIs (landing craft, infantry) crossing the English Channel in the first D-Day photo transmitted by military authorities to newspapers in the United States. The photographer was S. Scott Wigle of the Coast Guard, a former Detroit journalist. His camera was later sold for $8.5 million in war-bond purchases during a nationally broadcast "Victory Bond Auction."* (National Archives)

21 *The Stars and Stripes and the ships at sea.* (National Archives)

20

21

American troops were not expected to capture the port of Cherbourg until D-Day plus fourteen. Until then, how could the Allies manage a massive buildup of men and matériel amid the formidable Channel tides and strong currents?

The solution: They would bring their own harbors with them. Makeshift breakwaters were to be floated across the Channel, then set down off the Normandy shore.

There would, in fact, be two artificial harbors. Mulberry A would be erected off the American beaches and Mulberry B would serve the British and Canadians.

At the heart of the plan were a hundred giant blocks of hollow reinforced concrete, code-named Phoenixes. They were each two hundred feet long, sixty feet high, and sixty feet wide, divided into watertight compartments. They were about as heavy as Liberty ships and just as buoyant.

During the spring of '44, the blocks had been sunk into the mud at Selsey Bill, a promontory east of the Isle of Wight. Just before D-Day they were refloated.

Making only three knots at the rear of the fleet, they were towed across a hundred miles of rough Channel waters in batches of ten, each block pulled by a tug with a long line and each manned by a battery of soldiers wielding 40mm antiaircraft guns.

The Phoenixes were to be sunk again in two long strings—forming a pair of two-mile breakwaters—one at the American beaches, the other off the British and Canadian beaches.

The blocks were the most imposing components of Operation Mulberry, but there were other pieces to the puzzle: pierheads called Lobnitzes (named for their designer), able to rise and fall with the tide; pontoon roadways dubbed Whales; fin-tipped steel structures known as Bombardons, serving as deep-water wave breakers—and a motley fleet of old merchant ships, each of them loaded with explosive charges, and each to be scuttled to form additional breakwaters called Gooseberries.

Overseeing the American Mulberry's array of concrete blocks, decrepit ships, and nautical gadgetry was Navy Captain A. Dayton Clark, a hard-driving disciplinarian with a quick temper. From his perch in a 110-foot subchaser struggling with the high seas, he would shepherd the floating American harbor as it slowly made its way across the Channel.

As nightfall closes in on Sunday, June 4, the ships of the Bombardment Group for Utah Beach are under way toward the coast of France.

The skies are overcast, but they begin to thin as Rear Admiral Morton Deyo—the commander of the Utah bombardment force—brings the *Tuscaloosa* out of the Irish Sea, rounding the light at Land's End.

Then the cruiser changes course to parallel the coast of Cornwall. On Monday morning the sun breaks through for a while. In Admiral Deyo's mind "that flood of sunlight works magic against the chilly wind, hanging over everything. It seems a good omen."

Soon the parade of ships forms up, led by HMS *Enterprise*, maintaining a twelve-knot pace. At 10:45 A.M. Admiral Moon's attack transport *Bayfield* joins the procession off Plymouth. It carries Major General J. Lawton Collins, commander of the Army's VII Corps, and Major General Raymond O. Barton, whose 4th Infantry Division will assault Utah Beach just after dawn of the following day.

The transports *Barnett* and *Dickman* link up with the convoy off Dartmouth, and now eight destroyers are also in tow as the ships move into the Channel.

In late afternoon the destroyer *Herndon*—soon to be the first Allied fighting ship entering the Bay of the Seine—passes an LST that is loaded with armored vehicles and troops.

Someone from the *Herndon* yells, "Good luck, you poor bastards." A moment later, an afterthought: "They're probably saying the same thing about us."

There will be steak for dinner aboard the *Herndon* this night. The ship's radio, meanwhile, brings news from another world: Dixie Walker's five hits have sparked the Brooklyn Dodgers in their Sunday doubleheader against the Chicago Cubs. He is now batting .426 for the season. After dinner a few sailors take a nap on couches—above them a large photo of Utah Beach.

Aboard the cruiser *Quincy* the loudspeaker bellows at 10:30 P.M.: "All hands man your battle stations." A bugler blows general quarters. Among those jumping out of their berths is the correspondent Richard Lee Strout of *The New Republic*.

22 *The pontoon bridges of the American forces' Operation Mulberry following a storm two weeks after D-Day that wrecked the artificial harbor.* (National Archives)

22

It seemed to Strout that "all the world's ships were coming our way. Big ships, little ships, convoys with barrage balloons tugging them ahead. British ships, Dutch ships. Free French ships. Their names mingled like a chant. The British names came down through history. The *Black Prince*, for instance, buddying up with the old battlewagons *Texas* and *Arkansas*."

Only a few planes are spotted beneath the overcast—and they are friendly. The Luftwaffe has supposedly been crippled by months of bombing raids over France and Germany. But is it waiting for the right moment to strike?

The German Navy is nowhere in sight either. No U-boats have been spotted in the Channel, and the rough seas have discouraged the Germans from dispatching patrol boats.

The seven approach lanes of the fleet are now rearranged into ten channels swept for mines. Each of the five naval forces will use two lanes—one for fast vessels, the other for slow ones. Channels one and two are for Utah, numbers three and four for Omaha, the rest for the British and Canadian beaches.

HMS *Enterprise* finds the marker buoys—red for the starboard edge of its lane, green for the portside—and it slips into lane number one leading toward Utah Beach. Behind it the *Nevada*, and then the *Quincy* and the *Tuscaloosa*. Next, Britain's *Black Prince*.

At midnight the sky is overcast, and Richard Strout gazes up from the *Quincy* at a moon only a night away from full.

"Once it glows out and casts us in full relief in a silvery patch. Our ship is flanked by shadowy destroyers. There are only dim red battle lights. Suddenly over in France there is a spurt of tracer bullets and a falling meteor that I suppose is really an airplane. I keep thinking of home, where they are finishing supper at seven and getting ready for homework. We are probably all thinking the same things. We are talking in whispers."

Aboard the *Tuscaloosa* all is quiet on the flag bridge, and voices are hushed on the forecastle and upper deck, where the crews have taken their battle stations.

"One seems to feel the presence of millions of men," reflects Admiral Deyo.

To the east, in the convoy off Omaha Beach, the NBC correspondent John MacVane is crossing the channel on the Coast Guard ship *Samuel Chase*. He soon will board a landing craft to accompany the infantrymen of the 1st Division.

The panorama unfolding before him "could have been a study in gray by El Greco, weird streaks of black and light gray, gray seas with frothing peaks. It was a wild, dark, and oppressive scene."

Now, Eisenhower's message—"You are about to embark upon the great crusade"—is read to all the soldiers and sailors in the Channel.

Admiral Moon has some words of his own for the men of the Utah Beach task force.

"The greatest invasion in history is under way. We are honored to be an essential part of it. Soon we will meet the enemy in the most vital battle in modern times and we will defeat him. Victory awaits us at the other side of the Channel. Put home that Army touchdown. God speed and God bless all of you."

Colonel Russell P. (Red) Reeder, the commander of the 4th Division's three-thousand-man 12th Infantry, is no stranger to Army touchdowns: He had been a drop-kicker at West Point and later helped coach the football team. As his transport steams toward Utah Beach, he is presumably gratified by Admiral Moon's bow to Army gridiron prowess. But he has been given another message to read. About an hour after his ship leaves Plymouth, the captain asks him to convey Montgomery's farewell speech over the loudspeaker.

Monty has borrowed a passage from the marquis of Montrose, a British fighting man of the seventeenth century.

> He either fears his fate too much
> Or his deserts are small,
> That dares not put it to the touch,
> To gain or lose it all.

For some men, words of martial grandeur are hardly necessary at this late hour.

Brigadier General Theodore Roosevelt, Jr., destined to be in the forefront of the 4th Division's assault at Utah Beach, writes to his wife, Eleanor: "We had some proclamations read over the loudspeaker, pompous declarations about 'liberty' and 'rescuing the oppressed.' Afterwards I spoke a few sentences of plain soldier talk to buck up the men."

Aboard the destroyer *Herndon*, Thomas Wolfe, a Scripps-Howard correspondent, makes a notation in his diary at 1:40 A.M.: "C-47's (paratroops) low overhead. One flashes green light under wing: dit-dit-dit-dah—*V* for Victory. On the bridge, radar has picked up the coast of France."

The leading ships in the Utah convoy change course to portside, headed for the Transport Area—some eleven and a half miles offshore—where the landing craft will be lowered for the run in to the beach. Four large transports are carrying the 4th Division, and the destroyers *Jeffers*, *Glennon*, *Hobson*, and *Forrest* are accompanying them. The heavy ships *Nevada, Quincy, Tuscaloosa*, and *Black Prince* change course to starboard.

At 2:30 A.M. the *Tuscaloosa* temporarily drops anchor.

Admiral Deyo will remember his first glimpse of the French shore:

"All eyes have been drawn in astonishment to the tall lighthouse at Pointe Barfleur. Its light is serenely burning, beckoning to sailors as though no bloody conflict were scheduled for this very day!"

The *Tuscaloosa* gets under way again, and at 4:45 A.M. the big ships are in their exact positions for the shore bombardment. Now the *Tuscaloosa* detects German radar locking on to it.

The bombardment of German gun positions behind Utah Beach is scheduled to begin at 5:50 A.M.—eight minutes before sunrise and forty minutes before the first wave of troops will assault the beach.

But at 5:30, Britain's *Black Prince* comes under fire, tall splashes rising out of the water, though not very close. Then the *Quincy* is fired upon. Some ships ask Deyo for permission to reply. He does not grant it. Although the destroyers covering the troop transports will be close enough to see their targets, the admiral is waiting for spotter planes to pinpoint the German guns for the heavier ships.

Soon, all the big ships off Utah are targets of the shore batteries.

At 5:36, Deyo finally gives the order: "Commence counter battery bombardment."

Aboard the *Tuscaloosa* the three turrets—two forward and one aft—swing to face the German fortifications. Word comes to "stand by," and then a buzz, a flash, and acrid smoke passes Deyo's face.

For the admiral "the game has begun, the tension is over."

On the ten-thousand-ton *Tuscaloosa*, ears are plugged with cotton, helmet straps are buckled as the ship bounces to the gun blasts.

Off Omaha Beach, Lieutenant John Mason Brown climbs to the pilot house of the *Augusta* to describe the scene over the loudspeaker for the crewmen whose duties keep them belowdeck.

The German guns open up. To the drama critic turned naval officer, the blasts are like "very deliberate beats on a deep-voiced tom-tom."

"The *Texas* answers as quickly as an echo. She answers furiously with enough fire to avenge the Alamo. Great clouds of smoke pour out of her; flames spill from her like oranges from a broken crate. She is ablaze with her own fire."

Aboard the *Texas* Seaman Marvin Kornegay—startled by the massing of landing craft only a few hours earlier—now works the trays for the battleship's five-inch shells.

"The ship shook in the water," he will remember. "We fired until all the paint came off the gun, just about, from the heat."

Ernest Hemingway, on assignment for *Collier's*, is aboard a landing craft heading for the Fox Green sector of Omaha Beach.

He will tell of how the *Texas* bestowed a sense of comfort upon the riflemen—for a while.

"Those of our troops who were not wax-gray with sea sickness, fighting it off, trying to hold on to themselves before they had to grab for the steel side of the boat, were watching the *Texas* with looks of surprise and happiness. Under the steel helmets they looked like pikemen of the Middle Ages to whose aid in battle had suddenly come some strange and unbelievable monster.

"There would be a flash like a blast furnace from the fourteen-inch guns of the *Texas*, that would lick far out from the ship. . . .

" 'Look what they're doing to those Germans,' I leaned forward to hear a GI say above the roar of the motor. 'I guess there won't be a man alive there,' he said happily.

"As the craft got closer to the beach, the mood changed as the big ships ceased fire out of fear they would hit the troops on the beach.

"I never saw anyone smile after we left the line of firing ships. They had seen the mysterious monster that was helping them, but now he was gone and they were alone again."

Robert J. Casey of the *Chicago Daily News* felt a surge of emotion when he saw another of the American battleships.

Casey was aboard an LST. As it approached the shore—its tank guns focusing on the lighthouse at the village of Ver-sur-Mer—he thought back to dark moments from the early days of the war, to the retreat of the British Army from Dunkirk, and to a disastrous morning in Hawaii.

23

"6:35. There is no need for a diary entry to mark this moment in memory forever. Across the thinning gauze of the mist ahead of the charging infantry launches appeared a dim, horizontal streak.

"France!

"I was seeing it for the first time since we went over the Hendaye bridge in the great retreat four years ago. . . ."

"7:40. Off on the horizon to starboard a battleship suddenly appeared. I knew her for an American from the moment I noticed the color of the paint on her top rig. Almost before she had come over the rim of the sea she was blasting the distant cliffs with broadsides from her main battery. And I studied her through the glasses unbelievingly and felt an emotional surge that I knew I wasn't going to be able to share with anybody aboard.

"So help me! The *Nevada*. The last time I had seen that ship was the day she started to come up off the bottom in Pearl Harbor."

Just before 6:30 A.M., as the first troops approach the beaches, small boats called LCRs (landing craft, rocket) hurl projectiles at the German gun positions while the big ships cease their firepower to avoid hitting the GIs.

Aboard one of these rocket boats is a sailor who had once envisioned spending the springtime of '44 on a Navy baseball field in Virginia. He had been a member of the Norfolk Tars, a New York Yankee farm team, and had hoped to join the Norfolk Naval Air Station club that boasted such former big league stars as Phil Rizzuto, Dom DiMaggio, and Hugh Casey.

After joining the Navy he'd trained at Little Creek, Virginia, but he didn't make it to the diamond at Norfolk. One day when they asked for volunteers for rocket boats, the seaman raised his hand. Before long he was headed to Glasgow and then he was training for D-Day. On June 6 he found himself one of six machine-gunners on a rocket boat, and eventually they got close enough to shore to begin firing.

"Like most guys I have talked with, I don't know if I hit anyone," he would say.

But there is one confirmed "hit" before the LCR finishes its mission in the Channel.

"We all shot at the first plane below the clouds. We shot down one of our planes.

23 *Troops in a DUKW amphibious vehicle are dwarfed by the guns of the battleship* Arkansas *as they head toward Omaha Beach.* (National Archives)

24

"The pilot was mad as hell, and you could hear him swearing as he floated down in his parachute. Another rocket boat picked him up.

"We thought he was a German. He wasn't . . . and he was mad; I remember him shaking his fist and yelling, 'If you bastards would shoot down as many of them as us, the goddamn war would be over.' "

So it went for the United States Navy's machine-gunning Lawrence Peter Berra, soon to be better known as Yogi.

Off the British beaches there's a scare as dawn breaks. Three German torpedo boats out of Le Havre maneuver through a smoke shield and fire eighteen torpedoes. Two of them just miss the battleships *Warspite* and *Ramillies*. Another one sinks the Norwegian destroyer *Svenner*. But off the American beaches there's no sign of the German navy.

And the Luftwaffe will mount few challenges on D-Day. But the USS *Ancon*—command ship for Omaha Beach—has a close call at 5:40 A.M.

The Blue Network's George Hicks is standing on the *Ancon*'s bridge with a seventy-five-pound wire recorder at that moment. He will provide a stirring account of the tumult about to envelop the ship.

"It's planes you hear overhead now. They are the motors of Nazis coming and going.

"That was a bomb hit, another one. Flares are coming down now. You can hear the machine-gunning. The whole seaside is covered with tracer fire . . . going up . . . bombs . . . machine-gunning. The planes are coming ever closer, firing low. Smoke, brilliant fire down low toward the French coast a couple of miles. I don't know whether it is on the shore or is a ship on fire.

"It's quiet for a moment now. If you'll excuse me, I'll just take a deep breath and stop speaking. Here we go again! Another plane has come over, right over our port side. Tracers are making an arc over the bow now, disappearing into the clouds before they burst. Something burning is falling down through the sky."

(Now cheering can be heard over the narration.)

"They got one! The lights of that burning Nazi plane are just twinkling now in the sea and going out."

Hicks's account will be broadcast on all the American radio networks hours later—a rare "live" description of combat.

24 *The fourteen-inch guns of the USS* Nevada *blast German positions at Utah Beach.* (National Archives)

The Allied navies are indeed masters of the Channel. And overhead the American and British aircraft—the paratrooper transports and gliders, the bombers and fighters—rule the skies.

Back in London, Edward R. Murrow looks and listens. In the late afternoon, he broadcasts to America:

"Early this morning we heard the bombers going out. It was the sound of a giant factory in the sky. It seemed to shake the old gray stone buildings in this bruised and battered city beside the Thames. The sound was heavier, more triumphant, than ever before. Those who knew what was coming could imagine that they had heard great guns and strains of 'The Battle Hymn of the Republic' well above the roar of the motors."

CHAPTER SIX

"We Were Very Eager to Go In"

AT H-HOUR THE naval shelling had ceased, the bombers had paused. Now, at 6:30 in the morning—half an hour past sunrise—the infantrymen would begin to come ashore at low tide upon the beaches of Normandy.

For the men in the first waves—especially the troops of the 1st and 29th Divisions assaulting Omaha Beach—the final hours before the landing craft touched French soil were hellish.

The Channel was only moderately choppy off Utah Beach, but it tossed the small boats heading for Omaha as if they were roller-coaster cars. By the time the bluffs of France came into sight amid the haze of bombings and gunfire, the assault troops were shivering, drenched, and seasick.

That was indeed the case for Sergeant Bob Slaughter's heavy-machine-gun squad from D Company, 116th Infantry, 29th Division.

For Slaughter and his men it began at 2:00 A.M. aboard the British transport *Empire Anvil*, when the troops of the 29th Division's 1st Battalion were awakened.

Slaughter was only nineteen years old, but he had been in D Company for almost four years. Back in August 1940 he'd joined the unit in Roanoke when it was part of the Virginia National Guard. The Depression was still very real, so the few bucks earned by attending drills came in handy for a student in quest of spending money.

And good times beckoned too. The Guardsmen would visit the Virginia Beach resort area for their two weeks' summer encampment.

But six months after Slaughter enlisted in the Guard, a road far removed from the summery pleasures of Virginia Beach began to unfold. On February 3, 1941, as the nation mobilized, the 29th Division was placed into federal service. In September 1942, Slaughter climbed up the ramp of the *Queen Mary*, and the division set out for the British Isles.

There was much excitement ahead even before the men reached Britain. In a disaster kept secret until after the war, the *Queen* collided with the British light cruiser *Curaçao* five hundred miles off Scotland. The liner suffered only minor damage and had no casualties, but the *Curaçao* was sliced in half. Some men were plucked from the Atlantic, but 338 of the *Curaçao*'s crewmen were lost.

Soon, hard training began in England—some of it with American Rangers and British commandos—and the men of the 29th would make repeated assaults over the next year and a half on the beaches of Slapton Sands.

Now, in the predawn hours of June 6, the invasion was finally at hand.

Slaughter climbs up to the *Empire Anvil*'s deck on his way to the mess hall for a middle-of-the-night breakfast.

The ship is still twelve miles off the coast of France as the paratroopers drop and the night bombers raid the coastline. Planes drone overhead and there's a glimpse of light at the shore.

Slaughter sees fires burning, "like a tremendous gigantic sunset reflecting off the clouds."

So far the enthusiasm outweighs fear.

"We were very eager to go in," he would remember. "We'd been on that ship two or three days waiting out that storm. We'd been training for, heck, three years, for this one day, and it was real exciting for me. I was eager to go in. I didn't realize what we were getting into."

On many of the transport ships in the Channel the mess boys serve hearty breakfasts cynically dubbed "last meals"—steak and eggs, mounds of pancakes. But the fare aboard the *Empire Anvil* is an unidentifiable piece of meat with white gravy, white bread, and coffee or tea.

After breakfast Slaughter goes back to his stateroom and straps on his gear. He is burdened with more than sixty pounds of equipment strapped onto a heavy woolen uniform impregnated against a gas attack. He will take to France an assault jacket, a raincoat, a gas mask, a life preserver dubbed a Mae West, three days of K rations, a first-aid kit, grenades, bandoliers of ammunition, an M-1 rifle, and a half pound of TNT.

Slaughter chats with his fellow troops as they wait to scramble onto their British-built LCAs—landing craft, assault.

The men look for their buddies and shake hands. There are a few parting words: "See you on the beach" or "See you in Paris."

At 4:00 A.M. Slaughter walks over rails to his landing craft, and it is lowered on davits into the Channel.

Some thirty men are jammed aboard the LCA, and each one knows exactly where to sit—the loading has been practiced often enough.

There are two rows. Slaughter—the leader of his machine-gun squad—is on the left side, the sixth or seventh from the front. The platoon leader, Technical Sergeant Willard Norfleet, is in front on the right side with the British coxswain.

The Channel is rough—the swells perhaps seven to ten feet high, beyond anything encountered in the endless assaults of Slapton Sands. Many of the troops are already seasick from their hours on the *Empire Anvil*. But Slaughter feels just fine.

Moments later there is trouble in the waters around the British transport. The waves frustrate efforts to get landing craft away from the mother ship, and one LCA sinks. But its men are rescued.

As Slaughter's boat gets under way, the rocking is formidable, and the craft begins to take on water. One moment the troops are on the bottom of a swell and cannot see a thing. Then it seems as if they are on top of a mountain.

Sheets of water blow across the LCA, and the men are instantly soaked and freezing.

The pumps cannot keep up with the water coming in, and so the troops remove their helmets and start bailing with them. Slaughter uses his gas cape—a plastic bag designed to protect the skin from mustard gas—to shelter him from the spray and the cold. But the lack of oxygen under the cape quickly brings him into the ranks of the seasick.

Figuring he would be immune to seasickness, Slaughter has given his puke bag to a buddy who already filled one up, but now he surely misses it. He takes his helmet liner out and vomits into the shell. Then begins a ritual—throwing up into the helmet, washing it out, throwing up again. Before long he is vomiting all over himself as well.

Dozens of landing craft begin circling—this only makes the seasickness worse—and then they rendezvous, form up, and head for Omaha Beach. The roar of the diesel engines makes it difficult for the troops to talk to each other, but at this point there isn't much left to say.

25

D Company is scheduled to come ashore on the right flank of Omaha—at a sector called Dog Green—at H-Hour plus forty minutes, or 7:10 A.M.

The 1st Battalion of the 116th Infantry is to land at Dog Green in a column of companies—A, then B, then D, then C.

At 5:50 A.M.—Slaughter and his boatload have now been battling the waves for almost two hours—the fourteen-inch guns of the battleship *Texas* open up. The roar muffles the engines on the landing craft, and the swells created by the guns' recoil almost swamp the little boat. Twin-fuselaged P-38 fighter-bombers appear overhead.

Despite their misery the infantrymen are reassured—the big guns should be softening up the Germans. The landing will probably be an easy one.

About a mile from shore Slaughter's LCA stops to pick up a few soldiers whose assault boat has foundered. Others struggling in their Mae Wests will be left to bob around a while longer—there's no room to rescue everybody. At any rate the coxswains on the landing craft are not supposed to fish out men who are overboard—rescues are a job for the Navy or Coast Guard.

The companies in the 1st Battalion of the 116th are supposed to hit the shore in front of the Vierville draw—a path running from the beach toward the village of Vierville-sur-Mer. This little road through the bluffs overlooking Omaha is to be the troops' exit from Dog Green.

The coxswain of Slaughter's boat has been told to guide on the Vierville church steeple. But the tides take the landing craft perhaps three hundred yards to the east, and it approaches the shoreline near the adjoining Dog White sector. There's no steeple in sight.

The LCA is a few hundred yards offshore. Now, it becomes clear, the beaching will not be so easy after all. The Germans have opened up with artillery and mortars. Near-misses send plumes of water high into the air all around Slaughter's landing craft. The sheets of spray fall back upon the men in the little boat, compounding their misery.

Back in Weymouth some of the British coxswains had bragged about taking part in beach assaults during the war's early years. They had assured the green American troopers they would be in good hands when D-Day

25 *Landing craft carrying troops of the 1st Division's 16th Infantry are buffeted by the choppy English Channel as they head toward the Easy Red sector of Omaha Beach after being launched from the Coast Guard vessel* Samuel Chase. (National Archives)

26

arrived. But now the coxswain in Slaughter's LCA has lost his nerve. The boat is still in high water, but he tells the troops he's going to lower the ramp.

Sergeant Norfleet, the platoon leader, knows his men have little chance to get through the surf if they disembark so soon—their heavy weapons and equipment will drag them down.

He tells the coxswain to keep the ramp up and head closer to shore. The coxswain is practically moaning now, convinced that German fire is about to rake the boat. "We'll all be killed," he tells Norfleet.

"I don't give a damn, you're going all the way in," Slaughter hears Norfleet tell the coxswain.

The British sailor is still determined to put the ramp down.

Slaughter sees Norfleet unholster his .45 Colt pistol and put it to the coxswain's head. "All the way in."

The argument is over. The coxswain will keep the ramp up, and the boat keeps moving to the shoreline.

Some 150 yards from the beach, Slaughter raises his head despite a warning to keep down, and what he sees to his right unnerves him.

A little boat, evidently from B Company, is taking a pounding from small-arms fire. Tracer bullets bounce off the ramp, and as the boat bobs, the troops jump off the sides and the back.

A and B companies are supposed to have had the Dog Green beach sector secured by the time Slaughter and the other men from D Company arrive, but all is chaos.

Now the ramp goes down on Slaughter's boat amid a heavy surf. Mortar and artillery shells are exploding, automatic weapons fire is raining down from the cliffs—the smell of cordite is everywhere. The water is turning red with blood.

The steel ramp is going up and down in the surf, rising six or seven feet in the air. It's like being on a bucking bronco, Slaughter thinks. One of the first men out of his LCA is killed when the ramp hits him in the head. Others leap off the side of the boat.

Slaughter tries to time the ramp's cycle of rising and falling so he'll jump off on the down side, but the water is so rough he can't get going, and he becomes a bottleneck.

26 *Assault troops are rescued by a Coast Guard boat after their landing craft hit a mine.* (National Archives)

After two or three cycles he manages to escape the boat. He finds himself in water up to his waist. Seconds later the shifting tide has brought the water to his armpits—and he is six feet five inches tall. He squeezes the inflation capsule on his Mae West and it explodes into a life jacket.

Now Slaughter tiptoes around in the water, trying to figure out what to do. Men are being shot down, and he hears cries. Burdened by their equipment, losing blood and in shock, even slightly wounded soldiers are beginning to drown.

Slaughter lends a hand to Private Ernest McCanless, his ammunition bearer, who is struggling in the water, still holding on to a box of .30 caliber ammunition.

The sergeant figures he'll take shelter behind a pole in the water, but then he sees a mine lashed to the top—one of the innumerable beach obstacles Rommel's men have planted. There are 150 or 200 yards of beach to cross before reaching shelter behind a seawall, but it seems an impossible task.

One man makes a dash along the beach from right to left—probably someone from the boat Slaughter had earlier seen being raked by fire. As the soldier stumbles, weighed down by his gear, he's shot. He yells for a medic. A first-aid man appears, and he, too, is hit by fire. Both of them lie screaming. Moments later they are silent.

Pushing aside what he has just seen on the sands, Slaughter knows he must get out of the water, and he begins to run. He tries to keep a low profile, though at six foot five it's a tough thing to do. About halfway across the beach he stumbles in a runnel and almost falls.

Before the troops left England, they had been ordered to encase their rifles in plastic bags to shield them from saltwater. But Slaughter had stripped the plastic and affixed a bayonet, to be ready for action instantly.

As he trips, he almost shoots himself, firing a round next to his foot. But

27 *A Coast Guard vessel heads back from a beachhead after German machine-gun fire caused a grenade to explode, setting the boat afire. The coxswain, Delba Nivens of Amarillo, Texas, and the engineer managed to put the blaze out.* (National Archives)

28 *Seaman Second Class John Kelly, eighteen years old, of Brooklyn, and his lucky helmet. The Coast Guardsman was climbing out of a landing craft when machine-gun fire inflicted a dent. He suffered only a scratch on the back of his head.* (National Archives)

27
PA26-15
703

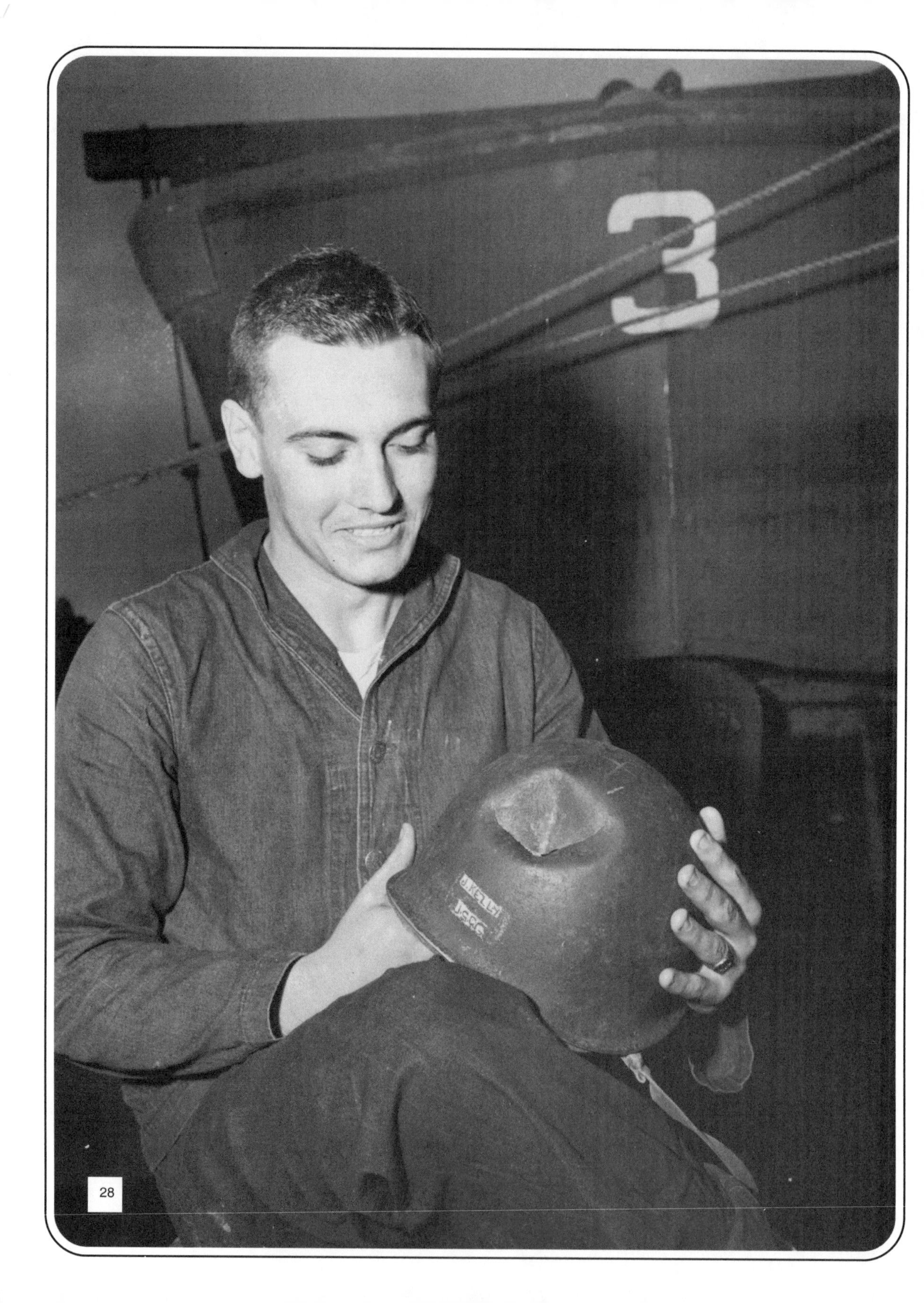
3

he keeps going, and later he thinks, *I probably looked like a buffalo with all that equipment.*

He makes it to a seawall without being hit.

Just behind him are three others from his squad.

The number-one gunner, Private First Class Walfred Williams, is still carrying his fifty-one-pound tripod for the squad's machine gun. A thick-chested nineteen-year-old from Chicago, Williams is famous among his fellow troops for his strength and endurance. He can do at least two hundred push-ups with ease, and on one training exercise he had carried that tripod on his back together with all his other equipment for twenty-five miles, refusing relief. He'd built himself up by cradling an old iron cook-stove in his arms and walking around a low-ceilinged basement back home. That tortuous exercise is serving him in good stead.

But the number-two man, Sergeant Sal Augeri, is not faring as well as Williams. He has lost his 33½-pound machine-gun receiver in the water.

The number-three man, McCanless—the soldier Slaughter had helped stay afloat—has lost a twenty-pound box of ammunition along with his water carrier. But he is still hanging on to his other box of ammo.

Now Slaughter and the three men in his squad are huddled behind the seawall, clinging to a fragment of shelter from the German gunners above them. Slaughter finds that his rifle will not fire again—it is clogged with sand. He removes his assault jacket and raincoat, spreading them out. He places his rifle down on the makeshift blanket and cleans it.

And then he notices small tears in both garments—they are bullet holes. He lights a cigarette that has been wrapped in plastic along with his matches. He is weak in the knees but unhurt.

It will seem unbelievable to Slaughter, but only a few men from his landing craft will not make it. One trooper had been crushed by the ramp. Private Robert Stover, who had been directly behind Slaughter in the boat, has been wounded, and he will die the following day. The medic, Private Roland Coates, was known to be a poor swimmer. Sergeant Slaughter never sees him again.

CHAPTER SEVEN

"In the Gray Light of a Summer Dawn"

FOR GEORGE MARSHALL and Henry Stimson, quitting time at the Pentagon Monday evening arrived at the quite ordinary hour of five o'clock.

A bit of socializing lay ahead for Marshall, however, before he returned to his quarters at Fort Myer, Virginia. A reception had been planned at the Soviet Embassy to honor the Army chief of staff for overseeing the second-front offensive Stalin had long been pleading for. Marshall would be decorated with the Order of Suvorov, First Class, one of the Soviets' highest military awards.

There were no special obligations this particular night for Stimson, and so the secretary of war went directly to his Washington apartment.

Elmer Davis, the chief of the Office of War Information—the government's propaganda arm—had an after-hours obligation at the National Press Club, and it kept him busy until 9:30. He did not head home afterward. Instead, Davis went to his offices at the Social Security Building near the Capitol.

In parlors throughout the country, millions of Americans gathered around their radios.

Shortly after eight o'clock Franklin D. Roosevelt went on the air in a fifteen-minute talk to hail the Allies' capture of Rome the previous day, the first Axis capital to fall.

"One up and two to go!" the President proclaimed. But the ultimate victory, he cautioned, "still lies some distance ahead" and "it will be tough and it will be costly."

In the midst of his speech Roosevelt turned briefly to the endeavor weighing on everyone's mind far more heavily than the events in Italy.

"Our victory comes at an excellent time, while our Allied forces are poised for another strike at western Europe, and while the armies of other Nazi soldiers nervously await our assault."

American paratroopers were hardly "poised" as the President spoke. It was past 2:00 A.M. on Tuesday in Normandy, and the men of the 82nd and 101st Airborne had been fighting for two hours in the fields of the Cherbourg Peninsula. But the infantry would not be landing on the beaches for another four hours, and so Roosevelt could say nothing of the great invasion already under way.

At the offices of the Columbia Broadcasting System on Manhattan's Madison Avenue, Ned Calmer was looking beyond the events in Rome. As 11:00 P.M. approached, he scanned the wire-service tickers for a clue that D-Day might be at hand. But there was nothing extraordinary amid the clatter of the teletype machines. When he went on the air for his nightly news wrap-up, Calmer reported that German defenses near the English Channel had been bombed for the previous four days but there was "still no hint as to when the great invasion will begin."

Then he returned to his glass work cubicle and, with one finger, pecked out in French the latest in a series of news reports for the French underground he was delivering over the CBS shortwave system on behalf of the Office of War Information.

A little later William L. Shirer, formerly the CBS correspondent in Berlin, took Calmer's place at the network microphone and analyzed the consequences of the capture of Rome. Then he nodded good night to Calmer, put on his hat and coat, lit his pipe, and went home.

Now it was past midnight. Jesse Zousmer, the night editor, was putting together Erwin Darlington's 1:00 A.M. roundup. George Herman, a newswriter, skimmed the bulldog, or early, edition of the New York *Daily News*. Darlington glanced over Zousmer's shoulder, seeking a preview of what he would be saying about the fighting in Italy. "You can't put that in," he told Zousmer, pointing to the name of an Italian town in the news report. "Why not?" asked Zousmer. "Unpronounceable," Darlington explained.

As Zousmer put the final touches on the broadcast, the CBS network was featuring Lennie Conn's orchestra, out of KNX in Los Angeles, the tune of the moment "I'll Always Remember the Forget-Me-Nots in Your Eyes."

And then the bells began to sound on the ticker of the Associated Press. One, two, three. Zousmer looked up. Two more bells. Zousmer, Darlington, and Herman moved quickly to the wire machine.

BULLETIN
LONDON, TUESDAY, JUNE 6, AP—THE GERMAN NEWS AGENCY TRANSOCEAN SAID TODAY IN A BROADCAST THAT THE ALLIED INVASION HAS BEGUN.

It was 12:37 A.M. in New York.

In London, it was thirty-seven minutes past six o'clock in the morning. Seven minutes earlier, the first wave of American infantrymen had spilled from landing craft onto the beaches of Normandy.

Zousmer ripped the bulletin from the wire machine and phoned his boss, Paul White. "No verification yet," Zousmer told White, remembering the phony "flash" sent by the Associated Press on Saturday. White told Zousmer to hold off on broadcasting the bulletin.

Moments later, the other American news agencies—United Press and the International News Service—also relayed the German report.

White decided that CBS could wait no longer, and he told Zousmer, "Get it on the air."

Zousmer handed the bulletin to Ned Calmer and told Jim Sirmons, the technician in the control room for Studio 9, to press the buttons that would put Calmer on the air.

Holding a yellow piece of teletype paper with the AP bulletin, Calmer slid into his chair, and at 12:40 A.M. the music of Lennie Conn's orchestra went silent.

"A bulletin has just been received from the London office of the Associated Press which quotes the German Transocean News Agency as asserting that the invasion of Western Europe has begun.

"This report, and we stress it is of enemy origin, with absolutely no confirmation from Allied sources, says that American landings were made this morning on the shores of northwestern France. There is as yet no reason to believe that this report is anything more than a German propaganda move or a fishing expedition for information. You will recall that Prime Minister Churchill warned us not long ago that the actual invasion would be preceded by feints and diversions. Nevertheless, until confirmation or denial of this German report is forthcoming, the CBS world staff is standing by and will bring you developments as reported."

On the stations of the National Broadcasting Company the accordion, organ, and guitar music of the New York nightclub trio the Three Suns had been competing for late-night listeners with CBS's Lennie Conn.

Now NBC interrupted its musical fare to broadcast the invasion bulletin. But it, too, warned there was no confirmation from the Allies.

At 12:43 A.M., United Press sent another bulletin: THE GERMAN RADIO SAID TODAY THAT GERMAN WARSHIPS ARE BATTLING ENEMY LANDING SHIPS AT LE HAVRE.

Zousmer began shuttling between the news tickers and Calmer's microphone as fresh bulletins came in.

In Washington, reporters were roused by their offices and hurried to the Pentagon to seek confirmation. But the War Department had nothing to announce. At the White House only a few lights shone, and the customary guards patrolled outside.

Joe Laitin, a United Press reporter, rushed to the Office of War Information at 1:15 A.M. But before he could question anyone, he was locked in the press room by Edward Klauber, the executive assistant to Elmer Davis. Three armed guards were posted to see that he didn't snoop around.

The OWI's own news ticker was usually quick to refute false enemy reports. But this time it remained silent.

Radio stations around the country began calling in their people. One NBC engineer hitched a ride to his studio aboard a milk truck. In Cincinnati, WLW staffers were winding up a farewell party for the station's promotion director, Chick Allison, who had enlisted in the Navy. Within fifteen minutes of the first bulletins they had dashed back to the newsroom.

Paul White, who would supervise CBS coverage, arrived back at his office, and he tried to reach Edward R. Murrow. White pushed a button activating a microphone and called out: "Hello, London. Hello, London. This is CBS. Hello, Ed Murrow. Hello, London." There was no reply.

CBS now began picking up evidence that the German report was true. A few moments before Calmer was to do a 1:30 A.M. update, the network's shortwave radio monitored the BBC warning French citizens living within ten miles of the English Channel to stay away from railways, roads, and bridges. Presumably, the bombs were dropping.

Among the CBS newsmen returning to the studio in the middle of the night was Robert Trout, who showed up wearing an old suit a few sizes too small. In his haste he hadn't devoted much time to wardrobe selection.

Trout soon went on the air, reading directly from the Associated Press, United Press, and International News Service tickers, a sixty-foot length of cable connecting his portable microphone to the network mike. He would broadcast almost continuously for ten hours.

Except for war-plant workers on the overnight shift, most Americans along the Eastern Seaboard slept through the first bulletins. But in Fort Lee, New Jersey, and across the Hudson River in the Washington Heights and Inwood sections of Manhattan, apartment lights were coming on. A siren had been sounded in Fort Lee, and many of those awakened figured it heralded the start of the invasion. Radios were tuned in, and bulletins were indeed arriving from London. But the siren had not been proclaiming D-Day. It had merely summoned volunteer firemen to fight a blaze at the Grant-Lee movie theater.

In Times Square there were only a few figures afoot in Tuesday's predawn hours. The usual packs of servicemen were looking to squeeze in a few more moments from their night on the town, and a couple of policemen walked their beats.

Near the New York Times building, a newsboy who heard of the radio bulletins from a newspaper deliveryman tried to dispose of his early editions, knowing they would soon be called back for an "extra." He figured out a way to get some instant sales. "Germans say Allies land in France," he shouted. The tactic worked. Two sailors rushed over to buy a paper, only to find nothing yet in print concerning an invasion.

The *Times* had been getting ready for D-Day since early April. Based on projections by Hanson Baldwin, its military analyst, a five-column drawing of likely invasion beaches had been made by Luke Manditch, a *Times* artist. Metallic maps were prepared and arrows were to be inserted pinpointing the actual landing spots.

A rewrite man had put together a brief history of the war, and a glossary of invasion terms had been prepared. Readers would be advised as to how an LCVP differed from an LCT, which differed from an LST.

For weeks the *Times*'s editors had kept the presses in readiness until the dawn hours in case the invasion were to come after the normal closing time for the final edition.

Ted Bernstein, the foreign editor, had taken a taxi home a bit after midnight Monday, and his wife greeted him with an accustomed highball. A moment later his phone rang. It was Clarence Howell, an assistant night managing editor. "You'd better come back. The German radio says the invasion's started."

Bernstein returned to the Times building and quickly decided to go with the unconfirmed invasion reports, inserting two pages labeled "A" and "B" carrying the initial dispatches and background material. At 1:30 A.M., the *Times* was on the street with an eight-column headline on page one:

GERMANS REPORT INVASION IS ON
WITH ALLIES LANDING AT HAVRE
AND NAVAL BATTLE IN CHANNEL

At 2:00 A.M., a couple of hours after the Times cafeteria had closed, two copyboys were sent out with fifty dollars to buy sandwiches and coffee. Wheeling a mailroom handcart along Eighth Avenue, they made the rounds of all-night eating places.

Two hours after the first German bulletin, Eisenhower's headquarters had yet to be heard from. But at 2:55 A.M. a brief dispatch from London over the wire-service tickers seemed to signal invasion: The largest assemblage of planes ever seen in the air over England had been moving out over the Channel.

At 3:15, a report from NBC: "Radio Berlin says Allied forces are being landed from the sea and dropped from the air near Cherbourg and Le Harve."

"We may be approaching the fateful hour," NBC's listeners are told.

At 3:27 A.M., Paul White answered a ring from one of the six telephones on his desk.

"War Department in Washington calling CBS. Stand by for an important message over CAX Army Signal Corps Channel at 3:32."

White pushed a button on his panel, opening the channel to London.

At 3:30, an excited voice over the NBC network from the New York newsroom: "We have just been informed we can expect, in a very few seconds, a very important broadcast from the British capital. And so, we take you now to London."

Two minutes later the voice of Colonel R. Ernest Dupuy, an Allied press relations officer:

"The text of Communiqué Number One of the Supreme Headquarters of the Allied Expeditionary Forces will be released to press and radio of the United Nations ten seconds from now."

Dupuy counted to ten.

And then:

"Under the command of General Eisenhower, Allied naval forces, supported by strong air forces, began landing Allied armies this morning on the northern coast of France."

D-Day was indeed at hand.

At the Senate House of London University, fifty correspondents had been locked up in a briefing room of the British Ministry of Information since being summoned at dawn. As American military policemen patrolled the grounds, press officers had told them of the invasion, and they took notes around two long tables.

Just before Dupuy's announcement, the chief briefing officer had dropped his arm as a signal that the rush to telephones could begin.

"In the next fifteen seconds the invasion flash will go out to the world," he said.

As Dupuy read his communiqué, the wire-service reporters were dictating their bulletins.

From the International News Service:

FLASH
LONDON—EISENHOWER ANNOUNCES INVASION BEGINS

Five minutes later the radio networks carried Eisenhower's Order of the Day. But it was not his voice. He had chosen Edward R. Murrow to read it for him.

"Soldiers, sailors, and airmen of the Allied Expeditionary Force. You are about to embark upon the great crusade, toward which we have striven these many months. The eyes of the world are upon you. The hopes and prayers of liberty-loving people everywhere march with you. . . .

"The tide has turned. The free men of the world are marching together to victory. I have full confidence in your courage, devotion to duty, and skill in battle. We will accept nothing less than full victory. Good luck. . . .

"And let us all beseech the blessing of Almighty God upon this great and noble undertaking."

At 3:47 A.M., Eisenhower himself was on the air, asking the people of occupied Europe to be patient until the signal came for them to rise up against the Germans.

"A landing was made this morning on the coast of France . . . the hour of your liberation is approaching . . . all patriots . . . continue your passive resistance, but do not needlessly endanger your lives until I give you the signal to rise and strike the enemy. The day will come . . . be patient . . . prepare . . . I call upon all who love freedom to stand with us . . . our arms are resolute—together we shall achieve victory."

The American writer Gertrude Stein, living in Grenoble, France, had listened to Ike's message, and she recorded her thoughts in her journal.

"Today we heard Eisenhower tell us he was here. They were here. Glory be. And we are singing hallelujah and feeling very nicely."

In occupied Amsterdam there was finally a glimmer of hope at a camouflaged annex where two Jewish families had been hiding from the Gestapo since July 1942.

They heard the first announcements by the BBC, and then Eisenhower's message.

A fourteen-year-old girl named Anne Frank made an entry in her diary:

" 'This is D-Day,' came the announcement over the English news, and quite rightly, 'this is the day.' The invasion has begun!

". . . According to German news, English parachute troops have landed on the French coast. English landing craft are in battle with the German Navy, says the BBC.

". . . General Eisenhower said to the French people: 'Stiff fighting will come now, but after this the victory. The year 1944 is the year of complete victory; good luck.'

"Great commotion in the 'Secret Annex'! Would the long-awaited liberation that has been talked of so much, but which seems too wonderful, too much like a fairy tale, ever come true? Could we be granted victory this year, 1944? We don't know yet, but hope is revived within us; it gives us fresh courage, and makes us strong again. . . ."

The first eyewitness report, pooled for all the American networks, came at 4:17 A.M. Eastern time. It was filed by Wright Bryan, the managing editor of *The Atlanta Journal*, who had also been accredited as a correspondent for station WSB, the NBC affiliate in Atlanta. He had just returned to London after getting a ride aboard a C-47 named the *Snootie* that had dropped a stick of paratroopers, among them Private Robert Hillman, the soldier bearing a parachute his mother presumably had packed.

"I rode with the first group of planes from a troop-carrier command to take our fighting men into Europe.

" 'Are you all set?' asked the colonel. 'Get this thing hooked for me,' he said as he took his own place closest to the door. They blinked as the pilot threw his switch, and before I could look up they began jumping. The paratroopers shoved each other so swiftly and heavily towards the open door that they jolted against the door frame."

In Washington, the White House switchboard operator, Louise Hachmeister, went into action at 4:00 A.M., phoning members of the President's staff with instructions to report to work. "One knew that grim, awful things were ahead," thought William Hassett, FDR's longtime aide, upon being awakened.

War Secretary Stimson had not been telephoned, but at 4:20 A.M. he stirred from sleep and turned on his portable radio.

The next day he would tell a reporter: "I was as surprised as anyone else when I heard a news correspondent telling how he had just returned from an airplane trip from France where parachutists were dropped."

At Scott Air Field in St. Louis nobody would sleep through the night. Twenty seconds after the Allied invasion communiqué was broadcast, sirens began to whine. The base chapel quickly opened its doors.

In Marietta, Georgia, the bells of a Methodist church began to peal at 3:30 A.M. Within a half hour the lights were on at every church in town. In Coffeyville, Kansas, families in their nightclothes knelt in prayer on their porches.

At the huge Brooklyn Navy Yard, just as the shifts were changing at 4:00 A.M., an announcement was made over the loudspeaker: "The invasion has begun." The workers dropped their hard hats, a few men knelt, and some women wept in silent prayer.

At that hour the famous Bow Bells of London's St. Mary-le-Bow church, destroyed by German bombs in 1940, came to life again in Manhattan, heralding D-Day from St. Luke's Lutheran Church off Times Square. The sound of the bells was piped to the empty streets from a powerful amplifier broadcasting an old recording made by the BBC.

As dawn broke, *The New York Times* was out with its final edition of the night—a "6:00 A.M. Extra."

The latest page-one headline read:

ALLIED ARMIES LAND IN FRANCE
IN THE HAVRE-CHERBOURG AREA;
GREAT INVASION IS UNDER WAY

The lead story, from London, was written by Raymond Daniell.

SUPREME HEADQUARTERS ALLIED EXPEDITIONARY FORCES, Tuesday, June 6—The invasion of Europe from the West has begun.

In the gray light of a summer dawn Gen. Dwight D. Eisenhower threw his great Anglo-American force into action today for the liberation of the Continent.

29 *One word says it all.* (*Editor & Publisher* magazine)

30 *Getting a glimpse of the invasion bulletins.* (Office of War Information Collection, Library of Congress)

NEWSPAPERS DISPLAY INGENUITY IN INVASION FRONT PAGES

The Detroit Free Press EXTRA
INVASION!

ST. LOUIS POST-DISPATCH WAR EXTRA
ALLIES INVADE NORTHERN FRANCE
4000 SHIPS BACKED BY 11,000 PLANES
BEACHHEADS WON: GAINS INLAND

Daily Mirror 2
ALLIES INVADE FRANCE
EISENHOWER'S COMMUNIQUE No. 1

PHILADELPHIA RECORD
The Invasion Is On
WE SLASH INLAN
IN HEAVY FIGHTIN

San Francisco Examiner FINAL
IT'S OFFICIAL
INVASION ON
Paratroops Spearhead Landing in Normandy

St. Petersburg Times
INVASION
TROOPS LANDING IN NORTHER FRANCE, EISENHOWER ANNOUNCE

Muskogee Daily Phoenix
INVASION
llied Troops Begin Landings
n Northern Coast of France

New York Post
INVASION
SMASHING AHEAD!
Nazis Say We're 10 Miles

INVASION EXTRA
First Pictures of Invasion Takeo

EXTRA!
Los Angeles Times
INVASION!

EXTRA
Union City Daily Messenger
FRENCH COAST INVADED

The Detroit News
BEACHHEADS WON ON FRENCH COAST
Hitler's Wall Broken as Allies Move In

The Fort Worth Press EXTRA
EUROPE INVADED

3¢ DAILY TIMES
WAR EXTRA
INVASION!
WIN 2 FRENCH BEACHHEADS!

THE CHICAGO SUN FINAL
INVASION ON! ALLIES IN FRANCE

INVASION EXTRA
San Francisco Chronicle
INVASION!
ALLIED ARMIES ARE LANDING IN NORTH FRANCE!

The Philadelphia Inquirer WAR EXTRA
INVASION
Mighty Allied Armies Land in Fr
Fleet, Planes, Chutists Battling

ALLIES INVADE FRANCE
Daily News
Establish Beachheads In France, Push Forward

The Des Moines Register
INVASION!
Blue, Evans 6 in Republican Nominations

LLIES SEIZE BEACHHE
BATTLE 10 M IN FRANCE

MILWAUKEE SENTINEL EXTRA
Vast Armies Land in France
Invasion!

EDITOR & PUBLISHER for June 17, 1944

30
MAGIC
INVASION
NEWS
BUITONI

CHAPTER EIGHT

"I Am in Ste.-Mère-Église"

IN THE STONE-WALLED village of Ste.-Mère-Église, five miles inland from the beaches of the Cherbourg Peninsula, there's a sign in the church square reading AUBERGE JOHN STEELE—the John Steele Inn.

If a visitor glances across the street, he can see an image aloft in the church: the figure of a paratrooper, his chute billowing, perched at the top of the wall near the steeple.

Inside the church, two of the stained-glass windows contain representations far afield from religious imagery: they portray the arrival of parachutists.

The figure atop the church was placed by the townspeople in tribute to the man the inn is named for. In the early hours of D-Day, a thirty-one-year-old private of the 82nd Airborne named John Steele descended from the skies, machine-gun bullets blazing all around him, and became entangled in the steeple of that church.

Ste.-Mère-Église was the key D-Day objective of the 82nd. Located astride Route 13, the main road from Cherbourg to Bayeux, it was the district headquarters of the German Army and the hub of a network of largely metal-surfaced roads connecting with all parts of the peninsula, routes the Germans could use to summon reinforcements during the invasion's early hours. Cable lines connecting Cherbourg with the strategic town of Carentan ran through the village. And it occupied high ground, dominating the approaches to it.

The 82nd Airborne was originally to have been dropped farther west—near St.-Sauveur-le-Vicomte—in an effort to cut the peninsula in two and

31 *Figure of a parachutist atop the church at Ste.-Mère-Église, placed in tribute to Private John Steele of the 82nd Airborne, who became entangled in the steeple during the predawn hours of D-Day.* (Nancy Lubell)

31

block the passage of enemy troops moving north to reinforce Cherbourg. But the German 91st Air Landing Division moved into the area in mid-May, putting it between the intended drop zones of the 82nd and 101st. So the 82nd's jump was shifted eastward, to Ste.-Mère-Église.

The task of seizing the village—among the first important missions of D-Day—was given to the 3rd Battalion of the 505th Regiment.

The 1st Battalion was to capture crossings of the Merderet River at Chef-du-Pont and La Fière, thereby blocking German forces who might arrive from the west or southwest. The 2nd Battalion was to hold a line running through the little village of Neuville-au-Plain to the north of Ste.-Mère-Église, averting the German offensive from that direction.

After seizing Ste.-Mère-Église the 3rd Battalion was expected to set up roadblocks to the south and east, thus warding off counterattacks until the 4th Division forces arrived from Utah Beach.

But before all this happened, the pathfinders had to light up the drop zone for the main body of the 505th Regiment. Shortly after midnight they descended—right on target.

An hour later all was chaos in the church square of Ste.-Mère-Église. A home had caught fire—possibly from stray bombing incendiary—and more than a hundred townspeople, summoned by the tolling of the church bells and a frantic banging on their doors, had emerged from their houses to fight the blaze. The German garrison immediately lifted its curfew, allowing the villagers—many in their nightclothes—to form a bucket brigade. Water was passed from hand to hand as thirty German troops, armed with rifles and machine pistols, stood watch.

Moments later, with the church bells still tolling and the flames beginning to spread, the sound of airplanes could be heard. The pathfinders had completed their work, and now the C-47's carrying the main body of paratroopers from the 82nd Airborne were low overhead, en route to their drop zone.

And then—apparently caught by a gust of wind—a band of parachutists floated down directly into the church square.

Private John Steele found himself heading toward the church itself. He watched German soldiers and townspeople running around madly below, and then he felt something "like the bite of a sharp knife." He had been shot in the foot. Seconds later he was entangled in the steeple.

Steele tried to cut himself loose, but his knife slipped away and fell to the ground. As he dangled, more German troops were rushing to the square, and bursts of fire were everywhere. His fellow paratroopers—perhaps twenty descending into the square—were silhouetted against the flames, and many were shot down all around him. A dozen Germans emptied their guns into one trooper stranded in a tree.

Steele figured the only way he could survive was to play dead. When the Germans discovered he was alive, they took him prisoner and brought him to a regimental headquarters with about a half dozen other captives.

And then something truly bizarre happened: having completed their defense of the village, the German troops returned to their barracks and went to sleep.

In a field one mile to the west, Lieutenant Colonel Edward Krause, having taken a rabbit's foot shod with horseshoes to France, was feeling very lucky. Just before going out the door of his plane, the 3rd Battalion commander had spotted the green "T" lights set up by the pathfinders, convincing him he was over the correct spot for his landing. Indeed he was. He came down in a triangular-shaped, hedgerow-bordered field just south of his unit's drop zone—the exact point he had previously chosen for his command post.

Krause quickly divided up fifteen men into four groups, telling them to move out six hundred yards in all directions and pick up stray paratroopers. They were to be back in forty-five minutes.

Less than an hour later, Krause was ready to move on Ste.-Mère-Église with 180 troops. He also had one civilian with him—a drunken Frenchman who had been wandering around after curfew and had been picked up by one of the patrols. The man had some important news: the German infantry battalion that had been garrisoned inside Ste.-Mère-Église was now encamped on high ground south of it, having moved out of the village because of the constant threat of air strikes. Ste.-Mère-Église was occupied only by service troops—a transport and supply company. What Krause did not know was that American paratroopers had already been cut down in the town.

The Frenchman told of a way to get into Ste.-Mère-Église without encountering German troops: an almost unused trail led into the village from the northwest.

Krause put the Frenchman at the point, under Captain Walter De Long of H Company, and the man led the way through a path lined by hedgerows providing cover. The night was almost pitch black—although there was a full moon, heavy clouds hung over the area. The more experienced troops seemed willing to step out—aware they had the element of surprise with them—but the newer ones were more cautious, carrying their rifles at the on-guard position while the senior sergeants snarled at them.

As the paratroopers crept up on Ste.-Mère-Église, they saw no German soldiers, received no fire. After a half hour they were at the outskirts of the village.

Now they paused, and Krause told his troops he wanted no firing until daylight. They were to use only grenades, knives, and bayonets.

Patrols set up blocks on the roads going into the village, and Krause, briefed back in England on the exact location of the cable from Cherbourg, found the communications line and cut it.

When Krause's men entered Ste.-Mère-Église, it seemed empty. But then they were stunned.

Private First Class William Tucker, setting up a machine gun behind the church, sensed someone behind him. He whirled around and his eyes came level with a pair of boots. A dead paratrooper was hanging in a tree.

Soon the newly arrived troops saw the other parachutists who had been shot down all over the church square.

"Men just stood there staring, filled with a terrible anger," Lieutenant Gus Sanders would recall.

Krause's troops began searching the buildings around the square, and they made a startling discovery: the German soldiers were sleeping in their beds. About thirty surrendered, ten were killed, and the others escaped into the countryside. John Steele was freed.

Then Krause fulfilled the vow he had made in England just ten hours before. He went to the village hall, unfurled the American flag that had flown over Naples, and raised it up the flagpole.

Ste.-Mère-Église had become the first village in France to be liberated by the Americans.

It was 4:27 A.M.

A half hour later, Krause sent a runner to tell the regimental commander, Colonel William Ekman, "I am in Ste.-Mère-Église." But in the confusion of battle Ekman never received the message.

The capture of the village was one thing; retaining it was another.

By 9:00 A.M. three hundred paratroopers were in Ste.-Mère-Église, but they soon faced a counterattack as two German infantry companies tried to retake the village from the south.

The attack was launched behind a strange shield. The German troops herded cattle from nearby fields onto the main road, hoping they would set off any mines that had been planted.

Private Dominick De Tullio wrecked that bit of strategy. Moving out well in front of the American roadblock, he turned the cattle into another field, then threw grenades at the Germans driving the cows, killing one man, wounding another, and sending the rest fleeing.

(The next day De Tullio volunteered to approach a town pump under heavy fire in order to get water for some wounded soldiers. A high-velocity shell killed him.)

Troops from the 2nd and 3rd battalions of the 505th managed to drive the Germans back into a thick forest, quelling the counterattack by 11:30 A.M. But Krause was hit by a shell fragment in the lower right leg. Major Bill Hagen, his executive officer, took command.

The men of the 2nd Battalion had been as fortunate as Krause's 3rd Battalion in their drop, descending on or near their zones. But their commander, Lieutenant Colonel Benjamin Vandervoort, had broken a leg on impact.

Vandervoort was not the kind of man to let something like that interfere with a mission.

Lieutenant Tom McClean of D Company would watch Vandervoort in action that day, and he would remember how "a couple of men grabbed an ammo cart, and he jumped in and had them pull him into Ste.-Mère-Église. Then he got a pair of crutches from a Frenchman. He was going around on them, with his leg in a cast, until they finally got a jeep up there."

As far as McClean was concerned, "Vandervoort was the best man I have ever run across. There was never any wavering on his part. He knew what he wanted to do and he was there with the troops to do it. Not behind, directing them, but with them."

Vandervoort and his battalion helped repel the counterattack on Ste.-Mère-Église. But their prime mission was to secure the northern approaches to the village. To do that, Vandervoort had earlier ordered that a roadblock be established a mile away at Neuville-au-Plain, along the main road from Cherbourg.

A platoon of forty-four troops from D Company was given the job sometime after 8:00 A.M. amid a flurry of contradictory messages on whether Ste.-Mère-Église had actually been captured. In command was Lieutenant Turner Turnbull, a half-Cherokee known as "Chief." A powerfully built six-footer, Turnbull was an officer highly regarded by his men and considered fearless.

Turnbull positioned ten paratroopers along an orchard on the left flank at Neuville and placed the rest on the right. Two riflemen and a bazooka man were sent back to the houses to set up a roadblock if enemy tanks arrived. Now they would wait.

Thirty minutes later, 180 soldiers from the German 91st Air Landing Division came marching down a road. But it seemed as if they were headed for a dance. They strolled along in a column of twos, singing and whistling, their helmets off.

When they got into range, Turnbull's machine-gunners opened fire. The German troops, their reveling over, scattered into ditches.

As the Germans returned fire, Lieutenant Isaac Michaelman, the platoon's number-two man—in charge of the squad at the orchard and observing from the upper portion of a farm building—was shot through the buttocks.

But it almost certainly wasn't the Germans who hit Michaelman—it was evidently one of his own troops, Private First Class Stanley Kotlarz.

"We were inside of a hedgerow," Kotlarz remembers. "We were told to set up a line right there and don't move beyond that.

"When you've got hedgerows around you, communications are pretty hard. In some places they're like trees. You've got a mound of dirt that stands three and a half, four feet tall and these hedge bushes are planted on top of that.

"Lieutenant Michaelman went out ahead to observe. None of us knew it. He must not have said anything to anybody. He climbed up a fire-escape ladder. I thought it was a German soldier because we were told not to go beyond this line."

Kotlarz fired, and even after Michaelman was hit, Kotlarz didn't realize who his target was. A few days later, both of them landed in the same hospital in England, Kotlarz having subsequently been wounded as well.

As Kotlarz recalls it:

"Michaelman was limping around. I said, 'Man, what the hell happened to you, Lieutenant?'

"He said, 'A sniper got me.'

"I said, 'Where'd he get you at?'

"He said, 'That farmhouse.'

"I didn't say anything then, but it was my slug that got him."

Soon after Michaelman had been hit, Vandervoort had arrived at Neuville in a jeep towing a pair of 57mm antitank guns taken from a glider.

By this time the Germans had moved into nearby fields, trying to turn the flank on Turnbull's troops.

Vandervoort sent a runner to ask Turnbull: "How are you doing? Do you need help?" He responded: "Okay and everything under control."

Still unsure whether Ste.-Mère-Église had been captured, Vandervoort headed back there, leaving the antitank guns with the troops at Neuville.

As he departed, the Germans intensified their attack, opening up with mortars and a self-propelled gun. Turnbull's bazooka man was killed. His antitank gunners were driven from their weapon, taking temporary cover among the houses. But soon they resumed firing, knocking out the Germans' self-propelled gun and a tank behind it.

As the battle continued, German reinforcements began arriving. Turnbull's men continued to hold the Germans off, but eventually they slipped into an open field at the Americans' rear and threatened to shut off Route 13, the paratroopers' only avenue of retreat toward Ste.-Mère-Église. By the afternoon Turnbull's situation was desperate. He had only twenty-three men able to fight. Eleven others were stretcher cases and nine had been killed.

"I have heard about spots like this," Turnbull yelled. "We're surrounded. There's one thing left for us to do. We can charge them."

"I'm ready," responded one soldier. But another one, Private Joseph Sebastian, urged a retreat before the men were totally cut off. "I think there's a chance we can get out—that's what we ought to do," he told Turnbull.

"What about it?" Turnbull asked his troops while making it clear that the wounded would have to be left behind if there were a retreat.

The men decided to try a breakout to the rear.

Corporal James Kelly, the medic, volunteered to stay with the wounded. Sebastian, having proposed the retreat, said he would remain behind as well, covering the withdrawal with his Browning Automatic Rifle. Corporal Raymond Smitson said he would stay, too, supporting Sebastian with a sack of hand grenades. Sergeant Robert Niland moved toward one of the machine guns, intending to help as well, but as he did so he was cut down by fire from a machine pistol.

As Niland was killed, someone yelled: "Let's go! For Christ's sake, let's go!"

Turnbull and the remnants of his platoon retreated. They expected to be quickly shot down, but they emerged unscathed, thanks to fire from the 1st platoon of E Company, which had just arrived, and to covering firepower from Sebastian and Smitson, who were later captured.

Otis Sampson, an E Company sergeant, would remember how "I grabbed a mortar and went out into the high grass. I had a field day with it—we just worked them over. One of their mortar shells landed in our command post, but nobody was killed. We didn't lose a man."

Turnbull's men and the troops from E Company who had reinforced them then headed down the road to Ste.-Mère-Église.

"I walked along with Turnbull," Sampson recalls. "He was very depressed, losing all those men."

Turnbull's troops had been outnumbered by four to one at the outset of the fighting—more so later on—but had held the Germans off for eight hours, even managing to destroy two armored vehicles.

And so they saved the men at Ste.-Mère-Église from being attacked from the north while they were facing German reinforcements coming from the south.

The battle of Neuville-au-Plain seemed a small one in the scheme of things. But it symbolized the heroics of the paratroopers in those early hours on the Cherbourg Peninsula. Often outnumbered and inferior in firepower, the airborne was nonetheless beginning to fulfill its mission.

Lieutenant Turner Turnbull would have little time, however, to savor his deeds.

Stanley Kotlarz would recall what happened the following morning at Ste.-Mère-Église:

"We decided we'd try and make advances. I was in a mortar squad. There was a gunner and an assistant gunner and two ammunition bearers, and Turnbull was right behind us. We hadn't gone about fifty feet, and the Germans were coming in with 88's—they travel so fast, you can't duck. The shell exploded right in our vicinity. I got hit by a piece of shrapnel in the wrist.

"Our first sergeant came up and said, 'Where's Lieutenant Turnbull at?'

I said, 'He's down there right behind us.' He went down there, and Turnbull was laying there. The 88 just took the whole top of his head right off. It sheared him right at his eyebrows."

Three weeks after the battle for Ste.-Mère-Église, the mayor of the town, Alexandre Renaud, sent a letter to the 505th's Colonel Ekman.

The mayor was looking back on how the Americans had beaten off yet another German attempt to retake the town the night of D-Day.

He wrote:

"On the evening of June 6, from the ditch where I had taken cover, I heard the battle drawing closer to us. The Germans came back as far as the outskirts of the town. There was hand-to-hand fighting.

"In the morning I had heard paratroopers say: 'We are attacking; the forces coming by sea will be here in six hours.' In the evening, however, they still awaited reinforcements. One of your men told me: 'The sea was too rough.' The women of the town cried and prayed. 'Don't leave us!' I heard them say to the men. One of the paratroopers replied with a smile and a laugh: 'We will never leave you. We are staying right here.' "

32 *Winged imagery in stained-glass window at the Ste.-Mère-Église church honors the arrival of the airborne. Inscription at the bottom reads:* "Ils Sont Revenus . . . *They Have Come Back.*" (Nancy Lubell)

6
JUIN
1944
6
JUIN
1969
ILS
SONT
REVENUS
THEY HAVE
COME
BACK

CHAPTER NINE

"Grandfather Puffed a Bit"

THE FATHER WAS the warrior-statesman, a champion of American power in international affairs, a booster of the strenuous life for individuals. "Speak softly and carry a big stick," was his credo.

The son could never hope to attain the heights of adulation the father had known, but he would truly be his father's son, and more, in the tests of battle.

On the eve of D-Day, Brigadier General Theodore Roosevelt, Jr.—age fifty-six, slowed by an arthritic hip that required him to use a cane—was about to lead men in an affair whose consequences would infinitely surpass the Battle of San Juan Hill.

As H-Hour approached, Roosevelt was aboard a transport ship moving through the darkened English Channel, headed toward a stretch of the Cherbourg Peninsula's eastern coastline code-named Utah Beach. With him were the men of the 4th Infantry Division. To the east his son Quentin was also crossing the Channel, preparing for the assault at Omaha Beach with the troops of the 1st Division.

Roosevelt paused to compose a letter to his wife, Eleanor.

"We are starting on the great venture of the war. We are attacking by daylight the most heavily fortified coast in history, a shore held by excellent troops. I go in with the first assault wave and hit the beach at H-Hour. I'm doing it because it's the way I can contribute the most. It steadies the young men to know I am with them, to see me plodding along with my cane.

"Quentin goes in, I believe, at H plus sixty. That's bad enough. Frankly, it may be worse than when I go in.

"We've had a grand life and I hope there'll be more. Should it chance that there's not, at least we can say that in our years together we've packed enough for ten ordinary lives. We've known joy and sorrow, triumph and disaster. We have been very happy. I pray we may be together again.

"The ship is dark, the men are going to their assembly stations. Soon the boats will be lowered. Then we'll be off."

The eldest son of Theodore and Edith Roosevelt was no stranger to warfare in France.

During World War I he commanded the 26th Regiment of the 1st Division. He had been gassed in the lungs and eyes at Cantigny, but led his men through heavy bombardment, refusing evacuation, and he received the Silver Star.

His brother Quentin—for whom the son poised off Omaha Beach was named—had been one of those dashing young airmen at the dawn of military aviation. In July 1918 Quentin was killed in action, his plane shot down over German lines. That was a more chivalrous time. The Germans buried him with full military honors, and the broken propeller and wings from his plane were placed near a cross marking his grave in the village of Chamery.

When the war was over, Ted turned to political affairs, serving in the New York State Assembly and then as assistant secretary of the Navy, a post his father as well as his cousin, Franklin D. Roosevelt, had held before him.

In 1924 he ran for governor of New York—narrowly losing to Al Smith—then served in the Hoover Administration as governor of Puerto Rico and governor-general of the Philippines before entering the business world in the 1930s as board chairman of American Express.

In the spring of 1941 Roosevelt returned to active duty with his old 26th Regiment, training at Fort Devens, Massachusetts. Before the year was over, there was a promotion to brigadier general and assistant commander of the 1st Division. His youngest son, Quentin, then twenty-one, had also enlisted, and was assigned to the division's field artillery.

Roosevelt was back in combat during the fall of '42 as the 1st Division invaded North Africa. In the summer of '43 the division moved on to Sicily. But now his star would go into eclipse.

Omar Bradley had been concerned about lack of discipline in the 1st Division going back to the North African campaign. Bradley would write in his memoirs how both the division commander, Major General Terry Allen, and Roosevelt "were exceptional leaders revered by their men, but both had the same weakness: utter disregard for discipline, everywhere evident in their cocky division."

Following the battle of Troina, in which the division suffered initial heavy losses, Bradley removed both Allen and Roosevelt and named Major General Clarence R. Huebner, a World War I veteran with a reputation as a disciplinarian, as the division commander.

But Bradley knew that Roosevelt was a leader, the kind of man who could inspire confidence in soldiers about to experience combat for the first time. So he assigned him to the 4th Division, which had arrived in England—untested by battle—in January of '44. He would serve under Major General Raymond O. Barton.

As D-Day neared, Roosevelt sought permission to hit the beach with the division's first wave of infantrymen. Barton turned him down, but Roosevelt persisted.

Finally, Barton relented despite Roosevelt's age and his frail hip. But, the division commander would recall, "When I said good-bye to Ted in England, I never expected to see him alive again."

Roosevelt would be accompanying the 4th Division's vanguard in the assault upon a nine-mile, north-south beachhead some three to four hundred yards wide at low tide.

First, the men would face gently sloping yellow sands, then a low concrete wall erected by the Germans in front of a stretch of dunes.

Behind the beach the going promised to be especially treacherous. The land was marshy—crossed at many points by drainage canals—and the Germans had flooded pastures in an effort to frustrate invading forces.

There would be just four routes off the beachhead—causeways with shoulders a few feet above the marshes. If the Germans could control the causeway exits, which were about a mile from the high-water mark, they could push the assault forces back. And so the paratroopers—despite fears they would suffer heavy casualties—had been dropped five hours before the first ground troops were to arrive at Utah. The 101st Airborne was given the mission of seizing the causeway exits.

The 4th Division's 8th Infantry, commanded by Colonel James Van Fleet and accompanied by one battalion of the 22nd Infantry, was to make the initial beach assault. Twenty landing craft, each carrying thirty-man assault teams, were to arrive in the first wave at 6:30 A.M. A total of ten boats from E and F companies were to come ashore at a sector called Uncle Red, in front of the causeway leading to Exit 3, near the village of Audouville-la-Hubert. Another ten boatloads, from B and C companies, were to land on their right flank at the Tare Green sector, closer to the causeway leading to Exit 4, at St.-Martin-de-Varreville.

Directly behind the first companies would be eight LCTs carrying a total of thirty-two "Duplex Drive" or "DD" tanks (they had twin propellers) designed to swim through the tides almost totally submerged, then come up firing on the beachhead.

After the first wave of infantrymen, and their accompanying armor and demolition teams, had arrived, the remainder of the 22nd Infantry, commanded by Colonel Hervey Tribolet, would assault the beach, coming in 85 minutes after H-Hour. The 12th Infantry, commanded by Colonel Russell P. (Red) Reeder, would land afterward.

The first troops to hit French soil in the Utah Beach landings actually arrived before sunrise. The Germans were believed to have set up an observation post on the tiny St.-Marcouf islands, two spits of land four miles off the coast. To avert premature detection of the Utah naval force, a detachment of 132 men from the 4th and 24th Cavalry squadrons was landed on the islands at 5:30 A.M. But they found no Germans. Their only casualties—two dead and seventeen wounded—would come from land mines, booby traps, and artillery fire hitting the islands in the afternoon.

At 5:36 A.M. the battleships, cruisers, and destroyers of Admiral Moon's task force opened up on the German fortifications. A half hour later a force of 360 Marauders from the Ninth Air Force began dropping 4,400 bombs on German positions. And, when the first wave of troops reached a point 700 yards from shore, 17 rocket boats delivered a final blast of covering fire.

In those frenzied moments the only effective German response came not from the troops defending the beach, but from underwater mines. The American landing craft had to pass directly across a minefield laid along the Cardonnet Bank, but none of the mines there were detected before H-Hour since they were of a type that required successive sweeps.

The two control vessels for the Uncle Red sector—boats that the invading forces were to guide on—were put out of action. One of them fouled her screw on a chain buoy. The other was *PC-1261*, the 173-foot primary control boat, which was to serve as a guide for four LCTs—vessels carrying four "DD" amphibious tanks apiece—and for the waves of infantrymen that were to come behind them.

Shortly after 5:30 A.M., the quartermaster aboard *PC-1261* stepped down into the chart room to report that gun batteries ashore had straddled the boat. Just then the vessel was ripped by an explosion. It had struck a mine.

Glass came crashing all around the crew, gear tumbled on the decks, lights darkened, and the boat listed fifty degrees to starboard.

Most of the crewmen took to life rafts while others hung on to the upturned hull. As the sailors waited to be picked up by rescue craft, an explosion erupted alongside them. A landing craft carrying at least thirty men was blown a hundred feet in the air, perhaps hit by a mine, perhaps by German fire.

Fifteen minutes later one of the four LCTs en route to the Tare Green sector on the right flank struck a mine, and it went down almost immediately, taking its four "DD" tanks with it.

While all this was happening, the Navy guns were blazing away. None of the ships was busier than the destroyer *Corry*, its guns firing eight five-inch shells a minute. But the Corry was receiving fire in return. Smoke-laying aircraft had been assigned to put down a protective screen around the destroyers, but the plane that was supposed to shield the *Corry* had been shot down. The *Corry* was the only destroyer the German batteries could clearly detect.

The skipper, Lieutenant Commander George Hoffman, tried to maneuver his ship to avoid the incoming shells, but it was a tricky business in shallow water filled with sharp reefs. Finally, he broke clear and began to tear away, doing more than twenty knots. Then, shortly after 6:00 A.M., a blast shook the destroyer.

The *Corry* had struck a mine, and its deck was ripped by a gash more than a foot wide. A boiler blew up, scalding the men attending to it, and both firerooms along with the forward engine room became flooded. The bow and the stern pointed upward at a bizarre angle. After tearing along for a thousand yards, the destroyer came to a halt. Now the Germans zeroed in, sending shell upon shell into her, blowing up the ammunition. At 6:41, Hoffman ordered his crew to abandon ship. The destroyers *Hobson* and

Fitch lowered rescue boats and they put down covering fire upon the shore as the men dived into the water, some of them choking as a German shell set off a smoke generator.

The *Corry* sank, but her mainmast and part of the superstructure remained above the water. As rescue boats picked up survivors, a lone sailor stayed behind. He retrieved the ship's ensign, then ran it up the mainmast. Finally, he swam away.

Thirteen of the *Corry*'s 294 crewmen were killed and another 33 were wounded in the only major naval loss for American forces on D-Day. But even as the *Corry* died, her flag still snapped in the breeze.

Moments before the *Corry*'s sailors began diving into the Channel, the men of the 8th Infantry had begun to scramble ashore from twenty landing craft. The first wave—six hundred troops—waded through a hundred yards of surf and was delighted to encounter virtually no enemy fire. "God damn, we're on French soil," yelled one soldier.

Some fifteen minutes behind them were the "DD" amphibious tanks, launched from a mile offshore in relatively calm water.

There had been great concern over the seaworthiness of these innovative tanks, which were equipped with canvas collars, or "bloomers," supposedly enabling them to swim—virtually submerged—through the Bay of the Seine. Lieutenant Francis Songer, the commander of the 70th Tank Battalion's B Company, had been so wary of the tanks that he had his troops reinforce the collars' seams by sewing in catgut with needles—items purchased at his own expense.

When the thirty-two "DD" tanks were five thousand yards offshore, the Navy sought to have them launched from their LCTs, fearing that these carriers might hit mines farther in. But Songer protested that the seas were too rough so far out and insisted on holding back until the tanks were a mile off Utah Beach. Although one LCT did hit a mine—taking four tanks down with it—twenty-seven of the twenty-eight tanks subsequently launched from the other carriers successfully swam to the beach.

33 *The destroyer* Corry, *which would be sunk by a mine off Utah Beach on D-Day.* (National Archives)

34 *Troops of the 4th Infantry Division go ashore at Utah Beach.* (National Archives)

33

34

Accompanying the first infantrymen ashore—as promised—was Theodore Roosevelt, Jr., the only general officer arriving with first-wave troops on D-Day.

After a three-hour run-in aboard his landing craft, a shivering and soaked Roosevelt splashed through about a hundred yards of surf, waist deep. He ran up four hundred yards of beach—"Grandfather puffed a bit" he would write to his wife—and reached the seawall.

Now, however, Roosevelt realized that something was very wrong.

A house stood behind the wall, but his maps showed no building should be there. Then he scrambled up on the dunes and found a windmill he recognized from the intelligence reports. Suddenly, Roosevelt knew—the men had been put ashore two thousand yards south of where they should have arrived.

There had been few terrain features, such as buildings and distinctive hills, for the coxswain to guide on, and the smoke and dust of battle had obscured what landmarks did exist. The inability of the coxswains to orient themselves, combined with a southeasterly current and the loss of two control boats, had taken the first wave far off course. The units who were to have left the beach on the causeways leading to Exits 3 and 4 were, instead, in front of the causeway toward Exit 2 at Houdienville.

Roosevelt had a crucial decision to make. Should the succeeding waves about to come ashore be directed to Exit 2 as well, or should they be sent toward the causeways to the north as previously envisioned? Roosevelt ran among his company commanders, telling them where they were, and then—in view of the lack of enemy resistance—he decided to start the war from where the first troops had landed.

For the rest of the morning he would range over the beach and beyond, directing newly arrived troops to move inland from the causeway south of their planned beach-departure route. "I must have walked twenty miles up and down that beach and over the causeways," he would recall.

Coming ashore at H-Hour with the troops on the right flank was Kenneth Crawford of *Newsweek* magazine, who was certain that things were proceeding on schedule.

Wearing a watch given to him by the famed combat correspondent Ernie Pyle the previous Christmas in North Africa, Crawford knew he was on time "because my wristwatch, guaranteed to be waterproof, shockproof, and otherwise indestructible, was nothing of the kind. It stopped at exactly

6:30 when I stumbled stepping off a landing barge into four feet of water. That watch was nevermore to run."

Crawford came in on a Higgins landing craft—named for its American designer—with thirty-two seasick men of the 8th Infantry and two Coast Guardsmen, the beach clouded amid dust, smoke, and fire. He watched as a barrage from the American rocket boats offshore passed uncomfortably close overhead before a smoke signal went up to call off the supporting fire.

"Packs were being fastened. There was a stream of curses as straps soaked with seawater refused to come unbuckled. Six inches of bilge, compounded of seawater and vomit, sloshed forward and aft.

". . . Even then there was time for a kid called Red, who was more green than red after holding his head in a bucket throughout the trip, to offer up an American wisecrack:

" 'That son of a bitch Higgins,' he said, 'hasn't got nothing to be proud about inventing this boat.' "

Crawford and his boatload made it safely to the seawall, where the correspondent found Roosevelt—wet, shivering, and wrapped in an Army blanket—sitting cross-legged in Indian fashion. Two aides were trying to fix a balky radio.

Crawford was happy to see the general, in part because "he had dry cigarettes, having had the forethought to wrap them in a rubber receptacle ordinarily used for quite another purpose."

Roosevelt wouldn't stay at the seawall for very long, as Crawford would recall.

"The general wondered what was going on in the little cluster of houses and barns across the meadow behind the dunes, about a mile away. I volunteered to take a look. As I stood on the dune looking, a captain called me a fool and ordered me down. He said I'd draw fire.

"I reported to the general that his men were already visible in the village.

" 'I'll take a look myself,' he said.

"He mounted the dune, stood erect, and looked. I gave the captain what I hoped was a withering glance. Shortly, though, there was a whine

35 & 36 *After their landing craft sinks, infantrymen aboard a raft make it to Utah Beach.* (National Archives)

35

36

and we all hit the dirt. For a grandfather, the general turned out to be extremely agile. The captain had the bad taste to laugh raucously."

Roosevelt was wounded slightly in those first hours, but that slowed him not in the least.

Crawford would remember how Roosevelt "made morale his business and promenaded the beach talking with soldiers. When a steel fragment nicked his hand, he wrapped the slight wound in a handkerchief, transferred his walking stick to the other hand, and hid his bloody one in his pants pocket."

Soon after Roosevelt's arrival at Utah Beach his jeep, Rough Rider, came ashore, and he got to the division command post as night fell. Still soaking wet, he took off his shoes and socks and went to sleep on a bedding roll in his quarter-ton trailer, not bothering to shed his uniform. He awoke three hours later, dried out.

Amid the light opposition at the beachhead there were some odd moments.

A soldier from C Company of the 8th Infantry ran over to his commander, Captain Robert Crisson, in great excitement.

"I have two women over here!" the GI said.

"Where?" asked the captain.

"In a ditch."

"What the hell are you doing with two women in a ditch?"

"I don't want them to get shot."

At this point a sergeant interjected, "How old are they?"

Before things could get out of hand, Captain Crisson had the women moved to a safe spot.

Despite the damage done by the mines, everything was going the Americans' way in the beach landing.

They had achieved surprise thanks to the Germans' failure to garrison the St.-Marcouf islands. The first troops ashore had no serious problems with the surf as they debarked. And the misdirected approach of the landing craft proved a fortunate error since the southerly beach sector at which the 8th Infantry arrived was only lightly defended.

The German command had considered the Cherbourg Peninsula an unsuitable spot for amphibious landings, so it had positioned only a second-rate unit at the coastal defenses. The fortifications were manned by one regiment of the 709th Division, a "static" force composed largely of reservists and non-Germans—average age thirty-six—with no great fervor for their task.

The American air bombardment at Utah had limited impact, the cloud cover forcing sixty-seven planes to return without dropping their loads and others to miss their targets. But the Navy sent effective fire against the more remote and large-caliber batteries that the ground forces would have had trouble knocking out. And the overall fury of the combined air and naval firepower stunned the German defenders in those first hours. Although they willingly blasted away with artillery, the Germans quickly surrendered when the 4th Division's troops moved in close.

And the beleaguered coastal defenders received no reinforcements. They had little communication with higher headquarters, their lines having been destroyed by the bombing or cut by the paratroopers. The commander of the German Seventh Army, General Friedrich Dollman, would not even realize until late in the day that a seaborne landing had occurred at Utah.

The American combat engineers and underwater demolition teams had an easier job than expected. One German artillery round did, however, find a target just after H-Hour. As a boatload carrying demolition units stopped in the sand at 6:35 A.M. and its ramp went down, a shell blasted the bow, killing six men. But the others scrambled into three feet of water, carrying sixty pounds of explosives apiece, and began to blow gaps.

The German beach obstacles designed to impale landing craft proved to be much sparser than anticipated, and most of the devices weren't mined. The demolition teams had planned to blow fifty-foot gaps, but they abandoned that idea in favor of a more ambitious project—clearing the entire beach on the first tide. They finished the job in about an hour. The engineers blew gaps in the seawall behind the beach and cleared minefields amid only intermittent shelling.

Though the beach landing proved relatively easy, it was only a first step. The troops had to get inland quickly, and for that they needed help from the paratroopers.

While the 82nd Airborne moved to capture Ste.-Mère-Église, the 101st set out to link up with the 4th Division by seizing the inland exits of the four causeways—dirt roads topped with asphalt running from the beaches over salt marshes into farm country.

The 502nd Regiment was assigned to capture the two northerly exits while the 506th Regiment was to take Exits 1 and 2 to the south.

Under the original plans—sent awry by the southward mislanding—the first troops ashore were to use causeways leading to Exits 3 and 4.

The best causeway—number 4—ran through the village of St. Martin-de-Varreville, past a German coastal battery and into the barracks area housing its gunners, a position designated as WXYZ.

These guns were considered a major threat. Because the area was so flat, they could fire on the troops at the beach. But paratroopers arriving at the battery site found that it had already been hit by aerial bombing.

The barracks area—a group of thick-walled stone farm buildings strung out over seven hundred yards of road—nevertheless was an obstacle to movement between Exit 4 and the airborne landing zones. Its capture was important.

The commander of the 502nd's 1st Battalion, Lieutenant Colonel Patrick Cassidy, gave the job to Staff Sergeant Harrison Summers of B Company and assigned fifteen men to go with him.

Over the next few hours Summers would emulate the World War I hero played by Gary Cooper in the 1941 movie *Sergeant York.*

"Summers at the threshold of WXYZ was a slender, quietly bashful soldier, Laughing Boy in uniform, anything but a warrior type," the military historian S.L.A. Marshall would write. "In sending him along, Cassidy was unaware that he had just given orders to a second Alvin York."

Few of the men assigned to Summers were from his own battalion, and the sergeant didn't even know his troops' names. As he deployed them for an assault, one thing was, however, perfectly clear—they had little enthusiasm for battle.

Summers decided to go it alone, hoping he'd inspire the others to follow.

First he sprinted to a small farmhouse, kicked in the door, and sprayed the inside with his submachine gun. Four Germans were killed while a dozen others escaped out a rear door to the neighboring house.

Summers looked around, but his men still lagged—they were in a roadside ditch. He charged the second house, diagonally across the street, but the Germans had fled by the time he got there.

One of Summers's troopers, Private William Burt, came into the open at this point. Burt set up his light machine gun to cover Summers, who ran to the third house, from which the defenders were firing with rifles and machine pistols. Now, accompanied by Lieutenant Elmer Brandenberger, who had just arrived to join the fray, Summers charged again. A booby trap knocked Brandenberger down, severely injuring an arm. But Summers kept going. He broke down the door, killed six Germans inside, and drove the rest out the back. Two paratroopers were wounded hustling Brandenberger away, but the remainder of Summers's men were content to stay in their ditch, supplying covering fire.

After resting a half hour the exhausted Summers encountered a captain from the 82nd Airborne who had been dropped far from his landing zone. "I'll go with you," the captain said. Seconds later the officer was shot through the heart, even before Summers could learn his name. Now Summers would again kick down a door and enter a building alone. He killed six Germans in the next house, and the others fled and surrendered to his men, who were finally creeping out of their ditches.

One of Summers's troops, shaken by the captain's death, approached the sergeant.

"Why are you doing it?" asked Private John Camien.

"I can't tell you," Summers replied.

"What about the others?"

"They don't seem to want to fight and I can't make them. So I've got to finish it."

"Okay," said Camien. "I'm with you."

The two men worked their way along five more buildings, resting between each and then swapping Camien's carbine for Turnbull's tommy gun as they took turns charging and providing covering fire. In their rear Burt blasted away with his machine gun at the firing slots in the stone walls. Another thirty Germans fell dead.

There were two more buildings to take. Summers kicked in the door of the first one, then made an astonishing discovery. Fifteen German artillerymen—oblivious of the furor all around them—were sitting at a table eating breakfast. As they started to rise, Summers shot them all down.

The last building was the biggest one in WXYZ, the two-story main barracks. By now, reinforcements for Summers's fifteen-man unit had arrived, and some of the troops who had originally come with him tried to assault the building. But snipers opened up, killing four men and wounding four others.

On one side of the barracks was a haystack and ammunition shed. Burt fired tracer rounds at the hay, setting it ablaze, and the flames quickly spread to the shed. As it caught fire, the ammunition began to explode, and thirty Germans who had been inside came streaming out. They were cut down trying to cross an open field.

At this point Staff Sergeant Roy Nickrent arrived with a bazooka. He figured that it couldn't penetrate the stone wall of that final building, so he fired at the roof, finally starting a fire after shooting off seven rounds. As the roof began to collapse, the Germans who had been shooting back from the lower level fled outside. They ran into gunfire from Summers's men, who were concealed in a hedgerow along with newly arrived troops from the 4th Division. Fifty Germans were shot down while some thirty others fled into hedgerows, then quickly surrendered.

Summers, bruised and bleeding from encounters with door frames and house walls—but otherwise unhurt—lay down in the building next to the burning barracks. He was totally drained after five hours of combat.

"I guess it's time for a smoke," he said.

A trooper asked him, "How do you feel?"

"Not very good," he answered. "It was all kind of crazy."

While Summers was performing his heroics on the road beyond Exit 4, Maxwell Taylor, the commander of the 101st Airborne, was moving with a makeshift party of troops toward Exit 1, the southernmost point off the causeways.

At first Taylor wasn't sure where he had been dropped, but when dawn arrived he recognized the church steeple of Ste.-Marie-du-Mont to the northeast, indicating he was approximately on the intended drop zone of division headquarters.

Taylor sent Colonel Thomas Sherbourne of his artillery corps westward to Hiesville with a detachment to set up the division command post while he moved out with a small group of troops.

Taylor and his men turned eastward and soon came to a farmhouse. They asked the farmer for the location of the nearest German troops and were told they were at Ste.-Marie-du-Mont.

"As I was about to go, the farmer asked me to wait a moment, went back into the house, and returned with a clip of World War I rifle ammunition," Taylor would remember. "He gave it to me with the injunction, '*Allez me tuer un Boche*' ('Go kill me a German')."

With the paratroopers widely scattered, these were moments for improvising. Taylor soon linked up with men from the 501st Regiment's 3rd

Battalion, led by Lieutenant Colonel Julian Ewell. Unsure whether the 506th Regiment was accomplishing its mission of seizing Exits 1 and 2—the regiment would in fact be delayed getting there—Taylor and Ewell's men headed for the outskirts of Exit 1.

The group was top heavy with brass. Going along on the patrol was most of the 101st Airborne's divisional staff, including the artillery commander, Brigadier General Anthony C. McAuliffe, to be immortalized six months later with his reply of "nuts" to a German surrender demand at Bastogne.

"Never in the history of military operations have so few been commanded by so many," Taylor would observe.

At about 6:00 A.M., the Taylor-Ewell contingent—numbering some eighty troops—embarked on a trek of three miles toward Pouppeville, a German strongpoint astride the road leading to Exit 1.

Moving along hedgerow-bordered fields, the men picked up a scattering of paratroopers along the way. Some of the new arrivals had come down atop the houses of Ste.-Marie-du-Mont and had managed to work their way out of the village. But two of the airborne troops who landed in the village had been captured and beaten. Another one, Private First Class Ambrose Allie, had been lined up against a wall with a second paratrooper. They were about to be summarily shot when several other paratroopers arrived and gunned down the Germans who had seized them. Now Allie joined up with Taylor's force.

By 9:00 A.M., after drawing scattered fire from outposts in ditches and fields—at one point shooting down six of seven Germans who had emerged from a dugout—the troops approached the outskirts of Pouppeville. By now there were 150 men in the group, more stragglers having been picked up.

A network of trenches ran along the landward end of the village, but the Germans had abandoned them and were in the houses within town. A

37 *Men of the 101st Airborne with villagers in Ste.-Marie-du-Mont after rounding up German prisoners.* (National Archives)

38 *Paratroopers on patrol at a churchyard in the village of St.-Marcouf.* (National Archives)

39 *A souvenir for the airborne at St.-Marcouf.* (National Archives)

37

38

39

few hours of skirmishing lay ahead, and Taylor almost became a casualty. One of his own men threw a grenade that bounced off the side of a window and landed near the division commander.

The paratroopers eventually drove the Germans from one house to another, and then only the village school remained in enemy hands. A bazooka round was fired at it—the final blow. The German commander emerged a few minutes past noon to surrender with his thirty-eight men of the 1058th Grenadier Regiment. The Americans had lost six dead and twelve wounded.

Taylor now sought to make contact with the 4th Division, whose troops could be heard about fifteen hundred yards away, coming up from the beach. The Pouppeville villagers told the Americans that the road toward the beach wasn't mined. Taylor sent Lieutenant Luther Knowlton and a sergeant down it. As they moved out, a tank headed toward them, coming around a bend in the causeway.

"German?" asked the sergeant.

"Damned if I know," said Knowlton.

"To hell with it, I'm firing," said the sergeant, and he did.

But then the two paratroopers saw an orange recognition panel displayed from behind the tank's turret hatch—it was an American Sherman. Knowlton threw an orange smoke grenade in reply. Little orange flags appeared above the lip of a roadside ditch, waved by troops of the 4th Division's 8th Infantry.

Captain George Mabry walked through the two-hundred-yard gap separating his ground forces from the airborne to shake Knowlton's hand, and they embraced.

The paratroopers and the infantry had linked up.

But once the 4th Division's troops moved beyond the beachhead, the going wasn't so easy.

Colonel Red Reeder, commander of the 12th Infantry, had approached the shore shortly after 11:00 A.M.

"The thunder from the warships was deafening," he would recall. "The acrid smell of the Navy's powder drifted into our motorboats."

Once a football player and then a coach at West Point, Reeder couldn't help but conjure a gridiron image as he touched down.

"Our boat grated on the sand. Its iron gate dropped. I felt as if I were in the kickoff of some terrible football game."

His men ran to the dunes overlooking the beach, and there they spotted small black-and-white markers with a death's head symbol and the warning MINEN!

But a more formidable foe than the mines would be the waters behind the beach, the mile-wide lake the Germans had created by flooding the lowlands.

Wading through mine-cleared areas bounded by white tapes the engineers had put up, Reeder's men held their rifles above their heads to keep them dry.

They were heavily burdened with ammunition, weapons, canteens, gas masks, and waterproof packs containing rations for three days along with a blanket and extra clothing. Some carried bundles of dynamite, wrapped in rubber and tied to long poles, to be used against pillboxes.

The Americans had been warned by the French underground that the Germans had bulldozed furrows in the water—the depth might suddenly drop from chest high to about ten feet. So the troops moved out wearing life preservers, and swimmers were paired with nonswimmers.

But Reeder would be heartened by the fortitude of his men.

"When I saw nonswimmers near me in the lake struggling to go forward, hanging on to their weapons and equipment, I knew that we would win the war."

Reeder and his troops emerged from the lake at the village of St.-Martin-de-Varreville where "ducks, angry at the intrusion, quacked along its cobblestone street."

Soon, fighting in the hedgerows would begin.

By D-Day evening, many of the infantrymen had reached their first objectives beyond the Utah beachhead, and troops had penetrated six miles inland. Casualties were much lighter than feared—197 dead in taking Utah Beach, about one-fourth the losses incurred in the raid by the German E boats at the Slapton Sands training exercises the previous April.

40 *Troops of the 8th Infantry Regiment, 4th Division—the first wave at Utah Beach—move inland.* (National Archives)

41 *A German soldier who had been defending a pillbox overlooking Les Dunes de Madeleine, behind Utah Beach.* (National Archives)

40

41

As the 4th Division advanced over the next month, General Theodore Roosevelt, Jr., would help direct operations from a mobile headquarters—a truck captured from the Germans.

On the night of July 12 his son Quentin stopped by to see him at his field camp. Quentin found his father to be tired but in good spirits, and left at about ten o'clock.

Less than two hours later, Roosevelt was dead. He had virtually challenged the Germans to shoot him, running along the dunes of Utah Beach to rally his men inland, and he had only been nicked. Now, five weeks after his D-Day heroics, he succumbed to a heart attack.

Roosevelt was buried in a temporary military cemetery in Ste.-Mère-Église. Patton and Bradley were among the pallbearers.

He would eventually lie alongside his brother Quentin, the remains of both men reinterred in the American cemetery overlooking Omaha Beach. The grave of Teddy Roosevelt, Jr., would be marked with a gold star. It was not put there because this was the resting place of a general. The star was emblematic of the nation's highest military accolade. For his actions at Utah Beach, Roosevelt was posthumously awarded the Medal of Honor. It was a citation his father had coveted, but never received, for the charge up San Juan Hill.

42 *Brigadier General Theodore Roosevelt, Jr., outside his command post in Normandy a few hours before his death from a heart attack.* (National Archives)

43 *General Roosevelt's grave at the American cemetery overlooking Omaha Beach.* (Courtesy of Maj. Gen. Albert H. Smith, Jr.)

42

THEODORE ROOSEVELT JR
BRIGADIER GENERAL U S ARMY
NEW YORK JULY 12 1944
MEDAL of HONOR

CHAPTER TEN

"Mission Accomplished . . . Many Casualties"

BLACKOUT CURTAINS were drawn. Maps and photographs were spread out on a large table in the second-floor conference room at First Army headquarters on Bryanston Square in London.

A thirty-three-year-old former football coach from rural Texas named James Earl Rudder had been summoned to the office this day in January 1944. He was about to be given what Omar Bradley would call the toughest mission ever assigned under his command.

Rudder had come up to London from Bude in Cornwall, where the lieutenant colonel had been climbing the cliffs of southern England with his men of the 2nd Ranger Battalion.

The Rangers were elite troops, their specialty the conquering of seemingly insurmountable heights—with free ropes, with ladders, even with knives securing handholds as they scampered up.

Since their arrival from the United States in December '43, Rudder's Rangers had trained hard with no idea when they would go into action or just what they would do—only that the task would be formidable.

Now, Colonel Truman Thorson, the chief of planning under Bradley, would give Rudder one of D-Day's most vital missions.

A Ranger force of 225 men was to set out during darkness in small boats, then arrive at H-Hour at a triangular cape three and a half miles west of the nearest landing sector at Omaha Beach and two miles east of the village of Grandcamp. The spot—distinctive for its inverted-V outcropping—was called Pointe du Hoc. It was an almost sheer cliff that rose one hundred feet high. Atop the cliff were positions for six 155mm howitzers that could bring devastation upon the invasion. The huge guns could hit Omaha and Utah beaches and even send shells 25,000 yards out to sea, far enough to blast the transports emptying infantrymen onto the assault craft.

The Rangers' assignment: get onto the narrow, rocky beach in front of the cliff, climb it under the sights of German defenders, rout the enemy, and destroy the big guns.

On that January day another lieutenant colonel of the Rangers, an Iowan named Max Schneider, accompanied Rudder for the unveiling of the plan.

"When we got a look at it, Max just whistled through his teeth," Rudder would recall. "He had a way of doing that. He'd made three landings already, but I was just a country boy coaching football a year and a half before. It would almost knock you out of your boots."

The road to Pointe du Hoc had begun at a muddy training ground in Tennessee called Camp Forrest. In the summer of 1943 Rudder arrived there to take over Ranger units already in training.

Richard Hubbard, who had been one of the first volunteers for the Rangers, would recall the scene:

"I was in the Rangers before Colonel Rudder came in, and living conditions were what we'd call today 'tent city'—it was horrendous. We had ten men in five-man tents with double bunk beds and mattresses that were stuffed with dirty, crummy, dusty straw. There was no attempt to make streets. It was just a mud slime hole. I guess the commander at the time felt the Rangers were supposed to live under combat conditions. It was pretty awful. Our mess hall was maybe a hundred or two hundred feet from the latrine. There was just a tarpaulin surrounding an open-trench latrine area. And they cooked in a field kitchen. The flies from the latrines were getting in our food. The first week there everybody in the camp had screaming dysentery.

"When Rudder came in, one of the first things he did was tell them, 'By God, we're gonna move that kitchen.'

"And the fellas were running around with makeshift uniforms, and he said he was gonna have none of that crap, we were going to have well-repaired shoes and uniforms. We were Class A soldiers, by God, we're gonna look like it.

"We all liked him pretty much—he got us out of that mudhole and eventually got us into barracks. We were convinced that he was on our side."

44 *The cliffs of Pointe du Hoc.* (National Archives)

44

Ralph Goranson—another of the Rangers and later the commander of C Company—found himself respecting the new leader from night one.

"We had a speed march at Camp Forrest. You do seven miles in one hour, which is part fast walking and part low-speed double time with full gear. The other leaders we had would train us from a jeep. Rudder was right out there with the troops. We knew we had a leader."

Rudder had graduated in 1932 from Texas A & M, where he played center on the football team, and then received a commission as a second lieutenant in the Army reserve. He spent the next six years teaching and coaching football at Brady High School in Texas, then coached at John Tarleton College in Stephenville, Texas. He seemed destined for a comfortable, if obscure life. Then the nation mobilized, and he was called up from the reserves, reporting for active duty in 1941 at Fort Sam Houston, Texas.

Two years later Rudder had risen to major and was assigned to select and train men for some of the most hazardous assignments the Army could devise.

Upon arriving in Britain the Rangers embarked on five months of grueling exercises, scaling cliffs at Swanage and Bude in southern England and heights on the Isle of Wight, sometimes making three climbs a day. Meanwhile, P-38 fighters were taking reconnaissance photos of Pointe du Hoc.

Among those who would be leading the Rangers up the cliff was a twenty-four-year-old first lieutenant from Margate City, New Jersey, named Ted Lapres, Jr.

Lapres shouldn't have even been in the Rangers since he was color blind, unable to pass the standard Army test requiring a recruit to distinguish colored numbers on a series of pages.

But he'd surmounted that obstacle.

"A sergeant had told me that the guy who's giving the test wasn't paying attention, he's just flipping pages. So if I didn't see a number, I made up a number—and I passed the test."

Lapres joined the Rangers at Camp Forrest, and in May '44 he'd learn what all that climbing had been a prelude to.

"It was probably a month before the invasion. Colonel Rudder and several of the officers of the battalion told us what the mission would be. They had pictures of the cliffs and where the guns were. My boat was supposed to go up right near the observation point and take out the guns closest to that. The muzzles were twenty to thirty feet from where we were supposed to climb up. It seemed like the blasts would knock you back off the cliff. I thought that not many of us would come out alive."

Richard Hubbard would recall trepidation about one particular element of the attack plan.

"We'd been trained to infiltrate behind lines and we thought we'd be landed in dark. And then they told us it was gonna be in daylight. We had a rather sinking feeling about that."

But Hubbard and the others were confident they could do the job.

"There never was a moment in anyone's mind that I ever talked to that we wouldn't be able to do what we trained to do. We just knew it was an isolated spot on the beach, it was a cliff, it would not be heavily defended—why would you defend a cliff that no one's gonna be able to get up anyway? We had all the confidence in the world that we could accomplish our mission.

"We never did look at it as a suicide mission. But we had never been in combat before. We might have just been too damn stupid to understand what the danger really was."

The Pointe du Hoc gun emplacements were hit three times by medium bombers of the United States Ninth Air Force as D-Day grew near. Hours before the Rangers were to arrive, British heavy bombers included the cliff in their strikes along the entire invasion front. And at dawn the battleship *Texas* fired 250 fourteen-inch shells at the Pointe while American bombers made a final sweep.

The last-minute bombardment might keep the German soldiers atop Pointe du Hoc holed up in their trenches, but the Allied planners hadn't expected the raids to take out the big guns, two of which had evidently been casemated. Only a ground force could do the job for sure—if it got to the top of the cliff.

To accomplish the mission the Rangers needed more than raw courage. They looked to technical wizardry—a series of ropelike devices that would be catapulted from their boats to the clifftop via rocket fire. Grapnels (six-inch-long shafts with petallike prongs) would catch on the cliff heights—or so the Rangers hoped—and then they would scamper up on the ropes and knock out the surprised German defenders.

The plan called for Companies D, E, and F of the 2nd Ranger Battalion—225 men—to head for the Pointe, arriving in an assault wave of ten British-made landing craft called LCAs accompanied by four DUKWs (amphibious trucks known as "ducks") and two LCA supply boats.

Each assault boat would be equipped with three pairs of rocket mounts wired so they could be fired in twos from a control point at the stern. One pair of rockets carried plain three-quarter-inch ropes. Another pair was attached to rope of the same size fitted with toggles, small wooden crossbars that could be inserted in a cliff space at one-foot intervals. The third pair was connected to light rope-ladders with rungs every two feet.

In addition, each boat carried a pair of small hand-projector rockets attached to plain ropes that could be carried ashore and fired from the beachhead itself.

The boats also had extension ladders for climbing the cliff—112 feet of tubular steel assembled in advance in sixteen-foot lengths that could be attached to each other.

The four DUKWs were equipped with donations from the London Fire Department—one-hundred-foot ladders. Atop each of the four ladders was something that no fireman had ever needed to use—a brace containing a pair of British-made Vickers machine guns. Staff sergeants, their helmets painted bluish gray to blend in with the waters behind them, would be perched atop the ladders, blazing away—a machine gun in each hand—to cover the Rangers as they went up the cliff.

During the many weeks of training, the ladders had become a most sensitive piece of equipment.

"They were supposedly a secret weapon," remembers Bill Stivison, one of the sergeants assigned to ride atop them in the assault. "We had nets put over the ladders to keep them camouflaged. When we'd go through town, people thought they were guns or something."

Companies E and F were to assault the east side of the Pointe, and Company D was to scale the west side. The first objective was to destroy the 155mm howitzers and fortifications. The next priority would be seizure of the coastal road between Grandcamp and Vierville, the village behind the westernmost sector of Omaha Beach.

The men were to go ashore at 6:30 A.M., and when they arrived, eight other Ranger companies—six from the 5th Ranger Battalion and Companies A and B from the 2nd Ranger Battalion—would be poised in landing craft, waiting for a signal.

If the first three Ranger companies succeeded in reaching the top of

Pointe du Hoc, they were to fire off two flares shot by 60mm mortars. Once the remainder of the Ranger force spotted the flares, those men would head for the Pointe and go up the cliffs as well. If no flares were fired by 7:00 A.M., the Rangers offshore would conclude that the assault at Pointe du Hoc had failed. They would then head eastward to Omaha Beach, go ashore at Vierville, then make their way overland to the Pointe along with troops from the 29th Division.

On the eve of D-Day a pair of British transports, the *Amsterdam* and the *Ben Machree*, carried the first-wave Ranger force toward the Pointe. Private Jake Richards decided he'd like a memento of the operation, so he took out a dollar bill and asked his fellow Rangers to sign it. Herman Stein became involved in a long chess game with his fellow Tech. 5, Preacher Davis. Finally, it was time for a few hours of sleep.

At 2:00 A.M. the Rangers were awakened for a flapjack breakfast, and, as Lieutenant G. K. Hodenfield of the servicemen's newspaper *Stars and Stripes* would recall, wisecracks flew on how "the condemned men ate a hearty meal."

Two hours later a command sounded over the transports' loudspeakers: "Rangers, man your craft."

"All aboard for Hoboken ferry—leaving in five minutes," remarked one Ranger.

The men were lowered into their assault craft some ten miles from shore. And then, everything began to go wrong.

The LCAs, designed with a shallow draft, hardly seemed a match for the four-foot chop. Eight miles from shore an assault craft carrying Captain Harold Slater and two dozen men of D Company was swamped by the waves. Four Rangers drowned. Rescue boats picked up the others after they'd bobbed in the water for two hours.

Ten minutes after Slater's craft foundered, one of the supply boats sank. Only one Ranger survived. The other supply boat was battered by the seas as well, and the crewmen threw packs belonging to D and E companies overboard in order to stay afloat.

The nine remaining assault craft weathered the seas, but their pumps became overwhelmed, forcing the Rangers to bail water with their helmets. The men were cold and soaked on their two-and-a-half-hour trip in, but fortunate in one way: only a few became seasick.

There was, however, plenty of trouble to come.

As they approached the Normandy coast, the Rangers could see the *Texas* firing shell after shell in the half-light, the sound of the blasts reaching them long after they spotted the comforting tongues of flame from the gun muzzles.

But they were not heading toward the strongpoint that was taking a beating from the *Texas*. Disoriented by the haze, the fifteen-knot winds and the strong current, the *Fairmile*, a British escort vessel leading the Rangers, had mistaken Pointe de la Percée—three miles to the east—for Pointe du Hoc.

The assault craft were almost at the wrong cliff when Colonel Rudder realized what was happening. He managed to turn the boats around, and now the Rangers headed westward along the coast toward their destination.

The navigational error was a costly one.

The element of surprise had been lost. Instead of arriving head-on, the Rangers were proceeding parallel to the shoreline—a few hundred yards off the coast—amid sporadic German fire from strongpoints along the stretch between Pointe de la Percée and Pointe du Hoc.

And the assault force would now be late. The first LCAs did not arrive at the beach in front of Pointe du Hoc until 7:08 A.M., thirty-eight minutes behind schedule.

The eight Ranger companies waiting offshore for the flare signaling a successful mission had seen nothing by the 7:00 A.M. deadline. They stood by for an extra ten minutes, then received the code word "Tilt" by radio, ordering them to follow their alternate plan. They would assault Omaha Beach, then try to get to the Pointe via land instead of coming in directly behind the first Ranger wave. Colonel Rudder's three companies would be fighting in the early morning on their own.

And the plan of attack had to be changed. Because the double column of nine LCAs was arriving from the east instead of coming straight in across the Channel, D Company would not be able to swing out of formation in time to reach the west side of the cliff while E and F companies were climbing up the east side. All three companies would be bunched together at the eastern face.

As they approached Pointe du Hoc, the Rangers faced a final consequence of their late arrival. The *Texas* had ceased firing, as prearranged, just before H-Hour—6:30 A.M. So the Germans atop the cliff had forty minutes to recover from the bombardment they had been catching.

The United States destroyer *Satterlee* and the British destroyer *Talybont* did supply last-minute fire support, but German troops were moving around on the cliff's edge as the Ranger boats arrived, and they began sending small-arms and automatic fire down on the landing craft.

The Rangers' misdirected approach was especially hazardous for the four DUKWs carrying the fire-department ladders.

Problems were foreseen for the seven-man crews even before these amphibious craft set out. They were slow—able to make only five knots—so they provided especially easy targets, even with the element of surprise, which they decidedly had lost. And it was questionable whether the ladders—to be lifted by hydraulic gears—could ever be stabilized. If they were out of alignment as they rose up, they would jam. So each DUKW had a pair of men flanking its ladder to adjust the center line.

As these boats approached the beach below Pointe du Hoc, the DUKW from E Company was suddenly dead in the water.

One of its Ranger crewmen was twenty-year-old Private First Class Richard Hubbard. He would have vivid memories of the moment.

"The driver, with a look of amazement on his face, turned to us and said, 'The engine quit.'

"Like big dumb asses, we said, 'Well, start it again.'

"But we'd taken machine gun bullets to the hood. We couldn't get out and raise the hood because it was waterproofed—it was sealed. So we just slowly drifted in the water and rotated around and around in a circle in the tide and the eddies, and we came under heavy machine-gun fire. They realized they had stopped us and so they put concentrated fire on us."

One of the Rangers on the DUKW was killed, Hubbard was hit in the back by shell fragments, and another man, Duncan Daugherty, was shot in the lung.

For Hubbard and the other survivors, desperate hours lay ahead.

"We eventually had to get out of the vehicle and get into the water, and we kept this dead floating vehicle between us and the fire that was coming from the shore. We used it as a barricade."

But when the men plunged into the water, there was more trouble.

"We had a safety belt—a flotation system—that was around our waist, not a Mae West. When we jumped into the water and tried to inflate these things with carbon-dioxide capsules, all we got was a bunch of bubbles came up. All the flotation devices had been perforated by the shell fragments—they were useless."

To make matters worse, Hubbard and the others were heavily burdened.

"Myself and another fellow, we jumped into the water with all of our ammunition still strapped to us. We had bandoliers of ammunition and an ammunition belt and a grenade bag. We were wondering why in the hell we were having so much trouble swimming, and we realized we were starting to swim with forty-five or fifty pounds of ammunition. We dumped that and we treaded water."

For at least an hour and a half, the Rangers drifted eastward toward Omaha Beach with their useless DUKW being carried by the tide. Eventually, a 29th Division landing craft that was returning from the beach picked them up.

Suffering from exposure, the Rangers were taken to a transport ship and then returned to England. Hubbard would make it to France a week later and would fight with the Rangers until the end of the war. But for him, D-Day was over.

The nine assault boats and the remaining three DUKWs with the high ladders made it to the edge of the thirty-yard-wide rocky strip of beach at Pointe du Hoc, encountering automatic weapons fire from the left flank as they arrived.

The lead boat was carrying Lieutenant Ted Lapres and his men from E Company. As it touched down, all six rope-bearing rockets were fired, but the ropes fell short of the cliff edge—they had been so thoroughly soaked on the trip in that they were too heavy to make the top.

As the Rangers of E Company crossed the beach, "potato-masher" grenades causing heavy concussions were thrown down at them, wounding two men.

With their boat rockets proving useless, Lapres's men had to rely on the hand-held rockets. The first one was fired fifteen yards from the cliff, and it succeeded in sending a hand line to the top. Private First Class Harry Roberts started up. He got about twenty-five feet above the beach, but then the rope slipped or was cut, and he slithered down. A second hand rocket was fired, and the grapnel on that one also caught the clifftop. Roberts tried again and this time made it to the top in forty seconds. Five men quickly went up behind him.

At the rear of the assault force came the three boats of F Company, commanded by Captain Otto Masny. In the last of these boats was twenty-three-year-old Herman Stein.

Stein watched as many of the waterlogged ropes of the preceding boats failed to catch the top of the Pointe, in part because they were being fired too far from the cliff.

"The goddamned sailors wanted to get the hell out of there and leave, so they were shooting them off when they felt like it," Stein would remember.

"Captain Masny did a great job. I was in that boat with him and Lieutenant Dick Wintz, and we saw all the ropes going up and they were all falling short, dropping into the water or onto the beach. Masny says, 'Get in there and tell that goddamned guy'—there were English sailors in charge of the boat—'not to send the rockets off till we give the word.'

"Dick Wintz went up and he held a gun to the guy's head and he says, 'Don't you shoot those things off till we say to shoot. Don't push that button.'

"We hit the shore before that guy hit that button. All our ropes went up on the top."

Stein would have preferred a single rope to a ladder rope, but soon he had no choice—and then came an embarrassing moment.

"I was looking for a single rope because I was one of the better climbers. And I got to a ladder rope, and Masny says, 'Get up that rope, son, get up that rope.' I had to go up the damn ladder rope. I got about halfway up and my Mae West blew up on me and almost pushed me off the cliff. I had knocked the thing that blew it up. It was just one of those stupid things. I finally realized what was happening and I deflated it."

F Company went up along a section of the cliff shielded from the German gunners.

"They had a machine gun on the far left side," Stein would recall. "They could fire on most of the guys, but we were in a nice little nook that they couldn't get the gun in to, so actually we didn't get any fire at all."

Fifteen Rangers had been cut down by German fire—most of it from the left flank—as they tried to cross the beach. But within about a half hour, some 190 men were atop the cliff.

The three DUKWs that survived the run-in could, however, do little, since the craters left by the aerial and naval bombardment frustrated attempts to anchor them on the beach. There wasn't much beachhead left, anyway, to set the DUKWs down upon. Because the Rangers had been delayed in arriving, the tide was starting to come in.

"There were just a lot of pockmarks on the beach," remembers Bill Stivison, the sergeant assigned to ride atop F Company's ladder, wielding twin machine guns.

His DUKW remained in the water, but he decided to give it a try anyway.

"I told John Gilhooly, my ladder operator, 'Run me up, I'll see how high I can get.' He ran me up about sixty feet. But with the choppy waters in the Channel, I was weaving. I was going back and forth so much, even if I had seen any targets, it wouldn't have done any good and the chances are I would have hit some of my own people. Finally, I said, 'John, take me back down, I'm not doing any good here.' So he brought me back down."

When the Rangers reached the cliff top, they encountered a landscape nothing like the scene they had studied in all those aerial photos. The bombing and naval shelling had created a wasteland—craters and mounds of wreckage were everywhere and the landmarks they expected to find had been obliterated.

But there was a much bigger surprise awaiting the men. When the Rangers reached their prize, the 155mm battery, they found the open gun positions and the casemates heavily damaged by bombing—but no sign of the howitzers themselves.

"When I got topside and found the guns weren't there, I thought the war was practically won," Ted Lapres would recall.

But could the guns be elsewhere, and still a menace?

The Rangers moved out, and the 2nd platoon of D Company set up a roadblock along a curve on the coastal road running behind the cliffs, hoping to cut off any German troops headed toward Omaha Beach from Grandcamp.

At 8:00 A.M., First Sergeant Leonard Lomell and Staff Sergeant Jack Kuhn of D Company went out on patrol to see if the big guns might be somewhere in the area.

They hadn't spotted anything in the surrounding fields so they moved

45 *One of the rope ladders used by the Rangers.* (National Archives)

45

to the south along a sunken lane bordered by hedgerows. Some two hundred yards down the path, they stopped.

"I just happened to look over a hedgerow," Lomell remembers. "It was pure luck. Lo and behold, there in a swale, a little valley, about ten, twenty yards away, were five 155mm coastal guns, neatly camouflaged with rope netting, all their ammunition in readiness, and not a soul in position at that moment. The guns were aimed at Utah Beach—they were ready to be fired."

They could also have been turned to blast the troops arriving at Omaha Beach.

Although Pointe du Hoc and the surrounding area had been heavily bombed, Lomell would remember how "there was not one shell crater near those guns—that's how cleverly they were positioned."

As Lomell looked over the hedgerow, he spotted some seventy-five to a hundred German soldiers about a hundred yards away.

"This officer was standing in a vehicle talking to them—we couldn't hear them. I don't think they knew that the Rangers climbed the cliffs, the way they were acting. It was their intention to come back to the guns, I'm sure."

Lomell went over the hedgerow and approached the howitzers as Kuhn covered him. If the Germans were to come forward while Lomell was concentrating on destroying the guns and he didn't see them, Kuhn would fire. That would alert Lomell and he would get away.

But the Germans never saw the two sergeants. Lomell set off thermite grenades in the traversing mechanisms for two of the guns, melting the gears, and smashed the sights of all five guns with the butt of his submachine gun as Kuhn covered him. Then he and Kuhn ran back to their roadblock to get more grenades. They returned within five minutes, each with a shirtfull, and Lomell set off the grenades in the traversing mechanisms he hadn't previously destroyed.

Lomell was crawling back over the hedgerow when "the whole place blew up. I went bounding down the rest of the hedgerow, into the road. Jack was tumbling down too. We couldn't hear each other because it was such a tremendous explosion. We ran like scared rabbits back to the roadblock. We didn't know if the end of the world had happened. We thought it was a short round from the *Texas,* which was our support fire."

An E Company patrol, led by Sergeant Frank Rupinski, had blown up the ammunition storage area for the howitzers, perhaps within fifty yards of where they had been hidden.

Soon, a runner was sent to Colonel Rudder's headquarters position informing him that the guns had been destroyed. (The supposed sixth gun may never have existed.)

The howitzers had evidently never been put into position atop Pointe du Hoc because of the heavy Allied bombing. They could still have been used with devastating effect from their spot behind the cliffs, but now they had been disabled before their crews could reach them.

Much hard fighting still lay ahead at the Pointe as German troops—operating from tunnels impervious to bombardment—sniped at the Rangers and later staged a series of counterattacks.

In the first moments after the cliff was scaled, Tech. 5 Herman Stein was paired on patrol with Private Jake Richards, the Ranger who had passed around that dollar bill for souvenir signatures on their transport ship hours earlier. Stein didn't have long to wait before going into action.

"As soon as I got up the top, Bob Youso was ahead of me. A kid who was with him got about sixty feet out, and he got a burst of machine-gun fire from the left side and he got killed. Youso yelled, 'Get down,' so we started to crawl. I had to wait for Jake to come up, I was assistant gunner to him. He had the Browning Automatic Rifle.

"We were checking things out and we thought we saw our guys, and he gave me the glasses and said, 'Check that.'

"I was on the edge of the pothole looking, and I said, 'Jeez, they do look like our guys.'

"And he said, 'Give me the glasses back, let me look at them again.'

"I said to him, 'Rich, you're out there like a sore thumb. You better get your ass down.' I no sooner said that than he got shot right through the neck. That was the end of him."

In another early encounter, Lieutenant Jake Hill of F Company used some choice language to taunt the Germans into showing themselves.

Trying to flush out a machine-gun emplacement, Hill had taken cover behind an embankment. Then he stood up to look at the position and shouted, "You couldn't hit a bull in the ass with a bass fiddle!"

That succeeding in drawing fire. Hill dropped back, then tossed a grenade that wiped out the machine-gunner.

A few minutes later, Lieutenant Lapres came down the road with a patrol from E Company. Hill's outwitting the Germans may have kept Lapres and his men from being ambushed.

There was plenty of action as well at a vantage point south of Rudder's command post. Sergeant Bill Petty and the nine men with him could see German troops—disorganized and possibly fleeing from the Omaha area—moving west along a country road toward Grandcamp. Petty had been turned down twice by Rudder when he tried to join the Rangers at Camp Forrest—he was a pale youngster from rural Georgia with no upper teeth—but he had persisted and finally won the commander over. Now, surprising the Germans with fire from his Browning Automatic Rifle, he cut down thirty of them during the afternoon.

But the Rangers were still fighting alone through the day, and they had little success communicating with the troops at Omaha Beach.

In the early afternoon Rudder sent out messages via radio and carrier pigeon: "Located Pointe du Hoc—mission accomplished—need ammunition and reinforcements—many casualties."

At 3:00 P.M. the 116th Infantry of the 29th Division replied, saying it had received a message but could not decipher it. About the same time a brief response came from General Huebner, the commander of the 1st Division: "No reinforcements available."

By nightfall more than one third of the two hundred Rangers who had arrived at Pointe du Hoc were casualties, among them Colonel Rudder. A shell—Rudder believed it came from a United States Navy ship—had killed an artillery captain and a Navy lieutenant acting as a spotter for the naval guns, and it knocked Rudder over, a piece of concrete from flying debris lodging in his arm. Then, while trying to direct fire, he had been shot in the left leg, a clean wound that entered and exited above the knee.

Captain Walter Block of Chicago, the battalion medical officer—a pediatrician in prewar days—found a subterranean chamber with sixteen bunks that had been abandoned by the Germans and began to work on the wounded, a flickering candle and a flashlight alongside him.

The Germans still held an antiaircraft position on the west flank of the Pointe as night came, and the Rangers were running low on ammunition, particularly grenades and mortar shells. A few Rangers who had lost their rifles were using German weapons, and the men at Rudder's command post also armed themselves with German "potato-masher" grenades.

The Germans would stage three counterattacks during the night, preceded by whistles and shouts apparently designed to frighten the Rangers.

By the following day Rudder was left with only ninety men able to bear arms, and, as Ted Lapres would recall, "We were pinned back close to the cliff and holding on for dear life." But with help from strong naval fire, the Rangers stayed put. That afternoon two boats arrived with food, ammunition, and a platoon of reinforcements.

On D-Day plus two the beleaguered force was finally relieved by fellow Rangers and units of the 29th Division arriving overland from Omaha Beach.

Even that had its harrowing moments. The Rangers had anchored an American flag to the cliff with rocks, but approaching American tank crews began firing, thinking the Rangers had been wiped out. Rudder waved the flag on a stick. The friendly fire ceased.

The flag still flew.

46 *The flag flies over Pointe du Hoc as the Rangers round up German prisoners.* (National Archives)

47 *The view from the top of the cliffs, ten years after D-Day.* (National Archives)

CHAPTER ELEVEN

"The Thin Wet Line of Khaki"

IT STRETCHED FOR seven thousand yards—a shoreline curving in a slight crescent—and behind it bluffs rose to 175 feet, dominating the landscape, then merging into cliffs at each end of the beachhead.

Lying in the surf before it were countless obstacles and mines. In the heights above it, a crack German division stood poised to defend Hitler's Atlantic Wall.

The American troops assaulting it would remember the place as "Bloody Omaha."

Spilling out of landing craft freezing, soaked and seasick, an assault force of 34,000 men hit Omaha Beach on D-Day—in Omar Bradley's words, "the thin wet line of khaki that dragged itself ashore."

The Allied brass had no fancy maneuvers in mind for these troops. Confronting the most heavily defended coastal sector in Normandy, they were sent in on a frontal attack evoking the image of the World War I Western front.

The men were expected to seize the beach, move up through the bluffs along five draws—or narrow roads—then occupy the villages of Vierville, St.-Laurent and Colleville, driving out the Germans as they penetrated inland. By nightfall, according to the plans drawn up in London, these troops would be occupying a coastal strip five to six miles deep.

The sectors on the right flank at Omaha Beach were assigned to two regiments of the 29th Division, its men untested by combat. They were under the overall command of the 1st Division, which was given the task of seizing the left flank. The "Big Red One" had made two previous beach assaults—at Arzew, Algeria, in November 1942, and Sicily in July 1943—meeting little opposition each time.

The troops would come ashore in assault sections—each landing craft generally holding an officer and thirty-one men—with a small but varied arsenal: rifles, bazookas, mortars, flamethrowers, and Browning automatic rifles as well as wire-cutters and explosives.

In the forty minutes preceding the touchdown of the first boats, the German fortifications would be drenched by an aerial and seaborne bombardment. B-24 heavy bombers were to saturate the coast, and a naval task force boasting the fourteen-inch guns of the battleships *Texas* and *Arkansas* would hurl shell after shell into the bluffs.

Earlier in the spring, Bradley had dismissed fears of huge casualties, calling such talk "tommyrot." The bombardment would soften up the German defenses—or so the GIs had been told.

"When we were briefed for the landing, they said there was a regiment of old Germans and Hungarians—something like that—defending the beach," recalls Isadore Naiman. "None of us were worried about anything."

Naiman had a formidable assignment for the morning of D-Day. The twenty-two-year-old sergeant from Cleveland was to arrive with B Company of the 112th Engineers at low tide, carrying blocks of TNT, then help blast paths through the beach obstacles Rommel had been so obsessed with.

"There were dragon's teeth—railroad ties crossed to a point—and there were floating mines," Naiman would remember. "If those little ships came in at high tide, they're going to hit that, they'd be torn right up."

Naiman had arrived overseas early in '42—among the first American troops in the British Isles—and he'd made numerous dry runs in exercises off Slapton Sands. He knew what was expected of him.

But as his boat approached the shore, he was stunned.

"Fifty yards to our left, a landing craft got hit by a shell. You could see the thing blow up—a yellow flash. The first thing we knew, these bodies were floating in the Channel, and they blew up like balloons.

"And there was live fire coming toward us. The whole picture changed. That started you thinking—it's not so easy."

All along the beach the 1,450 troops arriving in the first wave at 6:30 A.M. were in for the same sort of shock.

48 *Beach obstacles—poles with Teller mines atop them—in the waters off Grandcamp, west of Omaha Beach.* (National Archives)

49 *A mined obstacle at low tide.* (National Archives)

48

While German intelligence could never learn whether the invasion would come at Normandy or the Pas de Calais, the Omaha sector had been seen as a prime spot for an assault.

Since early April, Rommel's forces had been planting an elaborate system of beach obstacles to ensnarl landing craft.

Naiman and his fellow combat engineers had a formidable array of deadly devices to confront. Some 250 yards out from the high-water line they would find a band of gatelike structures of reinforced iron frames with waterproof Teller mines lashed to their uprights; a little farther toward the beach lay a band of heavy logs, their mine-tipped ends angled seaward; finally, hedgehogs, or crossed steel rails, whose ends could rip the bottoms of small boats.

If a landing craft wasn't wrecked by a pointed log or a mine—if an infantryman wasn't hit by the gunners in the bluffs just as the ramp of his boat went down—there were more hazards ahead.

After the GI reached the bank of shingle, or small stones, on the edge of the tidal sands, he still had to cross a shelf of beach flat to reach the draws in the bluffs. Along most of Omaha Beach the Germans had placed a row of concertina wire just landward of the shingle. At the western end of the beach, wire was laced atop a four-to-twelve-foot-high seawall of stone masonry and wood fronting the shelf.

The beach flat, dotted with large patches of marsh and high grass, and the bluff slopes were festooned with all sorts of booby traps: buttercup mines, mustard-pot mines, and, in a devilish flourish, devices called fougasses—charges of TNT covered by rock and set off by trip wire.

The Germans had set up strongpoints, most of them near the entrances to the draws, enabling them to bring direct fire onto the beachhead from the bluffs and cliffs. Each of the points was a complex system of pillboxes, gun casemates, open positions for light guns, and firing trenches. Connected with each other by deep tunnels, the firing positions were protected by minefields and barbed wire.

The Allies had expected to find these fortifications manned by only eight hundred to a thousand troops from the 726th Infantry Regiment, a strictly defensive unit with little mobility. As many as fifty percent of its men were believed to be non-Germans—mostly Poles or Russians—with a dubious willingness to risk all for the Third Reich.

But the American forces would also come up against a regiment of the

352nd Division. The full-attack infantry outfit, with a core of Russian-front veterans, had not been spotted by Allied intelligence until shortly before D-Day even though it had been in place for almost three months, having moved to the coast from the St.-Lô area twenty miles inland.

Beyond everything the Germans could throw at them, the American troops would be plagued by something nobody could control—the vagaries of weather.

The storm that had caused a twenty-four-hour postponement of D-Day had indeed abated, but the Channel remained choppy, the skies overcast.

The turbulent waters of the Bay of the Seine would deprive the infantry of support from the innovative Duplex Drive amphibious tanks the Allied planners had pinned such great hopes upon.

On his first inspection trip after arriving in England, Eisenhower drove one of the tanks around a British lake and was immediately impressed. Drawing on plans sent from Britain, the tanks were put into production in Ohio, then shipped overseas.

But not all of the brass was so sure the DDs could swim through the Channel waters. J. Lawton Collins, the commander of the VII Corps, overseeing the Utah Beach assault, took a look at the tanks when they were launched from Navy boats during an exercise and felt there was "too small a margin for safety" when the seas would be rough. Major General Charles Corlett—like Collins a veteran of amphibious attacks in the Pacific—also thought the DDs were potentially too unstable. He would later claim that warnings he presented to Eisenhower and Bradley were brushed aside.

The decision was made to employ the tanks, but their crews could not help feeling rather apprehensive. They were supplied with air lungs holding seven minutes' worth of oxygen, large knives to cut through the canvas collars if a quick escape were necessary, Mae West life vests, and rubber rafts. And Bradley had ordered that Army officers, rather than Navy men, should decide at what point offshore the tanks would be launched from the vessels carrying them.

As H-Hour approached, LSTs moved toward Omaha's westernmost sectors of Dog Green and Dog White—ahead of the 29th Division's first waves of infantry—with thirty-two DDs of the 743rd Tank Battalion on their decks. But the armor would not be sent into the waters. The battalion commander, Captain Ned Elder, who had been an instructor at the DD tank training school, and Naval Lieutenant Dean Rockwell, who had written a report expressing fears about the tanks' seaworthiness, decided the surf was too strong to risk launching them.

Those DDs would later be brought ashore by their carriers and would eventually supply vital firepower. But the 29th Division troops hitting the right flank of the beach at 6:30 A.M. would not get the immediate tank backing they had expected.

The combat engineers, meanwhile, were hard pressed to clear beach obstacles for the infantry in the half hour they had been given to do the job.

Weighed down by their equipment and explosives, the demolition units had little prospect of eluding the German gunners. The D-Day casualties for a special Army-Navy engineer task force at Omaha would exceed forty percent, most of the dead and wounded cut down during the first half hour.

And many of the engineer boats landed too far east, disrupting their assignments. As late as 8:30 A.M., an officer in the Dog White sector noticed two engineers carrying a heavy box of explosives along the beach. They stopped for a breather, and one of men, wiping the perspiration from his face, asked: "Where are we? We are supposed to blow something up near Vierville."

They picked their box up again and trudged westward toward the Vierville draw—where some of the morning's most intense fire was being brought upon the infantry.

Only six complete gaps could be blown through the obstacles on the first rising tide (low tide had come at 5:25 A.M.)—just two in the sectors of the 29th Division, the other four all confined to the 1st Division's Easy Red zone.

And the aerial and naval bombardment had provided little support in the early hours.

The Eighth Air Force sent 446 Liberator heavy bombers over the Omaha coast in a twenty-minute period beginning at 5:55 A.M. But the bombardiers were frustrated by the overcast—scattered clouds from three thousand to seven thousand feet above the Channel, even denser cover inland. Forced to operate with instruments, the planes were ordered to delay their bomb release by as much as thirty seconds to avoid accidentally hitting the troops in the landing craft. Only 329 planes were able to release their loads, and the thirteen thousand bombs dropped over Omaha would miss the Germans' coastal defenses altogether, instead falling as much as three miles inland. Many of the casualties were cows.

Some bombers never even crossed the Channel.

For Dick Wood, a radio operator and gunner with the 486th Bomb Group—his target the railroad yards at Caen in the British sector—there was a flush of excitement, but then frustrating hours in the skies over England.

"We were awakened real early, around two o'clock. They announced, 'The invasion is on, this is what you've been waiting for.' That made everybody gung ho: there was a big cheer.

"Then we sat around waiting for the signal to go. It seemed like forever before we got off. It was probably six o'clock, six-thirty. Then we climbed through the soup and were looking for the formation. We were flying up there by our lonesome. We never did find any other planes to form on. You're not going to go over there by yourself, that's for sure. Clouds all around, it was awful. We never did find the formation."

Wood's plane returned to his base at Sudbury, but there would be a second attempt hours later.

"In the afternoon, basically the same story, although we did find the formation that time, but it was having a battle with the clouds. Just about the time they were deciding, well, maybe we'll cross the Channel anyway, the whole mission was recalled.

"Frustration—put that in all caps."

The Omaha naval bombardment, which began at 5:50 A.M., had limited impact in the early moments of the invasion. Although many German rocket pits were knocked out, most of the coastal fortifications were well concealed from observation at sea.

And the infantrymen weren't getting artillery support either.

The 111th Field Artillery Battalion had an especially disastrous time of it. Its forward parties—including the commanding officer, Lieutenant Colonel Thornton Mullins—arrived between 7:30 and 8:30 in front of the Les Moulins draw. They found troops immobilized in front of the draw and were themselves met by heavy fire. Mullins realized that the DUKWs carrying his howitzers, scheduled to come in between 8:00 and 9:00 A.M., wouldn't be able to make it ashore. But his radios were disabled so he couldn't get a message to the boats.

"To hell with our artillery mission," Mullins told his men, "we've got to be infantrymen now." Although twice wounded, he began to organize small groups and led a tank forward, directing its fire against a German position.

Then Mullins started toward another tank along an exposed section of beach. A sniper killed him.

The thirteen DUKWs carrying Mullins's howitzers were soon launched from LCTs. Five of them swamped before they got a half mile toward shore and four more were lost while circling before their run-in. None of the thirteen would make it onto the beach. And only a single howitzer from the 111th—that one transferred to a rhino-ferry craft—would ever be fired.

The rough seas—northwest winds of ten to eighteen knots churned waves as high as six feet—had already taken their toll on the boats carrying the infantrymen. At least 10 of the 180 to 200 landing craft in the first assault group foundered on the three-to-four-hour run-in from the transport ships, a trip of ten to twelve miles. (Nearly all the men were rescued, but some spent hours in the water.)

Most of the infantrymen who made it to the beach were miserably seasick by the time they got there. Adding to their woes, a strong eastward current drove many of the boats coming in during the first hour far from their intended landing sectors. The current at Omaha was normally almost 2.7 knots some five miles offshore, but with the strong winds it was even faster the morning of D-Day. Some landing craft arrived at least a thousand yards too far to the east, and boats from the 29th Division became mixed with boats from the 1st Division. So as the troops hit the beach, they were not only shocked by the incoming fire, but confused—the landmarks in front of them, already obscured by the smoke of battle, were in many cases nowhere on their maps.

Of the eight companies in the H-Hour assault wave—four from the 29th Division and four from the 1st Division—only L Company of the 1st Division's 16th Infantry was ready to operate as a unit after crossing the beach. And that company had arrived thirty minutes late, had mislanded to the east of its assigned sector, and had lost 42 of some 170 men. The remnants had, however, arrived at a portion of the beach where the tidal flat almost reached a steep bluff, giving the men some protection.

One of the first units to hit the beach was A Company, 116th Infantry, 29th Division. The troops had crossed the Channel in the British transport *Empire Javelin,* then scrambled into seven British-built LCA assault boats, headed for the Dog Green sector. They arrived on time and, unlike most of the other boatloads, came in right where they were supposed to be. For A

Company that meant the beachhead in front of the draw leading to the village of Vierville-sur-Mer.

It was a disaster.

Some one thousand yards offshore, A Company's number-five boat was hit by artillery fire and sank with the loss of six men. Lieutenant Edward Gearing and twenty of his troops were picked up by rescue boats and missed the landing—they were the fortunate ones.

The number-three boat was hit by a shell while a hundred yards off the beach. Two men were killed outright and another dozen drowned.

At 6:36 A.M. ramps were dropped on the other boats and the troops jumped into the water. German gunners atop the bluffs, having already fired mortars, now opened up with machine guns.

As he scrambled into the surf, Lieutenant Edward Tidrick of boat number two was hit by a bullet in the throat. He collapsed in the sands ten feet from Private First Class Leo Nash. Tidrick raised himself up by his hands and gasped to Nash: "Advance with the wire cutters." But Nash had none—they had been lost in the chaos. Seconds later machine-gun bullets ripped through Tidrick's body.

The troops emerging from boats numbers one and four found themselves in water over their heads. Weighed down by their packs, many drowned. Others were quickly cut down. A few survivors clutched at the sides of their boats, struggling to stay afloat. Some made it to the beach by using the water as body cover, creeping toward the sands at the same rate as the tide. Packs, helmets, and rifles were tossed away to ease the burden.

Nobody from A Company ever saw what happened to boat number six. Half of its thirty-man load was later found drowned along the beach. The others presumably were washed out to sea.

Craft number seven, carrying a medical section with one officer and sixteen men, was raked by machine-gun fire just as its ramp was dropped.

One of the company's first-aid men, Cecil Breedin, stripped off his pack, helmet, and boots as he reached the sand. He managed to crawl back to the water and pull in wounded men about to be overtaken by the tide.

Within moments after the landing, most of the sergeants in A Company had been killed or wounded, and every officer had been hit. Only one officer—Lieutenant Elijah Nance—had survived. But he was shot in the heel as he left his boat and then, as he hit the sands, he was wounded in the

50

belly. The Germans evidently were concentrating their fire on the officers and noncoms, leaving the shocked survivors leaderless.

Fifteen minutes after the boats arrived at Dog Green, not a single shot had been fired by anyone in A Company.

Perhaps two thirds of the company would be lost—drowned or dead on the sands—within a half hour.

The survivors crawled to the foot of a cliff, finding a narrow area of cover, and there they stayed, immobilized by shock. After an hour and forty-five minutes, six men worked their way to a shelf. Four of them fell exhausted and got no farther. Two others—privates Jake Shefer and Thomas Lovejoy—joined a group of Rangers and fought on with them.

A Company's contribution to the first-wave assault: two men, two rifles.

The other three companies of the 29th Division hitting the beach around 6:30 A.M.—E, F, and G—landed to the east of A Company with mixed fortunes, but all were in poor condition.

Medics would do what they could, but many were cut down all along the beach with the men they were aiding, Red Cross armbands affording no protection.

Private Stanley Borok, a medic with the combat engineers, was going through his fourth invasion. He had survived Arzew in North Africa, Gela in Sicily, and Salerno in Italy.

"If you're shooting dice, how many lucky sevens can you roll before you crap out?" Borok told a reporter for *Yank,* the GI newspaper, soon after D-Day.

"The waves slapping and banging and the LCVP floating around in circles for two hours before H-Hour and everybody sits with a helmet between his knees, puking his guts out, so sick that he doesn't care what happens to him. But suddenly the boat starts moving in and somehow you stand up and swallow what you've got in your mouth and forget you're sick.

"I took five steps and this 88 lands about thirty feet to my left. Then I ran to the right and bang! Another 88, and this time my buddy is staring at his hand because his thumb is shot off. Then two more, just like that, and I found some backbone and ribs and the back of a skull with the whole face cleaned out, all of it right near the pack next to me."

50 *A soldier cut down at a beach obstacle.* (National Archives)

Borok's first patient was an infantryman who'd had his front tooth knocked out by shrapnel. His second one lay in a foxhole, buried up to his thighs.

"I didn't even notice it at first, but the blood was spurting from his chest. Two big holes. You can't plug up a guy's lungs, brother. We did all we could, though. I spotted this bottle of blood plasma we were giving some other guys and then I noticed this other one was dead, so I just took out the needle and put it in this guy's arm. But it didn't do much good. He died in my arms."

Moments after the survivors of the 116th Infantry's A Company had struggled onto the beach, a unit of elite troops approached Dog Green to the right of the Vierville draw. These were the men of C Company, 2nd Ranger Battalion. They had crossed the Channel on the British transport *Prince Charles,* then transferred to a pair of assault boats. There were sixty-four Rangers in all, and three-man British crews for each boat. Their assignment was to cross the beach, then move westward to knock out German guns atop Pointe de la Percée, the spot that the Rangers en route to Pointe du Hoc had mistakenly approached.

Like A Company, the Rangers of C Company landed exactly where they were supposed to touch down.

The company commander, Captain Ralph Goranson, a twenty-four-year-old from Chicago, was in the boat on the right along with his 1st platoon.

"We had excellent photographs from low-level aircraft right up to practically two days before the invasion," Goranson would recall. "I honed my boats in on a fortified house on top of the cliff. As we got in you could look up there and you couldn't see any people running around, but I saw the fortified house. I knew exactly where we were—that was my beacon."

And there weren't any obstacles in the water at that spot either. So far, so good, as the two boatloads of Rangers approached.

Then, a shock for Goranson and his men.

"When we got in close, all hell broke loose. It was coming in every which way.

"We were landing at low tide and were told we'd have plenty of cover going across the beach because there would be all kinds of craters from the

51 *Medics at work along a beach sector.* (National Archives)

51

Air Force—we could go from crater to crater. But there were none. That never happened because of the low clouds. The bomb line was moved several miles inland because of the possibility of killing so many of your own troops. So it was like a pool table where we landed.

"The minute the ramp went down in my boat it was taken off by either mortar or shellfire from Pointe de la Percée. The fire-control point—we found out later—was in the fortified house. They had eight positions sketched out, painted on firing tables. The next round took out the center of my boat and the third one hit the engine room in the back. There were three British sailors, two in the back and one in the front who was steering and lowered the ramp. The boat was destroyed and ten or twelve men killed in the boat, and the three sailors were all killed."

A machine gun was raking the other Ranger boat at the same time, cutting down fifteen men as they spilled off it.

When the ramp on Goranson's boat went down, Lieutenant Bill Moody, the commander of the 1st platoon, was the lead man out. He took the right sector of the beach area as the Rangers made their way across 250 yards of sand toward the cliff base. Goranson took the center of the sector. Lieutenant Sid Salomon, the leader of the 2nd platoon, was hit in the shoulder soon after leaving his boat. "I'm dead—take the maps," he called out to Sergeant Bob Kennedy. But Salomon was hardly done for—he could run, and he made it to the cliff. Some of the wounded Rangers were crawling toward shelter.

"There was a big pillbox in the middle of the Vierville exit and they just raised hell with the beach," Goranson remembers. "The idea was to get across the beach—if someone goes down, your best friend, don't worry, it's your job to get across.

"When we landed it was like I was on full automatic pilot. I did what we were trained to do, and that was get across the beach. I hit the beach once just to catch my breath, and machine-gun bullets started raising sand all around me. I picked up nine bullets in my gear that day. I didn't know it at the time."

The Rangers had lost thirty-five of their sixty-four men by the time they reached the cliff, but they would be an effective fighting force nonetheless—before the morning was over they would be the first unit to do direct battle with the Germans in their positions overlooking the beach.

Havoc lay ahead, meanwhile, for the companies of the 116th Infantry arriving at Dog Green behind A Company and the Rangers.

The boats from B Company came in scattered and under heavy fire. One of the boats of D Company, beginning to founder, was abandoned, and another one was sunk by a mine or a shell.

Only one company of the 116th's 1st Battalion would survive as an organized group able to pursue its mission. C Company, ashore at 7:15 A.M., was lucky enough to misland a thousand yards east of the Vierville draw. The troops found themselves concealed by smoke rising from grass fires on the bluffs and they faced only light opposition. With just a half-dozen casualties, the company was able to take cover behind the seawall.

At about this time, the boatloads of Rangers looking for the flares from Pointe du Hoc signaling them to proceed directly there could wait no longer. Assuming the assault at Pointe du Hoc had failed—though it had merely been delayed—the Rangers moved in toward Dog Green, planning to take an inland route to the Pointe.

But Lieutenant Colonel Max Schneider, in command of the Ranger flotilla—six companies from the 5th Ranger Battalion along with Companies A and B of the 2nd Ranger Battalion—quickly grasped the enormity of the chaos on the Dog Green beachhead. So he ordered his boats to swing eastward.

The 450 men of the 5th Rangers landed at the Dog White sector, then reached the seawall with the loss of only five or six men.

But the boats carrying Companies A and B of the 2nd Rangers didn't make it quite so far east. Going ashore at the edge of Dog Green, those Rangers suffered heavy casualties. One boat hit a mine, its 34 men forced to swim in under heavy fire. Small arms and mortar fire hit the other boats. Of the 130 men in these units, only 35 from A Company and 27 from B Company made it to the seawall.

There had been an unsettling prognostication for one of the men in a Ranger headquarters boat arriving with these two companies.

During the training days in England, Robert Lemin, the 2nd Ranger Battalion sergeant major, had visited a fortune-teller near Swanage. Lemin had told his fellow troopers that the seer informed him he was going on an ocean voyage and "wasn't going to make it" back.

Lemin was an experienced soldier and he wasn't the type—as his fellow

Ranger Richard Merrill would recall—who might "go off his rocker" at such news.

Merrill, then a twenty-four-year-old captain, didn't put much stock in fortune-tellers, either, but he had visited one in London. "I put my left hand down on a crystal ball. She told me, 'You're married.' Well, hell, I had my wedding band on."

But there were concerns that inexperienced troops would hardly have their morale boosted by dire predictions, so the military had put Lemin's fortune-teller out of business.

As the boat carrying Merrill and Lemin came to a stop on a sandbar, it was raked by fire. Merrill was the first man off. Behind him came another captain, a Texan named Frank Corder. "This is no place for Mrs. Corder's little boy Frank," he wisecracked as the ramp went down.

Merrill went to the left, Corder to the right.

Merrill made it across the beach unscathed, but Corder and the four men following him off the boat were all hit—two killed, the others wounded.

The next time Merrill saw Corder, it was along a road up from the beach, and he recognized him only by the sound of his voice. He'd lost an eye and most of his teeth, and one side of his face had been shot away. Merrill helped Corder get onto the back of a tank that took him to an evacuation boat. He would survive.

Sergeant Lemin had been the third or fourth man to exit the landing craft.

The fortune-teller had been right.

After Lemin got off the boat, he was never seen again.

Soon after hitting the beach, Merrill would discover what a close call he himself had experienced. Instead of a pack, he was wearing a newly designed vest that had a series of pockets. A folding shovel protruded from the rear. When Merrill finally took a breather and removed the vest, he noticed a bullet hole through the shovel's wooden handle. A round had entered three inches from his back.

While the 29th Division and the Rangers were catching fire on the western half of Omaha Beach, the 1st Division was meeting heavy opposition as well.

Captain Ned Elder—the officer who had refused to launch the DD tanks off their carriers in the 29th Division's sector—would be killed in action less than two weeks later, leaving a wife and a son he had never seen. But his decision had saved the lives of his tank crews. That much would become clear in light of what happened at the eastern end of Omaha Beach, where the 741st Tank Battalion was supposed to swim in with DD tanks in support of the 1st Division.

The seas were far rougher than anything those tankers had trained in, and the winds were considerable, but the battalion's officers—captains James Thornton and Charles Young—ordered their DDs launched almost six thousand yards off shore.

Because of an accident, one LST could not offload its tanks, and it eventually brought them ashore. But the other twenty-nine DDs, carrying 145 men, were sent off their carriers.

It was a catastrophe. The waves poured in over the canvas collars and tore their seams apart. The tankers tried to escape, but the DDs were being sucked down. All but two of the twenty-nine tanks quickly sank and many of the crewmen drowned.

And so, the infantrymen of the 1st Division—like the troops of the 29th Division—would have no effective armored support in the early morning.

Many of the "Big Red One" boatloads came ashore far from their intended sectors, bringing the same confusion that had resulted from mis-landings among the 29th Division. And the misfortunes of these first troops would snarl the assault of the units to follow.

The 1st Battalion of the 1st Division's 16th Infantry, reinforcing the initial wave, arrived between 7:00 and 8:00 A.M.

The men had spent three days aboard the Coast Guard vessel *Samuel Chase*. Weapons had been cleaned, final inspections had been undertaken, and the company commanders had rehearsed their attack plans on terrain models in the ship's hold.

On that final weekend the troops wrote letters, they read, and they gambled—card games and dice.

"No one really wanted to win at the gambling," Al Smith, the battalion's executive officer, would recall. "They didn't want to be lucky at cards and unlucky on D-Day."

Most of the winnings were turned over to the chaplain, earmarked for charity.

The men were awakened at 2:00 A.M. and had breakfast an hour later.

They could order anything they wanted, so Smith feasted—steak and eggs with pancakes on the side.

And it was service with a smile.

"The mess stewards were kind and solicitous," Smith remembers. "I guess they were glad they could remain aboard."

Twelve miles off the sector called Easy Red, Smith and thirty-five others from battalion headquarters transferred from the *Samuel Chase* onto an LCVP, a forty-five-by-fourteen-foot boat with a steel ramp. These American-built craft were bigger than the British LCAs, but they were scant defense against the churning seas. Smith's boat hadn't been in the water for ten minutes when everyone was soaked and cold, and just about all the men were seasick.

When the headquarters troops were a thousand yards off Easy Red—the beachhead barely visible through the smoke from grass fires—they heard what seemed a distant rumbling. But nobody sensed it was heavy gunfire.

"I had the impression all was going according to plan," Smith would recall. "I thought we had it made.

"Then we got about five hundred yards from where we touched down—and it was a disaster. Instead of LCVPs being forty or fifty yards apart, they were two to three inches apart, banging sides—five of them. I knew we were in trouble."

When Smith's assault boat shuddered to a stop at 7:15 A.M., its bottom scraping a sandbar, machine-gun fire battered the gate.

Smith yelled to the coxswain, "Hold the ramp"—and the sailor obeyed. Then, as a German gunner swept down the line of the five bunched landing craft, momentarily turning his attention away from Smith's boat, he allowed the gate to go down. Thirty-four men scrambled into waist-deep water. The last two couldn't get out quickly enough. Swinging back, the machine-gunner hit a pair of communications men.

At the beach Smith saw "dead and wounded from the first waves everywhere."

52 *As smoke rises from the naval bombardment, a landing craft carrying headquarters personnel of the 1st Battalion, 16th Infantry, 1st Division, approaches the Easy Red sector of Omaha Beach.* (National Archives)

53 *Troops of the 16th Infantry wade ashore.* (National Archives)

52

53

But he managed to move across the beachhead, and at about 8:00 A.M. he encountered Brigadier General Willard Wyman, the assistant commander of the 1st Division. Wyman, who had hit the shore moments earlier, was trying to reorganize his scattered and besieged forces.

The Army Infantry School taught that a combination of fire and movement was the best way to advance upon the enemy. So Wyman asked Smith whether the men were indeed advancing in that manner.

"Yes, sir," Smith replied.

But that wasn't exactly the way things were happening.

As Smith explained to Wyman: "*They're* firing and we're moving."

After making it through the surf and the beach shingle, Smith and another captain, Hank Hangsterfer, the commanding officer of the 1st Battalion's headquarters company, faced some precarious moments.

Trying to advance through uncharted swampy grass between the beach shingle and the bluffs, they found themselves in high water. They hadn't needed their Mae Wests when they got off their assault boat, but now they inflated them.

They finally reached a point near the top of the bluffs, arriving at a small grassy knoll where Smith—who would eventually command the 1st Division in Vietnam—took what he remembers as "the most pleasant five-minute break of my military career."

Smith and Hangsterfer sat down and ate some apples provided by the mess boys on the *Samuel Chase*. And then, "we had time for a wee nip of Scotch whiskey—my farewell gift from a little old English lady."

Al Smith's counterpart with the 16th Infantry's 2nd Battalion—executive officer Major Bill Washington—had hit the beach around 7:00 A.M.

Washington, like Smith, hadn't bargained for what was about to unfold.

"I wasn't worried," he would recall. "I had no concern at all."

But as he neared the shore, his outlook changed rapidly.

"I could see flashes of fire through the smoke that was hanging on the water. I thought it was our flamethrower teams going after the bunkers. It turns out it was small boats being hit and exploding.

"Now, you are four or five hundred yards off the beach, and we can see against the shingle just a mass of men. Everybody is lined up behind the protection of his row of stones."

For Second Lieutenant John Spaulding and his thirty-two-man boat section from E Company of the 16th Infantry, the first inkling of trouble came with the barrage from the Navy's rocket boats—Spaulding saw most of the rockets land in the water.

Then his LCVP passed several yellow life rafts. He didn't know who the men aboard them were and he wasn't permitted to endanger his approach by picking them up. Later, he figured they were crews from the DD tanks that sank.

Spaulding's assignment: land just to the right of a house that had been pinpointed on his maps, move across an antitank ditch, scale the seawall, then send patrols into the village of St.-Laurent-sur-Mer. There he was to make contact with E Company of the 29th Division's 116th Infantry, then push on to high ground.

At 6:45 A.M. his ramp came down, the Teller mines atop the obstacle logs clearly in view. Wading through the water, Spaulding and his men tried to avoid the mines while dodging machine-gun, mortar, and artillery fire.

A strong current was carrying the men to the left. Spaulding, a Kentuckian, was a decent swimmer and had tested himself against the Ohio River, but this was much swifter than anything he had ever seen. He managed to trigger the valve inflating his Mae West, but he lost his carbine in the process.

The water was waist deep at first, but then Spaulding stepped into a depression and suddenly he was over his head. "I had swallowed about half of the ocean and felt like I was going to choke," he would recall.

Spaulding's men were trying to salvage their equipment as they struggled to keep from drowning.

Technical Sergeant Philip Streczyk and Private George Bowen, the medic, were battling to hang on to their eighteen-foot ladder, to be used to cross an antitank ditch or similar obstacle. Spaulding tried to grab the ladder, but Streczyk yelled at him, "Lieutenant, we don't need any help." Spaulding was not, in fact, coming to anybody's aid—he was simply trying to grasp the ladder to keep himself from drowning. Finally, he told Streczyk and Bowen to abandon the ladder.

Sergeant Edwin Piasecki was about to drown as well, but his fellow troops rescued him.

The biggest burden was shouldered by Private First Class Vincent DiGaetano, who was carrying a seventy-two-pound flamethrower.

"I'm drowning," he shouted. "What do you want me to do with this flamethrower?"

Streczyk told him to drop it. He did, and he managed to get ashore.

The boat section lost many of its rifles, its mortar, and a bazooka and much ammunition before the men even got to the beach.

The first casualty came at the water's edge when Private William Roper, a rifleman, was hit in the foot by small arms fire. Just after the shore was reached, Private Virgil Tilley, one of the two men with a Browning automatic rifle, was hit in the right shoulder by a shell fragment.

And soon Spaulding would discover that he was not even at the spot where he was supposed to be. When he first saw the house he was guiding on—it had been wrecked by shells—he thought, *Damn, the Navy has hit it right on the nose.* But that house wasn't the one on his maps. He was, in fact, fifteen hundred yards to the east of his designated sector.

Now Sergeant Curtis Colwell blew a gap through barbed wire with a bangalore torpedo and the men dashed across the beach—seemingly in slow motion.

"They were too waterlogged to run but they went as fast as they could," Spaulding would remember. "It looked as if they were walking in the face of a real strong wind."

In those tumultuous first moments, Spaulding found himself doing something utterly bizarre. He had tried to raise the rest of E Company with his radio, taking it off his shoulder and working the antenna out as he made his way across the beach. But he picked up no one. Then he discovered that the mouthpiece had been shot away. Instead of throwing the radio aside, he carefully pulled the antenna down, put the useless radio back on his shoulder, and continued on his way.

Spaulding's men took shelter at the rubble of the demolished home, but as they arrived there, it was peppered by a German machine gun. The gunner left a series of dots along the wall as the troops crouched behind the building and the surrounding brush. The Germans would now get one man, killing Private First Class Lewis Ramundo with a burst of fire.

At this point nobody in Spaulding's boatload had been able to find out what had happened to the rest of E Company. The men looked back at the water and saw boats aflame. After a couple of glances they didn't want to look again—the carnage was too depressing.

At the Easy Red sector, reinforcements were facing heavy fire as late as four and a half hours after the first waves had arrived.

Lieutenant Max Zera was the assistant chemical officer for the 1st Division—concerned with defense against possible poison-gas attacks—and he also served as a liaison with the war correspondents. He wasn't due to arrive at Omaha Beach until the late morning, and he had expected to find little opposition.

"By eleven o'clock it was supposed to be shalom—you could go in there, kid," he recalls.

The reality was far different.

Zera was to go ashore from an LCI (landing craft, infantry). Since these were relatively large boats, carrying some two hundred troops apiece, they were tempting targets for the German gunners on the bluffs. Two of them, arriving at the Dog White sector at about 7:40 A.M., had, in fact, been hit by artillery fire or had encountered mines, and both had burned for hours, hardly a morale-boosting sight.

Among the men on board Zera's LCI was the inspector general of the 1st Division, Barlow Nye, who happened to be the brother of Senator Gerald Nye of North Dakota, one of the foremost isolationists in Congress.

As Zera recalls it, "Barlow Nye had no reason to be on this trip—what the hell is he gonna inspect? But he was in World War I and he wanted to go in.

"He saved all of our lives. The Navy was so ambitious. They wanted to take the LCI in, but it was impossible. So Barlow spoke to the captain of the LCI, and he said: 'No sense us going in. You'd better transfer these guys into smaller vessels.' They had all these little LCVPs with a gate, they had one man running it. It's like calling a taxi. They just came over to the LCI. There were so many of them, and these kids were just looking what to do. He put about fifteen or twenty guys in each boat. I was in command of my little boat."

But disaster still seemed near for Zera and his men as they approached Easy Red.

"I now see there's shells falling short and long. The next one is gonna be for you."

Zera figured that even if he survived, he'd surely be in Nazi hands before long.

"I was regretting I was Jewish because there was no way you were going to get the hell off the beach. You could never believe we could have done it. I thought I was gonna be a prisoner."

As Zera and his troops leapt into the surf, the landing craft was indeed hit, and Lieutenant Peter Paris, a combat correspondent for *Yank*, was killed. Zera struggled through surf over his head, then found some shelter on the beach. There he stayed for three hours—enveloped by a sense of utter isolation—before scrambling toward a bluff.

"You couldn't communicate with your adjacent platoon or battalion or company. It was bedlam. You had nobody to console you, nobody to talk to you. The leaders didn't know what the hell was going on. On D-Day you instinctively did what you felt had to be done. You just wanted to live."

Zera did have an edge over the average soldier when it came to providing reassurance for his family. His work with the war correspondents would earn him favors from Don Whitehead, an Associated Press reporter, and from Ernie Pyle.

"When I saw Don Whitehead, I said, 'Don, tell my mother I'm okay.' And his story said, 'Mrs. Zera, your son Maxie is all right.'

"Ernie Pyle actually came to tell my mother that I'm all right. I said, 'Ernie, if you get back to the States, call my mother.' He went up to my mother's house in the Bronx, it must have been in July when he went home.

"In the midst of all this horror the soldiers were thinking of their parents."

Whitehead, in turn, received assurances from the military that his own needs would be met. But the commander of the unit he accompanied ashore was evidently not too sanguine about the correspondent's prospects. The officer told Whitehead:

"We are ready to help you. The people at home won't know what is happening unless you are given information, and I want them to know. If you're wounded, we'll take care of you. If you're killed, we'll bury you."

The *Life* magazine photographer Robert Capa would experience a close call accompanying the first waves at Easy Red. But he emerged with some of the most memorable combat pictures of World War II.

As his landing craft touched down and the gate was lowered, machine-gun bullets were flying everywhere. The troops waded through waist-deep water, carrying their rifles over their heads. Invasion obstacles and the smoking beach loomed ahead. Capa took his Contax camera out of its waterproof oilskin and prepared to shoot. He paused for a moment on the gangplank, and then "the boatswain, who was in an understandable hurry to get the hell out of there, mistook my picture-taking attitude for inexplicable hesitation, and helped me make up my mind with a well-aimed kick in the rear."

Now Capa was out of the boat, and he headed for shelter behind the nearest obstacle, the beach more than a hundred yards away and bullets ricocheting off the freezing water. He was wading ashore "very elegant with my raincoat on my left arm," but soon decided he didn't need that accoutrement and tossed it into the water.

"I saw men falling and had to push past their bodies. I said to myself, 'This is not so good.' I hid behind some tanks that were firing on the beach. After twenty minutes I suddenly realized that the tanks were what the Germans were shooting at so I made for the beach. I fell down next to a guy who looked at me and said, 'You know what I see up there? I see my old mother sitting on the porch waving my insurance policy at me.' "

Capa took pictures for an hour and a half, then climbed aboard an LCI that had discharged a group of medics, who in turn had been cut down just as they left the vessel.

Now Capa felt a shock and he found his eyes covered with feathers. He thought: "What is this? Is somebody killing chickens?" Then he saw that the landing craft's superstructure had been shot away—the feathers were the remnants of lifejacket stuffing from men who had been riddled with bullets. "The skipper was crying because his assistant had been blown all over him, and he was a mess."

Amid all this, blood transfusions were being given to the wounded, and Capa got a picture of that.

He would take a total of 106 photographs. But only a few would ever be published—a darkroom assistant in London turned on too much heat while drying the negatives, ruining almost all the shots.

The next morning, the correspondent who seemed a friend to every infantryman arrived at Omaha. He was forty-four years old, a little man—he weighed maybe 110 pounds—and he was forever coming down with a bug of some sort. The foxholes of World War II hardly seemed the place for him. But his syndicated column, appearing in more than two hundred American newspapers, saw the war through the eyes of the ordinary foot soldier.

54 *Wounded troops are evacuated.* (National Archives)

Ernie Pyle walked the sands of Omaha Beach on D-Day plus one.

"There in a jumbled row for mile on mile were soldiers' packs. There were socks and shoe polish, sewing kits, diaries, Bibles, hand grenades . . .

"There were toothbrushes and razors, and snapshots of families back home staring up at you from the sand. There were pocketbooks, metal mirrors, extra trousers, and bloody, abandoned shoes. There were broken-handled shovels, and portable radios smashed almost beyond recognition, and mine detectors twisted and ruined. . . .

"As I plowed out over the wet sand, I walked around what seemed to be a couple of pieces of driftwood sticking out of the sand. But they weren't driftwood. They were a soldier's two feet. He was completely covered except for his feet; the toes of his GI shoes pointed toward the land he had come so far to see, and which he saw so briefly."

CHAPTER TWELVE

"Now Let's Get the Hell Out of Here"

ATOP THE CLIFFS to the west of Omaha Beach's Dog Green sector, the German commander in charge of the big guns at Pointe de la Percée had a wonderful view of seven thousand yards of beachhead. As he looked down at eight o'clock in the morning—an hour and a half since the first infantrymen had hit the beach—he was delighted by what he saw.

Scores of Americans lay wounded or dead, and those who had managed to escape the rain of firepower from above were huddled behind the shingle embankment, the seawall, the beach obstacles. The German officer spotted ten tanks and "a great many other vehicles" blazing.

He reported all this to the headquarters of the 352nd Division, the top-grade unit whose presence at the coastline had somehow escaped the notice of Allied intelligence. The division passed on the report to the 84th Corps in Normandy, and soon the news was on its way to Field Marshal Karl Gerd von Rundstedt, commander of all German forces in the West.

The Atlantic Wall had held: the invasion had been crushed.

But that wasn't exactly the way Captain Ralph Goranson's Rangers were seeing things. And the Germans' glee would have seemed a bit premature to Captain Joe Dawson's company, or to Lieutenant John Spaulding's platoon.

Amid the carnage and the confusion, small bands of American infantrymen were emerging from their tenuous shelter on the beach and beginning to make their way onto the bluffs and cliffs.

The artillery atop Pointe de la Percée had joined with the pillbox position at the Vierville draw to rake the boatloads arriving at the far right section of Omaha. But the two dozen survivors of Goranson's C Company, 2nd Ranger Battalion, made it off the beach.

Their mission was to take out the guns at Pointe de la Percée, and they had set out with two plans. If they didn't encounter heavy fire, they were to go through the Vierville draw into the village of Vierville-sur-Mer, then move west to the Pointe and take it out from the road running behind it. The alternative plan was Goranson's "hairiest one." If the Rangers couldn't get to the draw, they were to find a spot where they could climb the eighty- to ninety-foot-high cliffs overlooking the right side of the beach. Once atop the cliffs, they were to infiltrate through a minefield before reaching the road that would take them to the artillery fortification.

It quickly became clear to Goranson as he sprinted across the beach amid heavy fire that his men would never get to the Vierville draw—they would have to climb the cliffs.

Goranson looked toward Lieutenant Bill Moody, the leader of his 1st platoon, "and I just put up my two fingers and said, 'Go.' That meant go straight up where you are."

Covered by fire from their fellow Rangers, Moody and two of his men found a crevice in the cliff three hundred yards to the west, began to free-climb, and then, using bayonets for handholds, pulled each other up over the last ten or fifteen feet, the steepest section.

Atop the cliff, Moody attached four toggle ropes to stakes fifteen feet below the crest. He waved down, signaling the Rangers on the beach to follow him, and once the ropes were lowered, the other Rangers climbed to the top. By 7:30 A.M. all the survivors of C Company were above the cliff.

While they were heading for the top, Goranson had seen another boatload of troops landing—men from B Company of the 116th Infantry. He sent a runner to get them, and they followed the Rangers up.

The Germans were in a zigzag maze of trenches and dugouts lined with machine-gun nests and mortar positions firing down on the beachhead. To the right of the trench network was an abandoned stone building—the so-called "fortified house" Goranson had guided on when he approached the shore—and to the right of that was a set of abandoned trenches. The Germans had not feared an attack from there, figuring the cliffs leading to that spot couldn't be climbed.

The Rangers occupied this right flank, then staged a series of assaults on the German trenches.

Three times the Rangers stormed the dugouts, and three times they cleaned them out. But each time, German reinforcements arrived through communicating trenches from the Vierville draw and beat the Rangers back. Finally, by late afternoon, the Rangers gained the position—the Germans would counterattack no longer.

"When it was all over, they counted sixty-nine dead," Goranson remembers.

The Rangers suffered only two casualties, but one of them was Goranson's platoon leader, the first American officer to reach the heights above Dog Green.

"Lieutenant Moody had taken out the German commander topside. Probably minutes after I saw him, he got hit right between the eyes by a sniper."

Now the Rangers moved out toward their objective—Pointe de la Percée—leaving the men from B Company of the 116th Infantry to guard the spot they had taken. But by the time the Rangers arrived at the Pointe, there were no Germans in sight. The battleship *Texas* and the destroyer *Satterlee* had blasted away a chunk of the cliffside, perhaps wiping out that German commander who had been so pleased only a few hours before.

The Navy was still blazing away when the Rangers got there. They had no radio—the operator had been killed on the beach—so they sent up recognition flares, then tried to communicate with the ships by hand signals.

The Navy fire didn't kill any of the Rangers, but, as Goranson recalls, "a couple had their bells rung—they were goofy. I had one sergeant that accused somebody else of stealing his rifle—and he had it slung around his shoulder. But he was all right—he had a few loose teeth. The Navy took off the top of the dugout they were in."

About twenty minutes after Goranson's Rangers had gotten off Omaha's Dog Green sector, troops to their left began moving up the bluffs overlooking Dog White.

They were spurred on by a hero of the day—Brigadier General Norman Cota, the assistant commander of the 29th Division.

The fifty-one-year-old Cota was lucky to have even made it ashore. His LCVP had been hung up against a beach obstacle that had a Teller mine attached. The battering of the sea loosened the mine, but it failed to explode. Then, as Cota's ramp went down, his boat came under heavy fire, and three men with him, including the division's supply chief, Major John Sours, were killed.

As Cota arrived at the beachhead, he found troops crowded shoulder to shoulder—several rows deep—pinned down at the base of the timber seawall.

Waving his .45 caliber pistol, exposing himself to enemy fire, Cota began to run along the beach, demanding that the men get up and move out. He would lead by example, setting up the placement of a Browning automatic rifle, then directing the blowing of a hole through a belt of barbed wire with a bangalore torpedo. Cota was among the first three soldiers to go through the wire.

Putting himself at the head of a column of troops, he made his way to the foot of the high ground beyond the beach and started his men up the bluffs.

Once again Cota would narrowly escape death. As he was giving orders to a group of soldiers, six mortar shells came in. Three men were killed, two others were wounded. Cota wasn't even scratched.

Soon he would lead troops onto the St.-Laurent-Vierville road, crossing interlocking bands of machine-gun fire. Later he made his way back down to the beach, reorganizing tank units and demolition teams and getting bulldozers moving.

In the eyes of his aide, Lieutenant Jack Shea, Cota had this day proved himself to be "the best damned officer in the U.S. Army."

While Cota was racing along the sands, moving up and down the bluffs, virtually daring the Germans to shoot him, Colonel Charles Canham, the commander of the 29th Division's 116th Infantry—otherwise known as "Old Hatchetface"—was staging his own display of bravado to rally the men.

As Canham tried to get his troops moving across the beach, one of his senior officers—taking refuge from a mortar barrage—called to him from the shelter of an abandoned German pillbox.

"Colonel, if you don't get down, you're going to get killed," the officer shouted.

Canham—his wrist wrapped in a bloody handkerchief—yelled back: "Get your goddamn ass out of there and get these men off this goddamn beach."

The next day, Master Sergeant Gordon McDonald, the communica-

55 *Brigadier General Norman Cota receives the Distinguished Service Cross from Omar Bradley three weeks after D-Day.* (Dwight D. Eisenhower Library)

55

tions chief from 116th Infantry headquarters, saw Canham with his arm in a sling fashioned by Cecil Breedin, the A Company medic who had pulled his stunned fellow troops out of the water at H-Hour.

"What happened, Colonel?" McDonald asked.

"Oh, the bastards winged me."

Canham had been shot in the wrist as he raged along the beach the morning before.

The first soldiers to move out from the shingle at Dog White were the men from C Company of the 116th Infantry and the troops of the 5th Ranger Battalion.

A few GIs from C Company, which had arrived ahead of the Rangers, shook off the terror and tried to get going around 7:50 A.M. The first man to jump over the seawall was Private Ingram Lambert. He made it across a road, then set the fuse on a twenty-foot bangalore torpedo tube, trying to blow through a double-apron wire entanglement. Lambert pulled the igniter, but it failed to set off a charge. Seconds later he was killed by machine-gun fire. Lieutenant Stanley Schwartz, Lambert's platoon leader, took his place, and he, too, tried to set the igniter. This time it worked, and Schwartz blew a large gap.

The first man trying to go through the wire was shot down, but others followed, and soon troops were climbing the bluffs. Captain Berthier Hawks had suffered a crushed foot emerging from his landing craft, but he made it to the top of the bluffs with C Company, which had taken only six casualties after leaving the seawall.

By 8:10 A.M., 450 men of the 5th Ranger Battalion were also starting to cross the beach road, and they climbed the bluffs amid heavy smoke forcing some to don gas masks. Lieutenant Colonel Max Schneider, their commander, gave the signal "Tallyho" to his officers, ordering each platoon to make its own way beyond the bluffs to an assembly area south of Vierville.

Now individual soldiers were calling on their guile to survive, with or without a General Cota or a Colonel Canham to drive them forward.

First Sergeant Bill Pressley of the 116th Infantry's B Company, leading a group of soldiers up a narrow path on a bluff in the late morning, had come

56 *Lieutenant Colonel Max Schneider (far left) and men of the 5th Ranger Battalion, all of them wearing the Distinguished Service Cross. They were among the first troops to move inland from Omaha Beach.* (National Archives)

56

upon the body of an American naval officer, a large radio strapped to his back.

The soldiers moved higher on the bluffs, and moments later they spotted a mortar operator a hundred yards off, firing at succeeding waves arriving at the beach.

Pressley went back down the hill, took the radio from the dead Navy man, and made contact with a destroyer offshore, pinpointing the mortar's position. Soon five-inch shells were shattering the German emplacement.

On the eastern half of Omaha Beach the men of the 1st Division were beginning to move forward as well.

Samuel Fuller, a thirty-one-year-old corporal in the 3rd Battalion of the 16th Infantry, was hugging the ground, fire all around him, when an officer crawled over and ordered him to find the regimental commander, Colonel George Taylor, and tell him that demolition teams had cleared a path to the bluffs.

As Fuller recalled it: "There were bodies and blood all over—how was I supposed to run? I had a horror of stepping on corpses. But I finally reached him two hundred yards away. Then Taylor did an amazing thing. He stood up and shouted, 'Two kinds of people are staying on this beach, the dead and those who are going to die. Now let's get the hell out of here.' And he led us off."

(After the war, Fuller became a Hollywood director and screenwriter. He would chronicle the exploits of the 1st Division in his movie *The Big Red One*.)

Between the St.-Laurent and Colleville draws G Company and a section of E Company of the 16th Infantry led the 1st Division's advance off the beach from the Easy Red sector.

Captain Joseph Dawson's G Company was assigned to move on Colleville-sur-Mer, a village about a mile and a half inland, in the belief Germany artillery observers were using the church steeple.

G Company was one of the few units that hadn't gone off course approaching the beach. But Dawson's boat had a disastrous arrival. Daw-

57 *Colonel George Taylor of the 1st Division's 16th Infantry (shown after his promotion to Brigadier General): "Two kinds of people are staying on this beach, the dead and those who are going to die. Now let's get the hell out of here."*
(Courtesy of Maj. Gen. Albert H. Smith Jr.)

U.S.
1
57

son was first man off, followed by his communications sergeant and the company clerk. Seconds later a direct hit from German fire destroyed the boat and killed the other thirty-three men aboard, including the naval officer who was to control fire from the destroyers and battleships.

Dawson collected the men from his other platoons and they made it through the beach shingle. When the captain got over the lip, he found a minefield in front of him. In its midst was a narrow path where a dead American soldier lay. Using the body as a marker to tell him where the mines had been, Dawson threaded his men through them.

Under fire from artillery and machine guns, Dawson found a path toward the top of a bluff and began making his way up with his communications man. The rest of his troops went partway, then waited for him to survey the area.

As Dawson got near the top of the ridge, he heard voices. Then came the rattle of a machine gun. He looked up and saw the gun—six feet above him—but its crew couldn't see him. He threw a pair of grenades into the gun nest, silencing it.

Colleville lay to the left, but the direct route to it was through an open field. Crossing it would have left Dawson's men open to fire, so they penetrated through a wooded area.

About a half mile from Colleville, as they reached a large oak tree, Dawson encountered a Frenchwoman who "welcomed us with open arms."

The troops moved into the village, and—just as they'd suspected—an artillery observer was perched in the church.

Accompanied by a sergeant and a rifleman, Dawson went into the church. As the men entered, the Germans inside opened fire. No one was hit immediately, but when the three Americans moved toward the rear of the church, the observer in the tower shot and killed the rifleman. Dawson turned and shot down the German, and his sergeant killed the troops inside the church.

As Dawson ran outside, a German soldier evidently hiding behind a stone wall surrounding the church and its graveyard opened fire. He missed. Dawson, carrying a carbine he had picked up from his rifleman's body, fired back, and then the German fired again. The second shot shattered the stock of Dawson's carbine. One portion of the bullet went through his kneecap, another part penetrated the soft tissue in his leg.

At four o'clock in the afternoon the American troops in Colleville came under considerably heavier fire—from their own naval guns. For Dawson's company, those moments were "the most tragic occurrence that we experienced in the whole war." According to Dawson's count sixty-four American soldiers were killed by the shelling.

At about the time Dawson had led his men off the beach, Lieutenant John Spaulding's boat section from E Company was crossing the shingle, then taking cover at a demolished house.

The first objective for Spaulding's men was a pillbox whose machine-gun fire was mowing down F Company a few hundred yards to the left. They moved closer, managing to skirt terrain laced with box-type mines. "The Lord was with us and we had an angel on each shoulder on that trip," Spaulding would say. (A few hours later, H Company lost several men to mines coming through the same trail.)

Sergeant Hubert Blades fired his bazooka at the machine-gun nest above the men, but he was hit in the left arm by return fire. Private First Class Raylond Curley, a rifleman, was wounded seconds later. Then Staff Sergeant Grant Phelps moved into position with a Browning automatic rifle he had picked up when the man originally carrying it, Private First Class Virgil Tilley, had been wounded on the beach. Before Phelps could fire, he was shot in both legs.

Now the remaining men in the section decided to rush the machine-gun position, which was only fifteen yards away. As they ran toward it, the lone soldier manning the gun—a Pole—yelled, "*Kamerad*," and threw up his hands to surrender. Under questioning, the prisoner claimed there were sixteen others in a trench to his rear.

Spaulding's men, accompanied by some troops from G Company, went looking for the trench. They hit a wooded area, then found superbly camouflaged dugouts running zigzag fashion. The Americans moved along the top, spraying them with small-arms fire. But there was no one inside—the Germans had withdrawn.

Now Spaulding and his men headed west toward the village of St.-Laurent.

After crossing two minefields and trading fire in a couple of skirmishes, they came upon a construction shack at the rear of a strongpoint overlooking the beach. Sergeant Kenneth Peterson fired his bazooka into it, but no one came out.

Then Spaulding noticed a piece of stovepipe sticking out of the ground

58

seventy yards away. It led to a dugout. Technical Sergeant Philip Streczyk fired three times down the steps, then shouted in Polish and German for anyone inside to come out. Four unarmed men emerged, accompanied by several wounded soldiers. Inside the dugout Spaulding's men found a mortar, radios, and bunks.

Spaulding and Sergeant Clarence Colson then started down a line of empty trenches filled with Teller mines, grenades, and machine guns. It led them to a German position at the cliff edge. Coming up behind the Germans, they routed four from a hole, then engaged in a short firefight with thirteen others in a trench. Managing to dodge three grenades hurled at them, Spaulding and Colson killed one German and captured the others.

Then came an especially hair-raising moment for Spaulding as he proceeded with several of his men in the trenches. After losing his carbine in the surf upon leaving his boat, he had picked up a German rifle, but he was having trouble handling it. When he began to check the trenches, he gave the rifle to another soldier in return for a new carbine. A moment later he ran into a German soldier and pulled the trigger—but nothing happened. He had forgotten to take the safety off. Spaulding reached for the safety catch, but hit the clip release instead. Now his clip of ammunition hit the ground.

"I ran about fifty yards in nothing flat," he would recall. "Fortunately, Sergeant Peterson had me covered and the German put up his hands. That business of not checking guns is certainly not habit-forming."

In the moments following that, Spaulding and his men were ducking constant sniper fire as well as supporting American naval bombardment. The troops set off their last yellow smoke grenade—the recognition signal for the ships—to get the shelling to stop.

By midafternoon the men were on the right flank at Colleville (they numbered about forty-five, two thirds of them Spaulding's E Company troops, the others from G Company), but found themselves surrounded. They took cover in the drainage ditches of hedgerow-framed orchards.

At 3:00 P.M., German fire came in. Private Vincent DiGaetano was hit in the butt by shrapnel—the men had told him he was too big to be missed—and then Sergeant Fred Bisco was killed by rifle fire to the face and throat.

58 *Wounded troops of the 3rd Battalion, 16th Infantry, near the village of Colleville-sur-Mer.* (National Archives)

59

Now the troops looked back toward the beach and saw several squads of Germans approaching them. A runner from G Company started toward the Americans, but just as he got to the edge of their defenses, he was cut down, and the Germans kept blasting away, putting at least a hundred rounds of machine-gun fire into him. They wanted to make certain that any message he was carrying would not be found.

At this point Spaulding's troops were running low on ammunition—the lieutenant had six carbine rounds left—and they were still surrounded. But reinforcements would arrive, and they would make it through the night.

On the far left flank of Omaha Beach, L Company of the 1st Division's 16th Infantry got off the beach despite losing two of its boats.

Leading the way was a twenty-six-year-old first lieutenant from Low Moor, Virginia, named Jimmie W. Monteith, Jr.

"He was like a Tom Selleck, only Jimmie was redheaded," Al Smith, the 16th Infantry captain, would recall, likening Monteith to the Selleck character in the TV series *Magnum, P.I.*

"He had the same attraction for the women that Tom has, and he also had the loyalty of every soldier in L Company."

Monteith had arrived with his men at about 7:00 A.M., the rough seas and poor visibility causing them to be a half hour late and eastward of their intended landing spot.

The troops crossed two hundred yards of tidal flat at the Fox Green sector under intense fire, but found shelter beneath a cliff. The unit took numerous casualties, but unlike many of the other companies, its officers were still alive.

Backed by fire from a destroyer and a pair of tanks, the company quickly began to push inland around the west edge of the cliff, underneath a German strongpoint. But now luck was beginning to run out on the officers. The company commander was shot down exposing himself in order to direct the fire of nearby tanks. First Lieutenant Robert Cutler, Jr., the executive officer, took over.

Monteith, in command of L Company's second assault section, was ordered to move up through a small draw leading toward Colleville and engage pillboxes on the left strongpoint.

59 *German prisoners are marched along a beachhead.* (National Archives)

This is what the lieutenant did, in the words of the citation recounting his actions:

"Retracing his steps across the field to the beach, he moved over to where two tanks were buttoned up and blind under violent enemy artillery and machine-gun fire. Completely exposed to the intense fire, First Lieutenant Monteith led the tanks on foot through a minefield and into firing positions. Under his direction several enemy positions were destroyed. He then rejoined his company and under his leadership his men captured an advantageous position on the hill. Supervising the defense of his newly won position against repeated vicious counterattacks, he continued to ignore his own personal safety, repeatedly crossing the two or three hundred yards of open terrain under heavy fire to strengthen links in his defensive chain."

The account closes:

"When the enemy succeeded in completely surrounding First Lieutenant Monteith and his unit and while leading the fight out of the situation, First Lieutenant Monteith was killed by enemy fire.

"The courage, gallantry, and intrepid leadership displayed by First Lieutenant Monteith is worthy of emulation."

So said the citation accompanying the Medal of Honor, awarded posthumously on March 29, 1945.

Years later, Omar Bradley would look back with a feeling of relief over having sent the battle-tested 1st Division to Omaha Beach.

"As in the Sicily assault, the Big Red One once more bore the brunt of the enemy's fury. But I thanked God the division was there."

In the morning hours of D-Day, Bradley had found little to be thankful for.

Peering through his binoculars from the cruiser *Augusta,* he couldn't penetrate the smoke of battle. And no reports were being radioed from the beach.

Aboard the communications ship *Ancon,* Major General Leonard T. Gerow, commander of the V Corps, decided to send his assistant chief of staff, Colonel Benjamin Talley, to the beachhead for a firsthand report.

As he approached Omaha, Talley realized he would be able to see little—and would probably lose his radios—if he went ashore. So he or-

60 *Lieutenant Jimmie W. Monteith, Jr., awarded the Medal of Honor posthumously for his actions at Omaha Beach.* (Courtesy of Maj. Gen. Albert H. Smith, Jr.)

dered his DUKW to cruise up and down, a few hundred yards out in the Bay of the Seine.

The smoke and brush obscured the early progress made by small bands of troops. What Talley and naval observers could see was most disheartening—swamped tanks, sunken landing craft, bodies floating, furious machine-gun fire pinning down the infantry.

Talley provided only sketchy reports to Gerow, who passed these on to Bradley.

Bradley had expected the first waves to be forcing their way inland by 8:30 A.M. But he heard nothing until shortly before ten o'clock, when he received ominous news from Gerow: "Obstacles mined, progress slow . . . DD tanks for Fox Green swamped."

Eisenhower, too, was getting little information during the morning. An hour and a half after the first troops hit the beaches, he still had no idea what had happened. In a cable to General Marshall at the Pentagon he was somewhat optimistic—but unaware of the heavy fire coming from the German coastal batteries.

"Local time is now eight in the morning. I have as yet no information concerning the actual landings nor of our progress through beach obstacles. Communiqué will not be issued until we have word that leading ground troops are actually ashore.

"All preliminary reports are satisfactory. Airborne formations apparently landed in good order. . . . Preliminary bombings by air went off as scheduled. . . . In early morning hours reaction from shore batteries was sufficiently light that some of the Naval spotting planes have returned awaiting call."

As the morning grew longer, tensions heightened at Allied headquarters in London.

And in the Channel, Bradley began to fear "an irreversible catastrophe." When Gerow's headquarters reported at noon that the situation was "still critical" at all the beach exits, Bradley considered evacuating Omaha and sending the follow-up troops to Utah Beach or the British sectors. As he contemplated that bitter prospect, he prayed that his men could hang on.

61 *In a cable sent ninety minutes after the first infantrymen were scheduled to go ashore, Eisenhower tells General George Marshall, the Army Chief of Staff, that he still has no news from the beachheads.* (Franklin D. Roosevelt Library)

URGENT
GENERAL MARSHALL'S EYES ONLY

From: Supreme Headquarters, Allied Expeditionary Forces, London, England

To: War Department

Nr: 90016, 6 June 1944

90016 from SHAEF CP to AGWAR personal from Eisenhower to General Marshall for his eyes only.

Local time is now eight in the morning. I have as yet no information concerning the actual landings nor of our progress through beach obstacles. Communique will not be issued until we have word that leading ground troops are actually ashore.

All preliminary reports are satisfactory. Airborne formations apparently landed in good order with losses out of approximately 1250 airplanes participating about 30. Preliminary bombings by air went off as scheduled. Navy reports sweeping some mines but so far as is known channels are clear and operation proceeding as planned. In early morning hours reaction from shore batteries was sufficiently light that some of the Naval spotting planes have returned awaiting call.

The weather yesterday which was original date selected was impossible all along the target coast. Today conditions are vastly improved both by sea and air and we have the prospect of at least reasonably favorable weather for the next several days.

Yesterday I visited British troops about to embark

CM-IN-4441 (6 Jun 44)

DECLASSIFIED
E. O. 11652, Sec. 3(E) and 5(D) or (E)
OSD letter, May 8, 1972
By DBS Date APR 1 1973

EYES ONLY

30

300 France

SECRET COPY No.

43058AB 20000

THE MAKING OF AN EXACT COPY OF THIS MESSAGE IS FORBIDDEN

Indeed they could, and by midmorning the infantrymen were finally being supported by effective firepower.

Although the tanks that managed to make it ashore were scattered, and hampered in maneuvering by the beach shingle, they began to hit the German emplacements. As Major Sidney Bingham, the commander of the 116th Infantry's 2nd Battalion, would put it: "They shot the hell out of the Germans, and got the hell shot out of them."

Naval gunfire, limited in its impact before the first troops hit the beach, eventually found targets as communication between ships and shore improved. Two destroyers closed to within a thousand yards between 10:00 and 11:00 A.M. and put strongpoints from Les Moulins eastward under heavy fire. At noon the fourteen-inch guns of the battleship *Texas* opened up on the concrete casemates housing batteries on the western shoulder of the Vierville draw, the most massive firepower facing Omaha Beach. Soon, Germans at that strongpoint were emerging with their hands over their heads, surrendering to American demolition engineers, the first troops they could find. Next, the *Texas* blew apart the cliff housing the big guns at Pointe de la Percée.

When Gerow came ashore at nightfall, his first message to Bradley said: "Thank God for the U.S. Navy."

The engineers began to make progress as well. Bulldozers opened breaches in the shingle embankment during the afternoon and minefields were cleared. By evening, demolition teams had blown thirty-five percent of the beach obstacles.

While the Germans waged stubborn defensive actions, they would not manage a single strong counterattack against American forces all day.

(In preparing for the invasion, Rommel envisioned crushing the Allied troops before they could get off the beaches. He knew that German reserves would have a rough time rushing to the coast under the bombs of the

62 *A French farmer is questioned by a corporal from the 29th Division near Vierville-sur-Mer.* (National Archives)

63 *A Tri-Color welcome for the liberators.* (National Archives)

64 *Major Nicholas Keseric of Gary, Indiana, a medical officer of the 38th Engineer Regiment, has just delivered a baby born to a family living behind the beachheads.* (National Archives)

62

63

191661

dominant Allied air power. But Rommel's superior, von Rundstedt, had retained his reserve forces far to the rear, believing he could rapidly bring them into action to repel any forces beginning to move inland.)

And the Allies had absolute air supremacy. Not until nightfall was there appreciable German air activity near Omaha. Even then, with twenty-two planes attacking shipping, no serious damage was inflicted. The remnants of the German Navy could offer no challenge either.

The American troops would seize the coastal village of Vierville and they would move toward St.-Laurent and Colleville.

But it wasn't until early afternoon that Bradley's gloom had been relieved. At 1:09 P.M., the first favorable report arrived at V Corps headquarters:

"Troops formerly pinned down on beaches Easy Red, Easy Green, Fox Red advancing up heights behind beaches."

Just as Bradley and Eisenhower had known little of the real situation in midmorning, so, too, was there confusion in the heart of Germany.

At his mountain retreat of Obersalzberg, Hitler had gone to bed with his mistress, Eva Braun, at four o'clock in the morning. Around that time the top commanders at his Berchtesgaden headquarters, three miles away, had begun receiving reports on the paratroop drop. Von Rundstedt, at his command near Paris, asked Berchtesgaden for the release of two reserve divisions—the 12th SS and the Panzer Lehr—formally under Hitler's command. But Colonel General Alfred Jodl, Hitler's chief of operations, believed the airborne landings might be a diversion. He told von Rundstedt to wait. The divisions would not be released until 3:40 in the afternoon, and neither would arrive at Omaha Beach on D-Day.

Hitler slept through the first hours of the beach assaults—nobody at his camp had the courage to awaken him until 10:00 A.M. When he finally called his military chiefs together, he repeatedly told them he was certain this was not the main invasion. Then, after a few minutes, the conference came to an abrupt halt as Hitler shouted, "Well, is it or isn't it the invasion?"

Rommel was still at his home in Herrlingen, Germany, during the morning, celebrating his wife's birthday. At 10:15 A.M. the phone rang. It was Major General Hans Speidel, his chief of staff, with word that the invasion had evidently begun. The day Rommel had been zealously preparing for was at hand, and he was far from Normandy. "How stupid of me," he said.

By the end of D-Day the American troops assaulting Omaha Beach had gained a foothold beyond the shore—but only that—a huge contrast to the advances at Utah Beach. The main position behind Omaha was merely a narrow sector between St.-Laurent and Colleville, nowhere more than a mile and a half deep. The right flank, at Vierville, was isolated from the main body of troops. And cut-off German forces were still resisting behind the American forward positions while their artillery fire continued to hit the sands.

But the beachhead had been won, the Atlantic Wall pierced.

To the east, British and Canadian forces had made impressive gains. British airborne units seized the Orne River crossings north of Caen, and assault troops staged a wide breakthrough, moving as much as six miles inland though failing to capture their D-Day objectives of Caen and Bayeux.

The way was clear for massive reinforcements to come ashore for the Normandy campaign.

The United States 1st Army's after-action report would put American D-Day casualties at 6,603—a total of 1,465 killed, 3,184 wounded, 1,928 missing, and 26 captured.

Airborne casualties were estimated at 2,500. The losses at Utah Beach came to 197. Most of the remaining casualties were at Omaha.

Omar Bradley would remember those hours on Omaha Beach as "a nightmare."

Decades later, he would write: "Even now it brings pain to recall what happened there on June 6, 1944. I have returned many times to honor the valiant men who died on that beach. They should never be forgotten. Nor should those who lived to carry the day by the slimmest of margins. Every man who set foot on Omaha Beach that day was a hero."

65 *The buildup at the beachheads gets under way.* (National Archives)

66 *Eisenhower aboard the cruiser* Augusta *on D-Day plus one.* (National Archives)

67 *A field mass held July 14 in Ste.-Mère-Église at a hastily established American cemetery.* (National Archives)

65

99

67

CHAPTER THIRTEEN

"Let Our Hearts Be Stout"

ON THE AMERICAN homefront this was no day for celebration. It was a time for prayer, for an upsurge of patriotic feeling, for a renewal of unity.

And these were hours for the pealing of bells.

They would sound in churches throughout the nation, and as daylight arrived in the East, one particular bell would be heard by millions of Americans simultaneously.

At 7:15 A.M., Mayor Bernard Samuel of Philadelphia entered the foyer in the south end of Independence Hall and approached the Liberty Bell.

It had not been sounded since July 8, 1835, when it cracked while tolling to mark the death of Chief Justice John Marshall.

Now, holding a wooden mallet, the mayor prepared to tap the bell twelve times in a ceremony carried throughout the nation on the radio stations of the National Broadcasting Company.

"This great bell which you are about to hear was first rung in Independence Hall in 1753," said the mayor. "It bears the inscription from the Leviticus: 'Proclaim Liberty Throughout All the Land Unto All the Inhabitants Thereof.' Now, through radio, let it indeed proclaim liberty throughout the land and the return of liberty throughout the world."

At St. Patrick's Cathedral on Manhattan's Fifth Avenue, a crowd of several hundred gathered outside the great brass doors long before the first regular Mass at 7:00 A.M. By nightfall 75,000 persons had worshiped there. Five special masses were said in addition to the three scheduled services, and Archbishop Francis J. Spellman recited prayers over the radio networks.

At the Church of the Holy Cross on Manhattan's West Forty-second Street, votive candles were lit in the Victory Chapel, its walls lined with 7,967 service flags, each bearing the name of a man in the armed forces.

Most of the parishioners were women, their heads covered with scarves or handkerchiefs. As they prayed, a man approached Monsignor Joseph A. McCaffrey. "Pardon me, Father," he said. "Here's some money. I'm a Jew, but I'd like to say a prayer for my son. He's probably in the invasion." The priest explained to Aaron Moscowitz that no money would be accepted and then he lit a candle that would burn for seven days in honor of Lieutenant Murray Moscowitz.

Before the opening of the New York Stock Exchange, the Reverend Donald H. Morse of Lower Broadway's Trinity Church appeared on the trading floor to lead brokers in a six-minute prayer session. He read from the sixty-eighth Psalm of David, a favorite of Montgomery. On a secular note the invasion was good for the bulls. The market opened irregularly, but then moved up, led by automobile issues and other stocks with rosy prospects for postwar days when pent-up consumer demand could be satisfied. A total of 1.78 million shares changed hands, the largest one-day volume since the previous November 8.

On a Pennsylvania Railroad train bound from Washington to New York, a group of passengers hesitantly approached an Episcopal clergyman and asked him to lead them in prayers. The clergyman read from his Bible, then joined with the travelers in the singing of psalms.

In Corpus Christi, Texas, parents of servicemen—perhaps a hundred people in all—crawled two blocks on their hands and knees in penance.

The New York *Daily News* threw out its regular editorials and instead printed the Lord's Prayer.

A journalist at another newspaper used a little creativity to convey the solemnity of the day to his readers. *The Atlanta Constitution*'s city editor, Lee Fuhrman, had gone to the local bus station for early reaction, but none of the arriving travelers had heard about the invasion. Fuhrman was much in need of a photograph depicting people praying, so he commandeered the public-address system, announced that the invasion had begun, and asked for prayers. A *Constitution* photographer got a fine picture of the bus travelers with their heads bowed.

69 *A D-Day noon Mass at St. Vincent de Paul Church in Manhattan.* (Office of War Information Collection, Library of Congress)

70 & 71 *Services at the Emunath Israel synagogue on West Twenty-third Street in New York.* (Office of War Information Collection, Library of Congress)

69

THIS SYNAGOGUE
WILL BE OPEN FOR 24 HOURS
FOR
SPECIAL SERVICES ON "D" DAY
ALL ARE WELCOME
תלמוד תורה
TALMUD TORAH
EMUNATH ISRAEL

71

The Kansas City Star also manufactured a bit of drama. One of its reporters, Swede Knowlson, had been sent to Union Station for a reaction story, but he couldn't find much to write about there. He tried the airport next, and—like that Atlanta editor—took over a public-address system to announce the invasion. Still not satisfied, Knowlson returned to his office and advised Ray Lyle, a copyeditor, of his disappointment. Lyle felt that the people needed some waking up, so he called the engineer at an Armour meat-packing plant and persuaded him to toot its whistles to herald the invasion.

But there was hardly need for artifice in order to boost circulation. With their page-one headlines screaming INVASION in huge black and even red type, newspapers were barely able to print enough copies to meet demand. *The Daily Oklahoman* inserted a note in each copy urging readers to "share your paper please."

There inevitably would be snafus amid the frenzy. Some copies of the New York *Daily Mirror* reached the streets without page three, but with page two—reporting on the fall of Rome—duplicated.

The timing of the invasion wrecked *Life* magazine's production schedule. *Life*'s June 12 issue had closed on the previous Saturday. When the first bulletins arrived soon after midnight on Tuesday, 750,000 copies had already been printed. At 3:45 A.M. the presses were stopped, key employees were summoned to the office, and in the following twelve hours, twenty-five pages were changed to provide invasion-related material. A long article profiling Eisenhower's chief of staff, General Walter Bedell Smith, was inserted. The presses were started up again on Tuesday afternoon, and 3.25 million copies had the news of D-Day.

But the fragmentary early reports from the military—which said virtually nothing of casualties—brought a bit of lightheartedness to that issue of *Life* that would seem wildly inappropriate when the real story of Omaha Beach emerged.

Life ran an artist's rendering of the attack with ships, planes, and barrage balloons superimposed over a drawing of the English and French shorelines. The accompanying text told how the Allies "used the same short familiar route that travelers between England and France have used for centuries. One of the early reports even stated that the Channel was choppy and that some men became seasick, like tourists crossing for the first time."

Some radio commentary reflected an overly rosy view of the early hours.

NBC's H. V. Kaltenborn wildly exaggerated the effectiveness of the naval and air bombardment, gloating how "the initial success has been greater than we anticipated."

In some families there was a certain giddiness.

Mr. and Mrs. Lester Renfrow of Dallas celebrated the arrival of a baby girl on June 6 by naming her Invasia. Mr. and Mrs. Randolph Edwards of Norfolk called their new daughter Dee Day.

In Reno, the divorce capital of America, D-Day kept some collapsing marriages intact for at least a few extra hours—only fourteen divorces were granted. Some gambling houses closed, and in the ones that stayed open there were few customers.

The world of sports essentially shut down.

Major league baseball called off its schedule—night games between the Phillies and Dodgers in Brooklyn and the Reds and Pirates in Pittsburgh. But other big league teams went ahead with previously arranged exhibition games promoting baseball's self-proclaimed mission to provide entertainment for the troops. The Chicago Cubs played against a soldier team in front of GIs at Camp Shanks, New York, while the Cleveland Indians faced a minor league club in a game viewed by wounded veterans at Fletcher Hospital in Cambridge, Ohio.

Like baseball, the nation's racetracks would forsake profits this day. Only Delaware Park and northern California's Bay Meadows went ahead with their cards, but they donated receipts to war charities.

In Connecticut, however, it was business as usual for the boxing wars. Willie Pep, the featherweight champion and a hometown favorite, won a ten-round nontitle decision over Julie Kogon of New Haven at the Hartford Arena on D-Day evening. The crowd—7,751—was the largest to witness a Hartford fight in fourteen years. Lest the spectators feel guilty about being at the fights, they were asked to rise for a moment of silent prayer.

For radio comedians the show did go on, but the invasion was very much on their minds.

Red Skelton, making his last appearance before entering the Army, put on a skit in which a young boy questioned his mother about the invasion.

Bob Hope had planned to do his regular Tuesday-night show from a P-38 fighter field near Van Nuys, California, and he went ahead with it.

"Nobody feels like getting up and being funny on a night like this," he told his listeners. "But we did want to go through with our plans and visit with these fellows because they are the same kind of boys that are flying those eleven thousand planes in our big effort. God bless those kids across the English Channel."

For those who preferred dramatizations over D-Day bulletins, attention was focused on an extravaganza in the Pacific. It was directed not by Eisenhower, but Cecil B. DeMille, whose Technicolor movie *The Story of Dr. Wassell* opened at the Rivoli off Times Square. Gary Cooper was starring as Corydon M. Wassell, the sixty-year-old Navy doctor who had rescued wounded sailors in Java back in 1942. But movie attendance was light. As a theater manager remarked: "Everybody has someone in this and they are listening to the radio and getting bulletins. Who wants to see a picture show at a time like this?"

All eyes in Times Square were on the electronic bulletins winding around the Times Tower. A hopeful note came with the news that "Prime Minister Churchill reports Allied airborne troops have captured several strategic bridges in France before Nazis could destroy them."

Passersby paused and leaned against plate-glass windows as they looked up. A young sailor and his girl held hands tightly. An Army corporal in a Times Square bar remarked, "Well, we're rollin' and we're goin' to keep rollin.' " But the soldier's bravado seemed out of place. A traffic policeman at Broadway and Forty-sixth Street noted that his main chore this day was giving directions not to motorists but to people seeking nearby churches and synagogues.

The great Manhattan department stores either sent their workers home early or never opened their doors.

Walter Hoving, the president of Lord & Taylor on Fifth Avenue, closed down for the day and ordered that a twenty-seven-by-forty-foot American flag be flown from the third floor. The flags of thirty-three Allied nations were also displayed. In each window a sign read: "The invasion has begun. Our only thought can be of the men who are fighting in it. We have closed our doors because we know our employees and customers who have loved ones in battle will want to give this day to hopes and prayers for their safety."

72 *New Yorkers watch the D-Day bulletins winding around the Times Tower.*
(Office of War Information Collection, Library of Congress)

72

Macy's at Herald Square also shut down. Inside the store two announcers from WOR sat in a window and provided news reports over a loudspeaker as they received updates from a Dow Jones ticker. New Yorkers gathered at the north side of Thirty-fourth Street to see the broadcasters and hear the bulletins, children perching on their parents' shoulders. A chef leaned out of a third-floor restaurant across the street and a shoemaker hammering away paused at his work as the news reports sounded in the streets.

Some merchants saw an opportunity to win goodwill and coincidentally get in a commercial plug. An advertisement by Roberts Credit Jewelers in the Baltimore *Sun* exhorted: "Wake Up America. Back The Invasion To Win! No Sacrifice Is Too Great. No Cost Too High. The Battle Cry Is Do Or Die—Buy That Bond Today." Below this stirring plea the jewelry firm conveniently listed the addresses of its two stores.

But sacrifice did not seem to be the order of the day at certain war plants.

Production of airplane engines at Wright Aeronautical in Lockland, Ohio, was halted because 12,000 workers had walked off the job following the transfer of seven blacks from one shop to another. Company and union officials who sought to end the strike agreed it was a protest against mixing black and white workers.

Some 750 employees were on strike at a Springfield, Missouri, factory producing Army pants. About 2,500 workers at the Du Pont rayon division plant in Nashville, Tennessee, walked out, but they cited a patriotic motive: the company was refusing to dismiss two supervisors suspected of being shielded from the draft.

In contrast, 1,000 employees returned to work at the C. G. Hussey steel firm in Pittsburgh after striking to protest curtailed operation of a soft-drink canteen. They heeded pleas from the Army and Navy representatives to "back up the boys."

At the Bendix Aviation plant on North Sacramento Boulevard in Chicago, workers signed resolutions pledging not to be late or absent "until Europe is taken." At ITE Circuit Breaker in Philadelphia, Sarah Stewart, a riveter with five sons in the service, delivered a pep talk.

From the warplants, from youngsters, from ordinary families, telegrams and letters poured in to the White House.

His Excellency Franklin D. Roosevelt:
Forward to Gen. Eisenhower

Thousands of Negro shipyard workers pledge their unstinted support to those now engaged in the struggle to the death of democracy over fascism.

Ray Thompson, Chairman
Shipyard Workers Committee Against Discrimination
Berkeley, California

Dear Mr. President:

I am but a young girl. My heart along with millions of others today felt the great step that our forces took. Yes I felt tears, but I thought and realized tears could not help those I loved and the loved ones of others. Hope and prayers are what will help.

Today the Great God has heard countless prayers, which I know he will answer. And you as our leader by our side have given us hope.

I salute you Mr. President and May God Bless you.

Forever a Good American,
Mildred Schwartz
New York City

Hon. F. D. Roosevelt:

Wholeheartedly we pledge our support behind you in this great invasion.

The Spritz family
Philadelphia

An obvious way to support the boys was to shed some blood for them. In Baltimore a one-day record was set with the donation of 751 pints. Among those arriving at the Calvert Street center was Mrs. John Johnson, who had decided the previous Wednesday to make her donation this day—her Ouija board had predicted the invasion would come on June 6.

A smart defense lawyer might wave the flag on D-Day and find he was unfurling a wonderful summation.

In Baltimore Federal Court, an attorney representing one of several men accused of hijacking whiskey from a railroad car informed the jury that

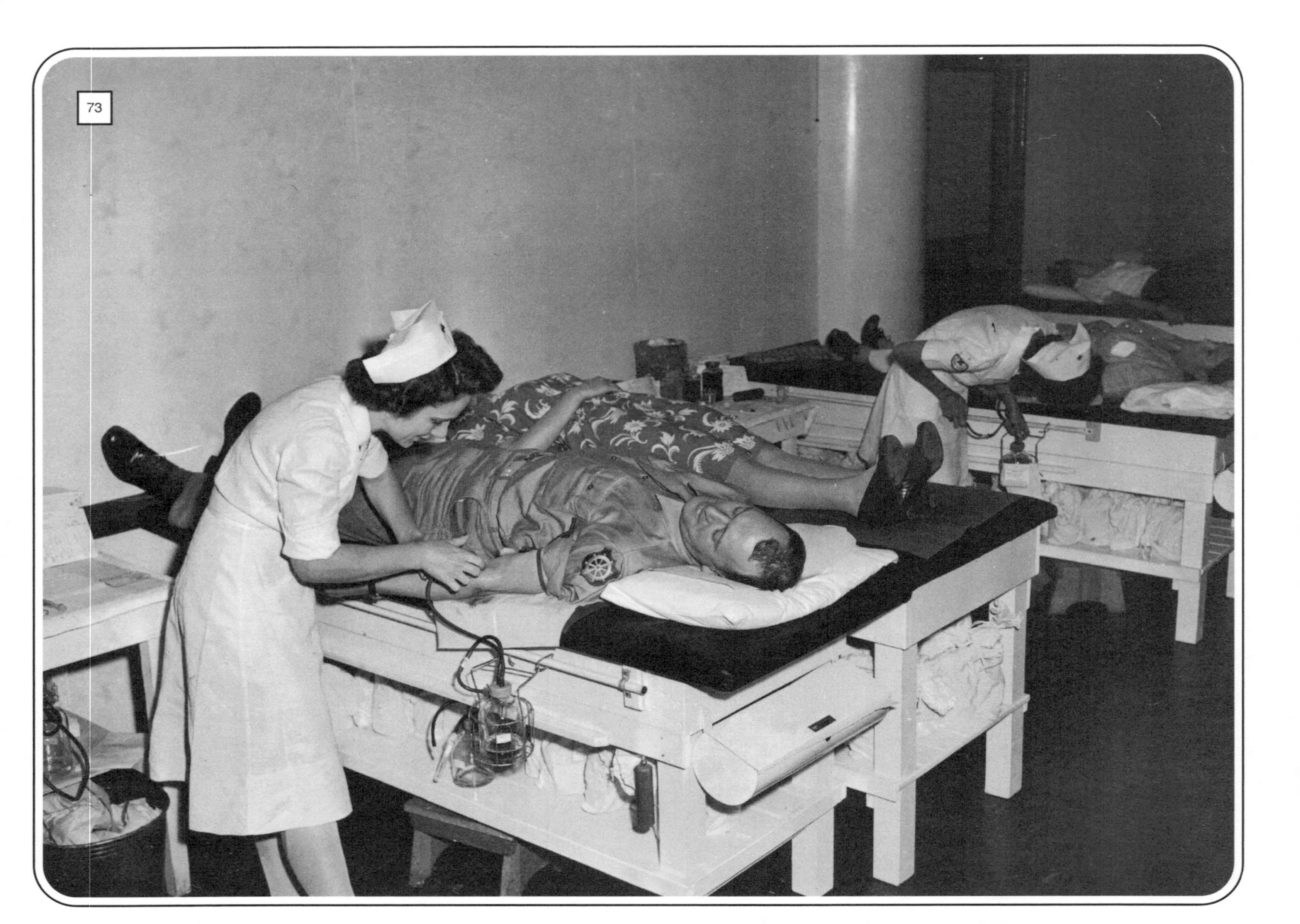

73

his client had been given a medical discharge from the Army. Otherwise, said the lawyer, the man might have been invading France at that very moment. The verdict: not guilty.

In Pittsfield, Massachusetts, a defendant fared less well in associating himself with the momentous events of the day. John Noxon, Jr., was being tried on charges he murdered his six-month-old mentally retarded son by electric shock. When Superior Court Judge Abraham Pinanski called a recess so jurors could attend a prayer service at the nearby Congregational Church, Noxon asked to come along. The request was denied.

The most direct way to support the war effort was, of course, to get into uniform.

Enlistments in the armed forces jumped on D-Day, and many women signed up for the WACS or WAVES.

Kathleen Sheehan, a forty-seven-year-old mother of two, appeared at a WAC recruiting office at Grand Central Palace in Manhattan. "My son is a paratrooper, and I know he is in this invasion, and D-Day was the final push," she told a reporter. She even vowed to donate a pint of blood to the Red Cross before beginning her training.

On this day, 474 second lieutenants began their Army careers in ceremonies on the banks of the Hudson River. It was graduation day at the United States Military Academy.

Over the previous few weeks there had been much speculation at West Point on when D-Day would come.

As George Pappas, then a twenty-five-year-old graduating cadet from Renton, Washington, would remember: "In our military history class we kept trying to guess when it would be. We knew they had to take into consideration facts like the tides and the wind and the moon. We thought it was gonna be the first week of June—maybe."

As graduation day—and D-Day—arrived, each cadet received an identical message of welcome into the armed forces:

> May the traditions of your alma mater sustain you and good luck be with you all.
>
> Dwight D. Eisenhower, '15.

73 *A serviceman backs the invasion from the homefront.*
(Office of War Information Collection, Library of Congress)

Twenty of the graduates were the sons of generals. One of them would receive a personal message from the Supreme Allied Commander.

He was twenty-two-year-old John Sheldon Doud Eisenhower.

Like his father, John Eisenhower was graduating in the upper one-third of his class—John was number 138—and he had chosen to serve in the infantry.

And like his fellow cadets, he had no inkling that D-Day was at hand when he awoke on a gray and muggy graduation morning.

He was already a celebrity. All during the June Week parades, dances, and receptions, John and the young woman he was dating, Kathie Whitmore, had been trailed by a photographer for *Life* magazine.

At 7:15 A.M., the corps of cadets, in dress grays, prepared to march off for breakfast at the huge Gothic mess hall before moving to the field house for graduation ceremonies. The Hellcats were tuning up their fifes and drums outside a historic little guardhouse. The 1st Regiment formed in the large central barracks courtyard. Alan Weston, commander of the 1st Battalion, fell in with his staff.

John Eisenhower, the battalion sergeant major, took his place behind Weston. Then, as the cadets were about to march away, Weston turned and looked at Ike's son. The cadet commander had a piece of news for him that would be kept secret from the rest of the cadets for the next three hours.

Long afterward, Weston would recall the moment:

"I told him, 'Johnny, this is the biggest day of our lives—we're graduating and at the same time D-Day has occurred in France.'

"I said we weren't supposed to let anybody else know because it was going to be announced to the corps as a whole three hours later."

After conveying his bulletin, Weston had faced forward and then barked out the order for the battalion to step off.

"I was stunned," Eisenhower would remember.

Weston, a twenty-four-year-old from the tiny town of Neosho, Missouri—appointed to West Point by a certain senator who would be his commander-in-chief a year later—had learned of the invasion before reveille.

"One of the tactical officers that I had to make a report to at the reveille formation had called me aside. He had information that had come from post headquarters. He told me to let Johnny know."

The commencement address was delivered at midmorning by General Brehon B. Somervell, the director of the Army supply forces.

His opening words would remain vivid for George Pappas.

"The first thing he said was, 'I want to officially inform you that this morning United States and British forces landed on the coast of France.'

"All hell broke loose. Everybody went just wild."

Weston would recall how "we all jumped to our feet and threw our caps in the air."

The informal motto of the class was "Win the war in '44."

But, as Pappas remembers, "Everybody was hoping the war wasn't going to be over before we got there."

After the ceremonies, John Eisenhower was besieged by photographers, and this time they wanted a shot of his mother as well.

Like millions of other women with husbands in the service, Mamie Eisenhower had experienced loneliness. She would write to Ike, send him dehydrated noodle soup on occasion along with pictures of John, and he would, of course, reply to her letters. But military security kept him from disclosing much about his activities.

They had last been together during the first two weeks of January. Ike had arrived in Washington on New Year's Day, bringing the gift of a Scottie pup to Mamie at her apartment in the Wardman Park Hotel. Seeking to keep his visit a secret so they could have some privacy, he had ridden up in the freight elevator to avoid the other guests, then had startled a deliveryman the next day when he appeared at the door in a bathrobe. The hotel worker hadn't recognized Ike without the stars on the collar and evidently wondered who Mamie's visitor was.

Then the Eisenhowers had paid a surprise visit to John. After that, Ike went to England to take command of Operation Overlord.

During the spring, Mamie had been sharing a large apartment at the Wardman with Ruth Butcher, the wife of Eisenhower's naval aide, Captain Harry Butcher. The women came up to West Point the day before John's graduation and spent the evening at the Hotel Thayer. Mamie's parents, Mr. and Mrs. John Doud, were in a nearby room.

Mamie and Ruth Butcher listened to the midnight news on a portable radio, heard nothing remarkable—the first bulletin was a half hour away—and then went to bed.

Around 7:00 A.M. the phone rang. Mamie's calls were being screened, but somehow this one had eluded the switchboard operator's vigilance.

"It was someone—a reporter, I guess—asking, 'What do you think of the invasion?' " Mamie would recall.

" 'What invasion'? I asked.

" 'They just landed in France.'

"I put down the telephone sort of stunned. I called the other room, told Poppa and Momma, and then turned on the radio again. Breakfast was a blur. The reality of the news was a shock."

The phone call had come from Alice Davidson, a reporter for the *New York Post.*

POST BREAKS THE NEWS TO GEN. EISENHOWER'S WIFE, the paper crowed that afternoon.

Mamie had seemed indignant that a newspaper reporter—and not the Pentagon—had given her the word. "Why hasn't somebody told me?" she asked Davidson.

After Mamie expressed skepticism, recalling the false-alarm "flash" sent out by the Associated Press the previous Saturday, the *Post* reporter told of personally hearing the London broadcast of Ike's first communiqué, then Eisenhower himself speaking to the people of occupied Europe.

"I believe I convinced her," Davidson told *Post* readers.

Throughout graduation day Mamie's thoughts were of her husband, "the awesome responsibility he held—to have to send all these men into action."

She had little concern about Ike's personal safety but she feared for John, should he see combat: if he were captured, he could be held hostage.

Following the graduation exercises, John posed with Mamie—facing an onslaught of forty photographers—but he had little to say.

"I felt a swelling of resentment, caused not so much by the photographers' peremptory demands or even by the irritation of the flashbulbs; I hated being singled out conspicuously from those whose comradeship I valued—my classmates," he would write years later.

After the cadets broke ranks at the field house, the photographers continued to pursue the Eisenhowers, insisting on a photo showing Mamie handing John the personal letter his father had written to him.

Almost immediately afterward, John lost the note amid the tumult and his rush to pack up: an Army car was standing by for a drive to New York City.

That night, Lieutenant John Eisenhower—under direct orders from General Marshall—shipped out on the *Queen Mary* with fifteen thousand other soldiers. He would be joining his father at his headquarters in England.

The other cadet graduates received thirty-day leaves, and some of them headed for honeymoons.

Twenty-seven wedding ceremonies were performed in West Point's three chapels on D-Day. Every half hour, between 1:00 and 8:00 P.M., a scene was repeated: the best man and ushers of a wedding party formed the traditional arch of steel with their crossed sabers, and a cadet and his bride passed under the bridge.

Cadet Fielding Greaves was married that afternoon to Elisabeth Jean Henshaw—both of them the children of Army colonels.

"We were waiting in the wings, and the next crew behind us was waiting for us to clear the front door and get out of the way," Greaves would remember.

As Mrs. Greaves recalled the moment, almost a half century later: "In my tender years I was torn between nervousness over having to walk down a long aisle and trying not to think about the fact that my husband was shortly going to do a disappearing act."

There would be a brief honeymoon, and then Lieutenant Greaves would report for artillery training in Oklahoma. He would head for the European theater the following January.

Two days after D-Day, General Bradley's only daughter—twenty-year-old Elizabeth, known to the family as Lee—was married at West Point to Henry Beukema, a graduating cadet who had just been commissioned in the Army Air Forces. In Bradley's absence, an old friend, Colonel Harris Jones, head of the West Point mathematics department, gave the bride away.

74 *John Eisenhower with Mamie at West Point during commencement week.* (United States Military Academy)

75 *Love in bloom on D-Day: Graduating cadet Richard L. Creed, Jr., of Center Rutland, Vermont, with his bride, the former Jeanette Elmer of White Plains, New York, at the United States Military Academy's Catholic chapel. Twenty-seven weddings were held at West Point following graduation ceremonies.* (United States Military Academy)

76 *General Omar Bradley's daughter, Lee, at West Point with graduating cadet Hal Beukema, whom she married two days after D-Day.* (United States Military Academy)

74

75

Several days after the wedding, an NBC correspondent caught up with Bradley on the Normandy beaches and presented him with a transcript describing the wedding ceremony. It had been narrated by NBC's Mary Margaret McBride, who had been a University of Missouri sorority sister of Bradley's wife, Mary. Copies of the transcript had been sent to NBC newsmen "to be handed personally to General Bradley if they should meet him."

At Annapolis, graduation ceremonies for 915 Naval Academy midshipmen were set for Wednesday.

On D-Day, a bit of traditional pomp and frivolity held center stage at Navy's June Week festivities: spectators lined Worden Field to watch the presentation of the colors and the "kiss."

The entire contingent of midshipmen—more than three thousand in all—wearing dark drill blouses and carrying bayoneted rifles, marched onto the field. Then the 20th Company, judged the outstanding unit among the graduates, stepped forward.

Mary Jessup of Roslyn, Long Island, dressed in a powder-blue gown and holding a bouquet of yellow roses, approached the company, escorted by Rear Admiral J. R. Beardall, the Naval Academy superintendent.

She presented the American flag and the Naval Academy colors to Midshipman Robert Beresford Williams, leader of the 20th Company, as the crowd applauded. The roars reached their peak when Williams kissed the color girl.

In San Francisco there was a ceremony of a different sort, a solemn moment filled with longing for a country that had been lost, but brimming with the promise of liberation. At five o'clock in the afternoon the captain of a French ship laid a wreath at a statue of Joan of Arc at the Palace of the Legion of Honor on behalf of the city's French colony.

Along San Francisco's market area the men and women running vegetable stands—French, Russian, Greek, even some Germans—erupted in cheers when copies of the *San Francisco Chronicle* carrying headlines of the invasion hit the streets. Bunches of carrots, celery, and turnips were tossed into the air in exultation.

Captain Pierre Gilly, in command of a French warship tied up at Boston harbor, told a reporter: "Now that the invasion has come, we are men full of hope; we are men of France again."

In mid-Manhattan a group of French sailors linked arms and danced down Broadway.

The French presence was felt in late afternoon as fifty thousand New Yorkers gathered at Madison Square Park beside the Eternal Light monument, its torch glowing in tribute to the dead of World War I, "the war to end all wars." It was New York's official D-Day observance.

Mayor Fiorello La Guardia opened the ceremonies at 5:30 P.M. by reading Eisenhower's Order of the Day, and then prayers were offered. Behind the speakers' stand a small elderly woman draped in black dropped to her knees for a silent vigil.

At the conclusion a singer named Lily Djanel, her arms outthrust, offered "*La Marseillaise.*" Beside her stood Major Jean de Lustrac of the French Military Mission to the United States, Lieutenant Georges Rossel of the French Navy, and six French sailors. Moments earlier, bearing the Cross of Lorraine on the flag of the Free French, they had been cheered marching down Madison Avenue. When Miss Djanel finished her rendition, two of the sailors wiped tears from their eyes.

In Washington, as throughout the nation, the day had begun on a prayerful note.

President Roosevelt had written a D-Day prayer he would deliver over the radio that night. A motorcycle messenger brought the text to Capitol Hill during the morning, and it was read in the Senate by David I. Walsh of Massachusetts and in the House of Representatives by its clerk.

But outside the Capitol building there was hardly a hint of the events transpiring across the ocean.

Allen Drury, covering the Senate for *The New York Times*, recorded the scene in his journal.

"Just a beautiful cool morning, the flag rippling in the wind, the sun slanting across the front of the huge old building, a few cars passing early from Union Station, green grass glistening, an air of quiet peace. Elsewhere time hung suspended and young men who would never see another day plunged forward into hell. On Capitol Hill at that early hour it was just another June morning, nature as always impervious to man."

77 *Youngsters attending L'École Maternelle Française in New York provide salutes for the French Tri-Color hours after Allied troops land in Normandy.* (Office of War Information Collection, Library of Congress)

78 *A march toward Madison Square Park, where Mayor Fiorello La Guardia presided over New York City's D-Day rally.* (Office of War Information Collection, Library of Congress)

77

78

The galleries were packed when the Senate and House convened—most of the seats filled by servicemen—but it seemed that nothing very extraordinary was at hand. Only eleven senators were at their desks, and there were many empty spaces amid the benches of the House of Representatives.

It was a stark contrast to the British House of Commons, where Churchill had appeared a few hours earlier. The prime minister had spoken first on the fall of Rome, and then, almost as an afterthought: "I have also to announce to the House that during the night and early hours of this morning, the first of a series of landings in force upon the European continent has taken place. . . . So far the commanders who are engaged report that everything is proceeding according to plan. And what a plan!"

In Ottawa, the Canadian Parliament delayed its business in order to hear King George VI read his D-Day prayer in a radio address to the British Empire and the Commonwealth. Prime Minister Mackenzie King then reported to the members on the progress of Canadian troops assaulting Juno Beach, and he read Eisenhower's Order of the Day.

Afterward, thoughts turned to the French people.

Maurice Lalonde, a French-Canadian representing a district in the Laurentian Mountains north of Ottawa, jumped to his feet and told the Commons, "It is fitting that a French voice should salute the hour of deliverance of France."

He broke into the strains of "*La Marseillaise*" and the other members of Commons and the spectators stood and joined in. Then the House sang "God Save the King."

When the United States Senate convened at noon, Chaplain Frederick Brown Harris called for God's blessing upon the forces of liberation. And then he asked for mercy toward "our enemies with calloused hearts and warped minds and poisoned conceptions."

"Forgive them, they know not what they do," said the chaplain.

That wasn't exactly the way Senator Tom Connally of Texas, chairman of the Foreign Relations Committee, saw it. Moments later he struck a discordant response to the chaplain's sentiments.

"Destiny is calling Adolf Hitler, calling him to the bar of judgment with his wicked designs and his bloody hands," Connally told his fellow senators. "He first drew the sword. Let him die by the sword."

In the House, Majority Leader John McCormack of Massachusetts delivered his own prayer, and then Minority Leader Joseph Martin, also of Massachusetts, had his moment.

Martin spoke of how "partisan politics, sectional and other prejudices disappear as we think of the heroic deeds of our men and women in every part of the globe, on land, on sea, and in the air."

But political maneuvering was not about to disappear for very long.

Dismissing Martin's oratory as "poetic license," the journalist I. F. Stone would note how "the Republican–Southern Democratic coalition soon got back to work in both houses with unabated enthusiasm."

In the House of Representatives the politicking focused on that other momentous day of the war—Pearl Harbor Sunday.

At issue was a Republican-backed resolution calling upon the Pentagon to finally court-martial Admiral Husband E. Kimmell and General Walter C. Short for negligence over the Pearl Harbor attack.

The politicians were not so much dwelling on the past as they were looking ahead—to the 1944 Presidential election. The Republicans had been accusing the Democrats of seeking to delay court-martial proceedings until after the election to avoid embarrassing Roosevelt. The Democrats claimed that the Republicans were trying to make a campaign issue out of a national tragedy.

Before the day was over, the House would direct the secretaries of war and the Navy to start court-martial proceedings within three months.

The Senate, meanwhile, was arguing over a bill that would extend emergency price controls for eighteen months, and Senator John Bankhead was feeling some heat from the White House. The Administration had accused the Alabama Democrat of seeking to raise prices for cotton goods in order to boost growers' profits. That evening it was politics as usual for at least one pressure group. The National Cotton Council sponsored a dinner at the Mayflower Hotel—the toastmaster, Senator Bankhead.

And D-Day or not, Sewell Avery was sounding off again.

The seventy-one-year-old chairman of Montgomery Ward appeared before a special House committee investigating the government takeover of the huge mail-order firm's Chicago properties. A month earlier, Avery had starred in what would become a famous photograph—he was shown being carried from his office by two soldiers who were under the personal direction of Attorney General Francis Biddle. The Army had moved in after

Avery refused to recognize a War Labor Board directive that he bargain with a freely elected union.

Now Avery was putting on quite a show once more. He told the House committee how troops had charged into his office in full battle array with bayonets fixed, standing "at the position of charge." Then he assumed the position himself, in case anybody hadn't been able to visualize his plight.

Avery reported receiving letters from around the nation supporting him in his battle against tyranny—the brand directed not from Berlin, but Washington.

"This indignation is easily interpreted," he said. "A free American people will not accept dictatorship."

Amid the politicking and the pressure of special interests, the Congress was faced with one matter it presumably could take up without partisanship.

On this day the War Department formally asked for funds to establish sixty-nine new national cemeteries.

At the White House, Roosevelt met for ninety minutes with his military commanders—General George C. Marshall, the Army chief of staff; Admiral Ernest J. King, chief of naval operations; and General Hap Arnold, the Air Forces chief. They had little to tell newsmen upon departing.

Colonel Oveta Culp Hobby, the director of the Women's Army Corps, arrived at the White House at 12:35 P.M. But she had no briefing to deliver. While Marshall, King, and Arnold were conferring with the President, she would have lunch with Mrs. Roosevelt, having been invited several days previously. Hobby, still serving as publisher of the *Houston Chronicle*, had received word of the invasion in a 6:00 A.M. call from her newspaper. The Pentagon hadn't bothered to phone.

Late the previous evening the War Department began to relay invasion reports to the White House. After speaking to the nation on the fall of Rome, Roosevelt had gone to his bedroom to put the final touches on his D-Day prayer. At 11:30 P.M. the first messages had arrived from the Pentagon, and the President was on the phone well into the night.

By the springtime of '44 Roosevelt had grown weary from his war burdens. And while the American people were kept in the dark, his health had become cause for alarm.

Back in January he had been suffering from the flu upon returning from the Teheran conference with Churchill and Stalin, and then he complained of headaches.

His longtime secretary, Grace Tully, began to notice how he occasionally nodded off while going through his mail or giving dictation. She became concerned by "dark circles that never quite faded from his eyes, the more pronounced shake in his hand as he lit his cigarette, the easy slump that developed in his shoulders as he sat at a desk that was always crowded with work."

In late March, Roosevelt went for a checkup at Bethesda Naval Hospital, and a cardiology consultant, Naval Lieutenant Commander Howard G. Bruenn, was called in.

Bruenn found the President was suffering from bronchitis, but there were more disturbing matters—an enlarged heart and high blood pressure.

Roosevelt seemed to take little interest in his medical condition—he evidently did not ask his doctors any questions—and apparently he was not told of its seriousness. Neither was the public.

In a news briefing on April 4, Roosevelt's personal physician, Vice Admiral Ross T. McIntire, reported that the President's health was "satisfactory." The only problems: bronchitis, a "respiratory infection," and a sinus disturbance.

Meanwhile, the doctors prescribed digitalis for Roosevelt's heart condition and advised him to curtail his daily activities, cut down on his smoking, and get more sleep. He was persuaded to take a long vacation at Bernard Baruch's 23,000-acre South Carolina estate, Hobcaw Barony.

On May 7, Roosevelt returned to Washington. His daughter, Anna Boettiger, arrived from Seattle about that time, at his request, to live at the White House. But her presence could offer little respite from the tensions as D-Day drew near.

Grace Tully would recall how "the Boss was keeping up a pretense of normal activity but every movement of his face and hands reflected the tightly contained state of his nerves."

The major Washington event of D-Day came at four o'clock in the afternoon, when Roosevelt held a news conference.

As the 181 reporters and radio journalists were about to enter the oval office, the President glanced at one of his aides, Jonathan Daniels.

"My Lord! All smiles, all smiles," said Roosevelt.

79 *The expectation of heavy casualties weighs upon the American homefront. A week before D-Day, President Roosevelt buys the first "buddy poppy" in a nationwide drive to raise funds for disabled veterans and their families. Doing the honors is Phyllis Fay Firebaugh, the daughter of a veteran.* (Franklin D. Roosevelt Library)

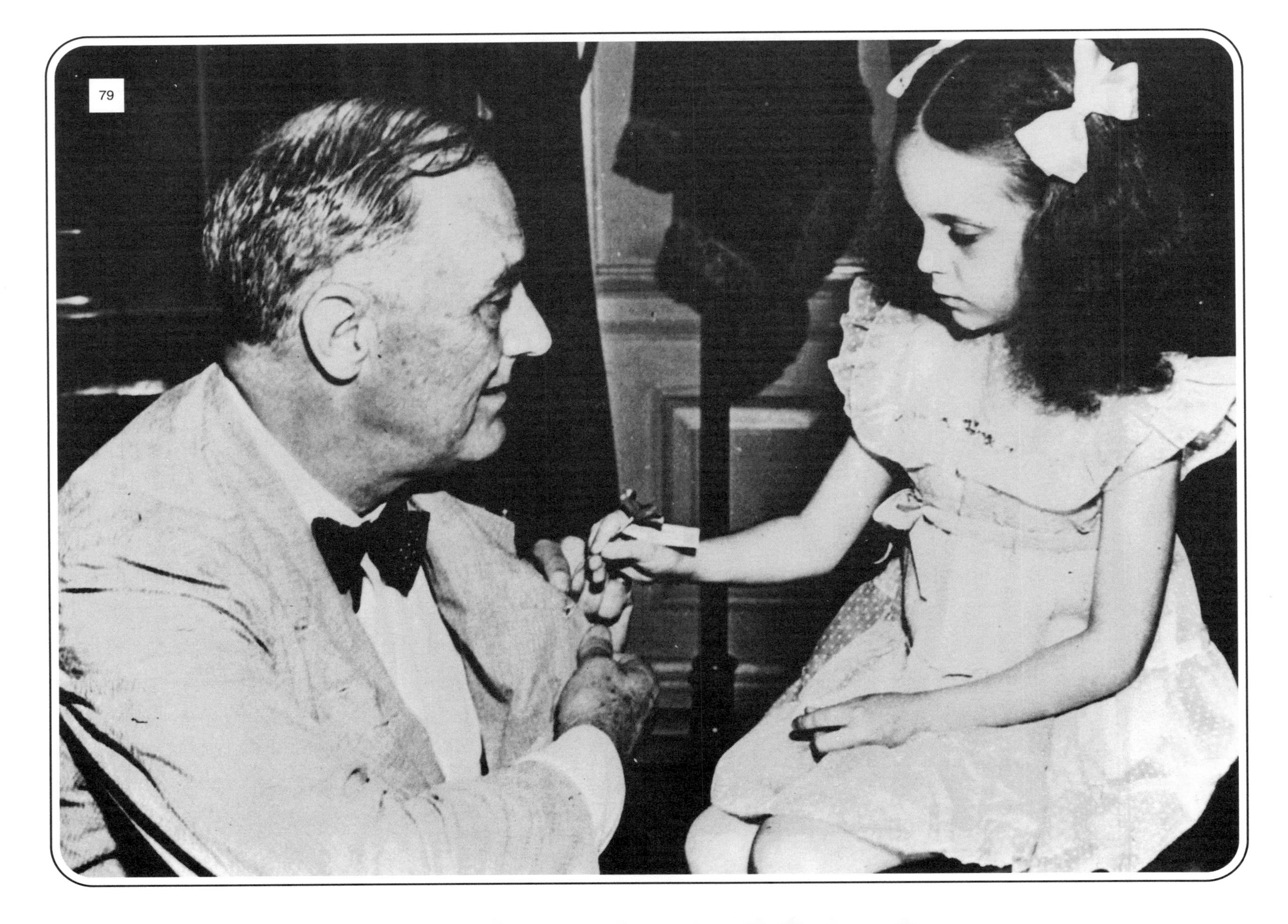

79

"You don't look like you're so solemn yourself, Mr. President," Daniels replied.

"No, I'm not so solemn, I suppose. All right. Bring the wolves."

Roosevelt sat at his desk in shirtsleeves, wearing a dark blue bow tie with white polka dots, and he puffed on a cigarette attached to an amber holder as the horde of journalists jammed around him.

D-Day almost proved disastrous to the President's Scottie, Fala, who was usually exiled to the lawn during news conferences. This time Fala was sitting beside Roosevelt's chair, and the first reporters into the office almost trampled him in vying for a good spot.

Roosevelt began by saying he thought it was a happy occasion. He spoke a bit of the planning for the invasion, noting that a half-dozen landing sites may have been considered.

Ordinarily, direct quotations of news conference remarks were not permitted, but this time Roosevelt said it would be all right in one instance, when he was asked how the invasion was going.

"Up to schedule," he said with a smile.

As of noon, the President said, Eisenhower had reported the loss of two American destroyers (only one, the *Corry*, had, in fact, been sunk) and one LST. Allied headquarters was also reporting one percent losses in air operations, but Roosevelt didn't make it clear whether that meant aircraft or paratroopers. He supplied no information on overall casualties and would offer no details on exactly where the landings had taken place. If Roosevelt was aware of how desperate the situation had been at Omaha Beach, he conveyed nothing of this.

"May there still be a half-dozen landing places?" he was asked. He replied that the question was improper and that the reporter knew that.

Amid the upbeat tenor Roosevelt cautioned against overconfidence. To make his point he employed one of his favorite tactics, a fictitious man-in-the-street anecdote: After the fall of Sicily, Roosevelt had encountered a man he knew who had a good job in a munitions plant on the West Coast. Asked what he was doing in the East, the man replied he had quit because "the war's over."

Roosevelt emphasized that neither the invasion—nor the war—was over. "You don't just land on a beach and walk through . . . to Berlin. And the quicker this country understands it the better."

As the news conference formally ended, a reporter shouted: "Just one last question, Mr. President. How are you feeling?"

Roosevelt laughed and said he was feeling fine. But, having been awake for a large part of the night, he confessed to being "a little sleepy."

I. F. Stone would note how "the President was happy and confident but tired, and he has aged. His hand shook a little when he lifted it to the same jaunty cigarette holder. He answers questions slowly."

But in the eyes of Eleanor Roosevelt, the launching of the invasion had rejuvenated her husband. In a D-Day letter to Joseph Lash, she wrote of how Roosevelt was contemplating Hitler's surrender.

"There is less tension but F keeps us all a bit undecided by saying that he doesn't know what he will do & when he hears Hitler is ready to surrender he will go to England at once & then in the next breath that he may go to Honolulu & the Aleutians! He feels very well again and looks well."

Mrs. Roosevelt held a regularly scheduled afternoon news conference for female correspondents—only women were allowed to attend her sessions.

Sitting at one end of a large divan in a second-floor White House conference room, she was peppered with questions on the invasion.

"This is no happy moment," she observed. "This is a moment when one step has been taken."

She confided that she had slept little after being told by her husband of the invasion late Monday night. Asked exactly what Roosevelt had said to her, she responded, "I don't remember." She would offer little else of note as the reporters' frustrations mounted.

At one point the questions and answers strayed far from the topic at hand.

"Could you tell us what you are going to do this summer?" a reporter asked.

After listing some engagements, Mrs. Roosevelt said she would be "the proverbial grandmother at Hyde Park."

Follow-up question:

"Are you going to do any home canning?"

The reply: "I always do some canning."

"That closed the subject of domestic science," Helen Staunton of *Editor & Publisher* magazine would observe.

The wives of the top military commanders spoke over the NBC network during the day.

Since Mamie Eisenhower was at West Point for John's graduation, a message from her was read by commentator Nancy Osgood.

"If we could ask our fighting men, they would tell us—ours is the job to fight, yours to help, by remaining as cheerful and as busy as possible," counseled Mamie.

As evening arrived, Roosevelt reintroduced a tone of solemnity after the smiles at his news conference.

The previous weekend he had gone to the Charlottesville, Virginia, home of his aide Edwin (Pa) Watson, accompanied by daughter Anna and her husband, Major John Boettiger. He'd read through the *Book of Common Prayer* in search of a theme for a D-Day message.

At ten o'clock Tuesday night Roosevelt sat in front of the radio microphones. Some 100 million Americans gathered around their radios to hear his prayer, and they could say it with him—the text had been printed in that afternoon's newspapers.

Roosevelt reported that the invasion had "met with success thus far." And then he offered the prayer—"Let Our Hearts Be Stout."

"Almighty God: Our sons, pride of our nation, this day have set upon a mighty endeavor, a struggle to preserve our Republic, our religion, and our civilization, and to set free a suffering humanity.

"Lead them straight and true; give strength to their arms, stoutness to their hearts, steadfastness in their faith. . . .

"Some will never return. Embrace these, Father, and receive them, Thy heroic servants, into Thy Kingdom. . . .

"And let our hearts be stout, to wait out the long travail, to bear sorrows that may come, to impart our courage unto our sons wheresoever they may be. . . ."

In New York Harbor there was a climactic tribute to the invasion force. It came at the symbol of freedom given to America as a gift from the nation soon to be liberated.

Since the war's early days the ninety-six floodlights of the Statue of Liberty had been darkened to conform with civilian defense dimout regulations. Only the torch had remained lit, and that merely to serve as a beacon for aircraft. But on D-Day, a half hour after sunset, the floodlights—a full 96,000 watts—blazed again. And for fifteen minutes the torch blinked repeatedly in a sequence of three short flashes and one long flash—the code proclaiming "V for Victory."

CHAPTER FOURTEEN

"These Are the Boys of Pointe du Hoc"

THE MORNING AFTER D-Day, an Army corporal named H. W. Crayton was walking along Omaha Beach when he found a Bible. He thumbed through the pages, looking for the name of its owner, and he found it: Raymond Hoback of Bedford, Virginia.

On July 9, Corporal Crayton mailed the Bible to the soldier's parents along with a note.

> Dear Mr. and Mrs. Hoback:
>
> You have by now received a letter from your son saying he is well. I sincerely hope so. I imagine what has happened is that your son dropped the book without any notice. Most everybody who landed on the beach D-Day lost something. I for one as others did lost most of my personal belongings, so you can see how easy it was to have dropped the book and not known about it. Everything was in such a turmoil that we didn't have a chance until a day or so later to try and locate our belongings.

The corporal would have sent the Bible to the Hobacks sooner, "but have been quite busy and thought it best if a short period of time elapsed before returning it."

Evidently the GI had been wrestling with a problem: What if he returned the Bible before the Hobacks had heard from their son? He didn't want to alarm them.

His fears were well placed. Seven days after Corporal Crayton sent the Bible back, telegram after telegram clattered out on the teletype at Green's Drug Store in the Blue Ridge Mountain village of Bedford. "The secretary of war desires me to express his deep regret . . ."

Raymond Hoback, twenty-four years old, and his brother Bedford, age thirty, had lost their lives as they came ashore in the very first boats at Omaha Beach.

They were among 35 men from Bedford—population 3,400—who had grown up together, then joined the 29th Division as National Guardsmen. They all hit the beach at H-Hour with A Company of the 116th Infantry—and 19 of them died.

A decade later, the townspeople of Bedford wrote to the French government, seeking a stone from Normandy for a monument. On D-Day's tenth anniversary, a granite block taken from a cave in Vierville-sur-Mer, above Omaha Beach, was placed on Bedford's courthouse lawn as a memorial. Some five thousand people crowded Main Street for the ceremonies, and the daughter of Earl Parker—one of Bedford's dead—only an infant on the day her father hit Omaha Beach, placed a bouquet of roses on the marker.

Every year on June the sixth memories come flooding back. The decades may pass, but the images do not fade away.

The chaplain of the battleship *Texas* saw it all—the first waves hitting the beach amid murderous fire, the bombers over the cliffs braving flak, the big naval guns blasting the pillboxes.

LeGrande Moody, Jr., had been asked by the captain of the *Texas* to ascend the bridge, take in the action with his binoculars, and describe the scene over the ship's loudspeaker to the crewmen belowdeck.

Remembering the dawn of D-Day from his home in Florence, South Carolina, almost a half century later, the Congregationalist minister needed no field glasses to see it all again.

"It looked like the biggest Fourth of July fireworks celebration that you ever dreamed about. We could see all those explosions, and we could see them shooting back with tracers. Once in a while you'd see an airplane hit, just out of the sky burning.

"And going in to the beach, the landing craft with troops. After it got to be daylight we could see what was happening. The horrible thing was, it looked like they were just mowing them down with these machine guns—like you'd mow down wheat."

Each year on D-Day the veterans return to Normandy. They visit the villages they liberated in those chaotic first hours—Vierville, Colleville, St.-Laurent, Ste.-Mère-Église. They walk amid the 9,386 white crosses and Stars of David at the American military cemetery overlooking Omaha Beach. And they try to find the spot where they first stepped on French soil.

Ralph Goranson went back to Dog Green on D-Day plus forty years with his fellow Rangers from C Company, 2nd Battalion.

"There were five or six of my men and I—Lieutenant Sid Salomon, and the guy that ended up as my first sergeant and several other men. We went down on the beach and we got into quite a spirited discussion—we finally determined where we went up. We went topside and the remains of the fortified house were still there—there was a campground beyond it, motor homes, and a hotel by the Vierville exit.

"I took my wife down there one evening at low tide and I said, 'See where that water's edge is—that's where we landed. The air was a little bit thick with lead.' "

LeGrande Moody, Jr., came back as well on the fortieth anniversary of D-Day, and he walked with his wife through the cemetery. Some years later he would recall how the visit brought back memories of a chaplain's task in June of '44.

"On the second day we got a call. They had a lot of wounded on Pointe du Hoc. I think there were twenty-seven Army Rangers that were brought aboard the *Texas*.

"The next morning Captain Baker called me and said, 'Chaplain, we have two Rangers that died during the night. We have sewed their bodies up in canvas and I want you to get a small boat. Take these two men ashore and turn them over to the Army graves registration officer, because someday their parents might have access to their graves or want to move their bodies back to the States. We're not going to bury them at sea.'

"We went ashore. It was very chaotic with so many troops landing. There was an Army captain who was directing traffic—troops, jeeps, and small guns that had to be towed. They were going on a little dirt roadway that led to Vierville-sur-Mer.

"I went up to this officer and I said, 'I'm the chaplain of the *Texas* and we have two bodies we've brought here to be turned over to the Army graves registration officer. Can you tell me how I can find him?'

"He says, 'Chaplain, I don't have the vaguest idea where you can find him.'

"I said, 'What'll I do with these two bodies?'

"He says, 'Oh, just put them over there with those bodies on that pile.'

"That was the most horrible thing I think I'd ever seen. None of those men had been sewed up in canvas or anything else. They had just been carried or dragged up and been stacked up, out of the way, so the troops could move and the jeeps could move with the guns. It looked like cordwood, maybe seventy-five feet down the beach. There must have been a couple of hundred, and they hadn't had time to bury these men. They didn't have anything to put over them, and the flies were everywhere. We just put our two bodies over there and started back."

As Moody walked through the manicured cemetery forty years later, the contrast to the scene along the road at Omaha Beach overpowered his emotions.

"In the cemetery all was beautiful. And on the graves they would give the man's name, his outfit, his hometown. And all of a sudden I saw one that didn't have a name, but it had an inscription.

"It was the inscription on the Tomb of the Unknown Soldier: 'Here lies in sacred honor a comrade in arms known but to God.' And when I saw that, I fell apart. It really did something to me, having taken two bodies over there—somebody's son, somebody's brother, somebody's husband."

While the images remain powerful for many, there are a few men who have themselves become symbols of D-Day—their own features captured in a fleeting moment by a photographer's lens.

As the fortieth anniversary of D-Day approached, Edward Regan was living in Atlanta, where he worked for the Social Security Administration. On the morning of D-Day he was a twenty-one-year-old private first class from the town of Olyphant, Pennsylvania, headed for Omaha Beach with K Company, 116th Infantry, 29th Division. As the troopship *Charles Carroll* started out across the Channel, he was "pretty much resigned to whatever my fate was gonna be—there wasn't a damn thing I could do about it one way or another."

Regan's landing craft was supposed to touch shore at 7:20 A.M. at the Dog White sector, but the currents took it off course, and when it scraped a sandbar, he was well to the east, mixed together with troops from the 1st Division.

He scrambled out of his boat only twenty yards from the beach, but the water was over his head and he was loaded down by his gear.

"When I got to that beach area, I collapsed—my combat efficiency was

80 *Back on D-Day plus one, LeGrande Moody, Jr. (right), the chaplain of the* Texas, *helped in the evacuation of a Ranger from Pointe du Hoc.* (National Archives)

80

zilch. And that's when that picture was taken."

The "picture" was snapped by *Life* magazine's Robert Capa, and it has become a "signature" portrayal of the D-Day infantryman. A soldier—his face clearly shown—is battling with the tides, surrounded by beach obstacles, as he gropes for his first few inches of French soil.

Regan does not recall encountering Capa at Omaha Beach. He did not even see the photo until the war was over, but he's sure it's him, and *Life* magazine agrees.

"When I washed ashore, I didn't see any photographer. I didn't know about the picture until I got home from the service. My mother had saved these pictures out of *Life* magazine and pointed this one out to me and said, 'Isn't that you?'

"I said, 'It could very well be me.' It looked like me. I remembered being in that position."

But by then, Regan was trying to put the war out of his mind.

"When I came out of the service, I had had it up to my ears with the military. The only time I would get to thinking about it was when I came across those pictures."

Capa's D-Day photos would flash in and out of Regan's thoughts.

"I saved those pictures, and over the years I'd come across them and take them out and put them away again. Eventually, the creases in them were beginning to split. I thought that I should write to *Life* and ask them if they would send me a print of that picture. Up to this time I was ninety-nine and nine tenths percent certain that it was me. They sent me a picture, and they had cleaned it up, the shadows weren't as pronounced. And when I saw that picture, I was convinced it was me."

In the spring of 1984, when *Life* began seeking out D-Day veterans for a commemorative pictorial feature, the magazine sent a photo specialist to Regan's home.

Regan showed *Life* a picture taken of him the night after he came out of the service, a studio portrait he sat for at his mother's request.

The *Life* representative compared that photo with the one taken on

81 *Soldier believed to be Edward Regan of K Company, 116th Infantry, 29th Division, struggling to get ashore at Omaha Beach. The photograph, taken by* Life *magazine's Robert Capa, is a renowned image of the D-Day infantryman's plight.*
(Robert Capa/Magnum Photos)

81

D-Day and agreed that Regan was indeed the Capa infantryman. *Life* paid Regan's way over to Normandy for the fortieth anniversary ceremonies and it ran the picture once more.

There is another "signature" photograph of D-Day: Eisenhower bidding farewell to the paratroopers.

The photo has been reproduced time and again, and it appears in the background of the Eisenhower postage stamp.

Ike is looking directly at a tall paratrooper with the number 23 on a card dangling from his neck.

The soldier would not dwell on that moment—he hadn't even realized that a photo was being taken and was kept busy by his combat duties. But one day Lieutenant Wallace Strobel of E Company, 502nd Regiment, 101st Airborne, was in a rear area, getting a bit of rest, when he looked through a copy of *Time* magazine. He spotted the photo of Eisenhower providing a personal sendoff to the airborne at Greenham Common field.

It was hard for Strobel to make out the face of the man Ike was speaking with—the photo was of poor quality—but he knew it was him from the number-23 tag.

Each of the C-47's carrying the paratroopers had been assigned a number. Since Strobel was the jumpmaster—or lead man—of plane 23, he wore that number to help his men find him as they formed up.

In July '44, when Strobel's company returned to base camp in England, one of the men at headquarters gave him a bunch of English newspapers that had used the picture. And the photo had appeared in *Yank*, the GI newspaper. It had already become a portrait for D-Day.

In the fall of 1952, Strobel was living in Saginaw, Michigan. One day, Eisenhower came to town on a presidential campaign whistlestop tour. Harvey Walker, the Saginaw County Republican chairman, a friend of Strobel's, got Ike to autograph the picture. Four decades later the photo was still hanging in the Strobel home: the Supreme Allied Commander chatting with the airborne lieutenant.

Even before the war in Europe had ended, thoughts of D-Day were evoking special moments. On the morning of March 29, 1945, Franklin D.

82 *Ike with Lieutenant Wallace Strobel and his fellow paratroopers of the 502nd Regiment in the lesser known of the two farewell photos. This one was taken by Mike Misura, the regimental photographer.* (National Archives)

82

Roosevelt was preparing to leave for a vacation at Warm Springs, Georgia. His secretary, Grace Tully, needed to see him on a matter far removed from the drive against Berlin. She had an idea for a set of birthday presents for the three children of Roosevelt's daughter, Anna. Sistie had celebrated her birthday earlier in March, Johnny was to be a birthday boy that week, and Buzzie had a birthday coming during April.

Tully brought three bound copies of Roosevelt's D-Day prayer to the President's office in hopes he would autograph them for the youngsters. But Roosevelt seemed tired and ill—as he had been so often—so the secretary decided to bother him only with a signature for Johnny, who had been bedridden for the past few weeks with a strep throat. The President inscribed the prayer and wrote a cheering message on the flyleaf.

It was the last signature he would ever affix in the White House.

On June 6, 1945, the first Normandy commemorative ceremony was held. A Liberty ship lay upturned off Utah Beach and an infantry landing craft, torn apart by German guns, remained at the edge of Omaha Beach as the American ambassador to France, Jefferson Caffrey, spoke at a plot of land where American soldiers had been buried.

In June of '46 there was a remembrance far from Normandy. The paratroopers of Lieutenant Colonel Robert Wolverton's 3rd Battalion, 506th Regiment, marked the moment when he led them in prayer at an orchard near Ramsbury, England, on the eve of D-Day. Wolverton had concluded by inviting his men to reassemble at the Hotel Muehlebach in Kansas City, Missouri, on the first anniversary of D-Day after the war. He had been killed in the first hours of the invasion—shot down as his parachute descended—and now his men had gathered for the reunion he'd decreed.

Forty-six veterans of the regiment—some now with their wives—met for dinner at the hotel, and then they assembled at a towering stone shaft where an eternal flame memorialized Kansas City's war dead. In the darkness, Colonel Wolverton's prayer was read once more.

By the tenth anniversary of D-Day, the memorial observances were being organized on a grand scale. Now political figures were at center stage

83 *Memorial dedicated on June 6, 1945, at the spot where the first German pillbox was captured at Utah Beach. The flowers were placed by villagers of Ste.-Marie-du-Mont in tribute "À Nos Liberateurs."* (National Archives)

IN PROUD MEMORY
OF OUR DEAD
1ST ENGINEER
SPECIAL BRIGADE
H-HOUR 0630
D DAY 6 JUNE 1944
207990

83

amid much pageantry. And they were focusing on the power equations of the moment. The ceremonies at Normandy became a forum for hailing the Western military alliance confronting the threat from the Soviets, the great allies of World War II.

Some 25,000 spectators stood on the sands of Utah Beach on the sunshiny afternoon of June 6, 1954, as 1,600 troops from the NATO nations marched in review. Jet fighters from the United States, Britain, and France streaked overhead.

President René Coty of France spoke with gratitude of the soldiers who "hung on by their fingernails," but he seemed just as intent on saluting the "military organization that unites us," and indeed, the NATO commander, General Alfred M. Gruenther, was present.

A one-sentence item appeared in the newspapers: "MOSCOW, June 6 (UP)—The Soviet press ignored the tenth anniversary of D-Day."

There were private moments, too, at the old battle sites that springtime.

James Earl Rudder, commander of the Rangers who stormed Pointe du Hoc, came back.

He returned to the cliff with his fourteen-year-old son, Bud, accompanied by a magazine writer doing an anniversary piece. Rudder looked at the heights once more and wondered how the deed had been done.

His youngster told a story about the American flag the Rangers had flown atop Pointe du Hoc and the medals his father had won.

Rudder had kept the flag, and when the war was over, he took it back to Brady, Texas, where he would serve as mayor before returning to his alma mater, Texas A & M, as its president.

The flag had remained for some time inside a wooden box in the den of Rudder's white limestone home. Along with it were a host of other souvenirs—two German pistols, two German chrome-plated 20mm shells, two German knives, a French beret—and the Distinguished Service Cross, the Silver Star, the Bronze Star with cluster, the Purple Heart with cluster, the Croix de Guerre and Légion d'Honneur.

Bud Rudder recalled how one day there was a final calamity in the saga of Pointe du Hoc.

The boy's mother had decided that the war decorations needed a proper place in the Rudder home.

"Mommy finally got a box with a glass in front and put the medals in it and hung it on the wall. Then it fell off the wall and broke to pieces, and after Mommy went to all that trouble, Daddy just laughed."

On the twentieth anniversary of D-Day, the generals returned to Normandy. Omar Bradley was there, and J. Lawton Collins, and Matthew Ridgway and Maxwell Taylor, by then chairman of the Joint Chiefs of Staff. Taylor flew over the old paratrooper drop zones in a helicopter, trying to locate the field he had landed in. But he couldn't find it. Everything "looked so different," he remarked.

Just north of Ste.-Mère-Église, parachutes were descending again. Robert Murphy, an eighteen-year-old pathfinder with the 505th Parachute Regiment on D-Day, was jumping into Normandy once more with his wartime buddy, John Lee. But this time their adversary wasn't the Germans—it was the French government.

Murphy, by then a Boston lawyer, and Lee, a Worcester, Massachusetts, steel executive, had international parachuting licenses, and Murphy had made more than two hundred sporting jumps since the war.

But when they arrived in Paris en route to their commemorative jump, the parachutes they brought with them were confiscated by French customs and placed in a barn near Orly Airport.

"Somebody in the French government put a kibosh on our jumping—they didn't give us any reason," Murphy would recall. He believed that the orders came from the top: "De Gaulle hated the Americans."

But Murphy received a sentimental assist, and the chutes didn't stay in the customs warehouse for long.

"Monique La Roche, a French woman skydiving champion I had met, talked to the customs man. She argued, cried, and said, 'These two men liberated France and were wounded in action, and you're holding their parachutes?'

"He took out his hanky and was just about crying and released the parachutes to us."

With help from Simone Renaud—the wife of Alexandre Renaud, the wartime mayor of Ste.-Mère-Église—Murphy and Lee obtained a small plane and made their jump. They landed in a field near Neuville-au-Plain, the spot where Lieutenant Turner Turnbull's platoon had made an all-day stand to save the troops at Ste.-Mère-Église from a counterattack, and they were saluted with flowers and champagne.

In this springtime of '64, the Supreme Allied Commander had also come back.

Ike walked along Omaha Beach, the cliff at Pointe du Hoc, the hedgerow country behind the beaches, and the cemetery, joined by Walter Cronkite for CBS's *D-Day Plus 20 Years: Eisenhower Returns to Normandy.*

"Everything had gone wrong that could have gone wrong," he reflected. "The thing that pulled this out was the bravery and the courage and the initiative of the American GI. That's what did it."

At the cemetery above Omaha Beach, Leon Durchin of Kelayres, Pennsylvania, looked on as French children placed small American and French flags on the graves of his uncles, Frank and Joseph Surek—anonymous GIs, the men Ike was remembering, brothers buried side by side.

For the fortieth anniversary a grand ceremony unfolded. President Reagan, Queen Elizabeth II of Britain, President Mitterand of France, Prime Minister Trudeau of Canada, Queen Beatrix of the Netherlands, King Olav V of Norway, King Baudouin I of Belgium, and Grand Duke Jean of Luxembourg gathered at Utah Beach.

A crowd of ten thousand watched from the dunes, and there was something of a festive atmosphere, the entertainment provided by a parachute jump. Honor guards from eight nations hoisted flags up tall poles, eight national anthems were played, and the French destroyer *Montcalm* fired a twenty-one-gun salute. French Alpha jets roared overhead, trailing streams of red, white, and blue smoke.

The only speaker at Utah Beach was Mitterand, a leader in the French underground during World War II. He looked to the present and the future. Yesterday's adversaries, he said, were now working together for "the Europe of freedom."

And, said Mitterand: "Let us salute the German dead who fell in this combat. Their sons bear witness as ours do that a new era may begin."

Amid the words of conciliation, one Western leader was not at Nor-

84 *French President François Mitterand and President Reagan lay wreaths before "The Spirit of American Youth Rising from the Waves" at Memorial Grove of the Omaha Beach cemetery. The inscription above the columns reads: "This embattled shore, portal of freedom, is forever hallowed by the ideals, the valor and the sacrifices of our fellow countrymen."* (Ronald Reagan Library)

mandy this day—Chancellor Helmut Kohl of West Germany had not been invited.

The exclusion did not sit well with some.

Alois Mertes of the Christian Democrats, the second-ranking official in the West German Foreign Ministry, warned that the D-Day events could be "a day of alienation between Germany and its allies" if they resulted in a feeling in his nation that "Germans were a vanquished people or a nation of guilty men between East and West."

Kohl—fourteen years old on D-Day—had reportedly sought an invitation to the ceremonies. The French newspaper *Le Monde* claimed that he brought up the matter in a conversation with British Prime Minister Margaret Thatcher. Kohl denied it. "There is no reason for a federal chancellor to celebrate when others mark a battle in which tens of thousands of Germans met miserable deaths," he said.

But a certain prominent German political figure endorsed the ceremonies and the exclusion of the Germans from them.

"It was better to lose the war with Hitler than to win it with Hitler," reflected the mayor of Stuttgart. "This is a very bitter idea, but it is a necessary idea."

So said Manfred Rommel, the son of the architect of Hitler's Atlantic Wall.

The Russians, having traditionally snubbed Allied D-Day ceremonies, this time sent a delegation headed by a general. But no significant political figures came along.

And there were some choice barbs out of Moscow at Reagan, whose D-Day was spent in Culver City, California, where he served as a lieutenant in an Army Air Forces film unit.

In the eyes of the Soviets, Reagan had come to Normandy simply to boost his standing for the following November's presidential election.

As *Pravda,* the Communist party newspaper, saw it: "Having weathered the war far from the front line, in the rear, Reagan suddenly decides four decades later to travel to the scene of fighting, seeking with the studied smile of a showman, and before the television cameras, not so much to dramatize the turmoil of war as to exploit the glory of the dead."

Reagan, like Mitterand, looked to the political themes of the 1980s while honoring the men of June '44. Speaking at Pointe du Hoc, he used D-Day as a forum to urge disarmament talks with the Russians.

So it was a day of "photo opportunities" for world leaders, a day for political jousting among great nations. And it was also a day to make a buck—or a franc. A café in St.-Laurent-sur-Mer, not far from the American cemetery, was selling white cloth bags labeled in both French and English: "Easy Gift to take Home—Sand from the Landing Beaches. 25 Francs."

But beyond all this it was a day for the veterans—for their reflections on the hours when all was smoke and fury, for greeting old buddies, for honoring those who never saw another dawn.

"These are the boys of Pointe du Hoc," said Ronald Reagan as he stood before the Rangers who had scaled the forbidding heights. They were men in their sixties now, laden with memories.

Ted Lapres, who had gone up the cliff with E Company, was back, and he thought of how Lieutenant Jake Hill had wiped out a machine-gun nest behind the cliff top not long before Lapres's patrol passed that very spot. "I never got a chance to thank him," Lapres would lament. "He was killed on D-Day."

Richard Merrill, who went ashore at Omaha Beach, then helped relieve the siege at Pointe du Hoc two days later, brought his camera with him for the fortieth anniversary ceremonies. When the film arrived from the developer, he was stunned.

"I took some pictures, but when they came out, my fingers and thumbs were in front of the lens."

The moment had been so overpowering, it had caused him to mishandle the camera.

Another former Ranger decided to commemorate D-Day by going into action once more.

A Ranger unit based in West Germany was preparing to climb Pointe du Hoc—under simulated fire—as part of the fortieth anniversary ceremonies. As Herman Stein—sixty-three years old—saw it: Once a Ranger, always a Ranger.

"I wasn't going to be denied. I got ahold of the captain who was

85 *President and Mrs. Reagan walk among the 9,386 crosses and Stars of David.* (Ronald Reagan Library)

86 *The emotions of the fortieth-anniversary reunion at Pointe du Hoc overwhelm Loring Wadsworth of Plymouth, Massachusetts, a veteran of E Company, 2nd Ranger Battalion.* (Ronald Reagan Library)

85

86
RANGER Bn
RBA
WW II
N.E.1

running the thing. I said, 'Do you mind if I climb with you?' He says, 'Do you think you can?' I says, 'Yeah, sure.' He says, 'Well, come on. The guys are practicing. Come on down with us, you can take a try.' I did it. It didn't take any time—about three minutes. And he says, 'Jesus Christ, you climb better than my guys.' "

For the men of the Army Air Forces there would be visits to England over the years, to the sites of the airbases they had departed from in their bombing runs over France.

Ray Zuker, who had piloted his B-24 *Lady Lightnin'* over the Channel at dawn on D-Day, went back to Sudbury with his son in 1988, looking for the base that had housed his 486th Bomb Group.

A brass marker affixed to a stone proclaimed the surrounding stretch of land the site of the 486th, and a memorial inscription graced the fifteenth-century church in town. But the runways were farmland now, and Zuker was finding little evidence of what once had been.

"The tower was gone. There were only two buildings left—two Quonset huts. One had been operations, the other the briefing room, and they were filled full of hay, both of them. All rusted."

Then he made a discovery.

"We got out of the car. I was scratching around in the weeds and found a darn D-ring. It had been put into the concrete with the chains they used to tie down the airplanes because the North Sea winds came across there pretty strong sometimes. Memory came flooding back."

At another farm—this one in Devon, off Slapton Sands—there would be disquieting echoes of D-Day.

As preparations were made for fortieth anniversary ceremonies, rumors flew that the bodies of some three hundred American servicemen lay in an unmarked mass grave on the property of a farmer named Nolan Trope.

Many of the soldiers and sailors who drowned in Lyme Bay during the early hours of April 28, 1944—victims of the German E-boat attack on the Operation Tiger exercise preparing for the Utah Beach invasion—had indeed been hastily buried on this farmland.

Most of the three thousand residents of the area—known as the South Hams—had been relocated in the spring of '44 because of the sensitive military activities there. Among those permitted to stay was a baker and his family. The daughter, Dorothy Seekings, then twenty-three years old, had helped her father deliver doughnuts to the troops.

Four decades later—the secrets of the Slapton Sands debacle having long been revealed—Dorothy Seekings was still living in Devon. She would finally talk about what she had seen in a meadow one day in April '44.

"The bodies were in American uniforms. There were great mounds of earth in the field and I was told they were going to be buried there."

Were the remains still in a common grave beneath the farmland? Nolan Trope took a dim view of the speculation. He closed his property off, threatening to bring trespass charges against anyone who came onto it seeking to locate the gravesite.

The rumors were, in fact, untrue. The bodies had been removed after the war and reinterred in various cemeteries. But off of Slapton Sands, the remains of the other 450 victims of Allied negligence and German opportunism still lie at the bottom of Lyme Bay.

For many veterans of D-Day there is a disturbing—and unanswerable—question. Why had they been fortunate enough to survive when so many of their buddies had fallen?

In 1988, Bob Slaughter—who had gone ashore at Dog Green with the first waves of infantry—helped unveil a monument to the 29th Division at Vierville-sur-Mer.

"It was an emotional thing," he says. "It brought back all my good friends that didn't make it. I felt remorse for them as well as feeling a little bit guilty I made it and lived such a full life and they didn't. It's not easy."

Frank Wawrynovic arrived at Omaha Beach in the late morning of D-Day with C Company, 115th Infantry, 29th Division.

Growing up in the town of Osceola Mills among the mountains of north-central Pennsylvania, Wawrynovic had been a crack marksmen, had once bagged thirteen rabbits with thirteen shots. On D-Day he had become the quarry, running across the beach "like a deer when the hunters are shooting at it."

Wawrynovic came through the beach assault with only a painful bruise on his left thigh from a piece of shrapnel. But there would be many a close call in the Normandy fighting to come.

On one occasion a sniper shot away a leaf inches from his head. Then, on June 19, he was wounded in the hedgerows near St.-Lô. Two medics and a battalion surgeon, Captain Elmer Carter—all of them wearing Red Cross armbands—rushed to his aid. As they worked on him, a burst of fire erupted from the edge of semidarkened woods. The medics and the doctor were killed. Then the German gunner fled without firing again. Wawrynovic was eventually rescued, and that night he was evacuated to England. He would spend a year and a half in Army hospitals, undergoing numerous operations on his right leg.

Decades later, when he visited the American cemetery, he would think of Captain Carter and the two medics. "These men had answered my call for help and died on account of me. This shadow will always be with me."

Wawrynovic would write in the 29th Division newsletter of how the combat veteran "as he slowly walks among the many crosses may become burdened by a feeling of guilt. For while he and his friends had shared so much together, they had died, yet he lives, but by living he feels that somehow he has deserted them."

Not all the men of the invasion were under arms. Among the more than five thousand boats in the English Channel were the merchant ships carrying a group of civilians who would arrive at Omaha Beach on D-Day plus one to set into motion Operation Mulberry. These were the seamen of the United States Merchant Marine, placed under military authority to help man the ships that were sunk off Omaha and Utah beaches to form the artificial harbors.

Four decades after D-Day, one of the seamen, a Seattle native named Raymond Carreau, launched a battle on behalf of his fellow Merchant Marine men.

Carreau had been aboard the merchant ship SS *Audacious*. "We were told the Army was taking over the ship, and we were under Army command," he would note.

He helped scuttle the *Audacious* at Omaha Beach for the "gooseberry" breakwater. But Carreau and the other Merchant Mariners were never granted veterans' status that would have entitled them to low-cost medical care, low-interest loans, and burial in military cemeteries.

Carreau petitioned the Pentagon for recognition, and he won. In December 1985, the Defense Department finally accorded veterans' rights to the civilian seamen of Operation Mulberry.

Just as the liberators remember D-Day, those who were liberated also mark the moment.

On the thirtieth anniversary of the invasion, a French delegation visited Arlington National Cemetery. The trip's organizer, Jean-Paul Roncoli, remembered one childhood day in June '44. "A GI put me on the fender of a jeep for a ride through town. He looked so tired, but he smiled and smiled. There was never a chance to say thank you—the soldiers went through so fast."

As the fortieth anniversary approached, Juliette Brault was living with her husband, Georges, and their cat—Airborne—near Utah Beach. For the Braults a personal anniversary was at hand—they had been married in June of '44. They would move up their celebration so the paratrooper veterans returning to Normandy could share in their joy.

Juliette was to have been married, at age sixteen, on June 6, 1944. The day before, she went to a dressmaker for a final fitting, then spent the night at her parents' home. Soon the bombs began to drop. In the morning the family took refuge on a farm and hid in trenches. Then, a piece of horrific news—Juliette was told that her fiancé had been killed in the bombings. But it wasn't true. Three days later, he turned up safe.

Forty Junes afterward, Juliette Brault would recall what happened:

"We had to go to another farm. Finally, Georges found me. I didn't want to be separated from him again.

"We took refuge near an American camp. I don't know how the Americans knew I was going to get married. My dress was riddled by shell fragments. I had lost my white shoes. The Americans brought me at least three pairs of shoes. One pair from a parachutist rose high over my ankles and wasn't pretty. Another was also too big. But the third was a pair of civilian shoes from an officer. I wore them for my wedding.

"The mayor who married us called it love in the ruins."

For her fortieth wedding anniversary she made parachute decorations for her cake and hung little chutes in her home.

And she displayed a banner: WELCOME, OUR BELOVED AMERICAN FRIENDS.

"If there were another war," said Juliette Brault, "I am sure the Americans would come again."

The sentimental personal touches, the pageantry, the speechmaking are worthy tributes. But it is all so different now at Omaha Beach.

"It wasn't anything like this, Emily—nothing at all," one veteran was heard to remark to his wife as they walked along the streets of St.-Laurent-sur-Mer, behind the beachhead, one June the sixth long after H-Hour of D-Day.

Drew Middleton, who covered the invasion for *The New York Times*,

LES FORCES ALLIEES
DEBARQVENT SVR CETTE
PLAGE QV'ELLES NOMMENT
OMAHA BEACH ET LIBERENT
L'EVROPE 6 JVIN 1944
THE ALLIED FORCES
LANDING ON THIS
SHORE WHICH THEY CALL
OMAHA BEACH LIBERATE
EVROPE JVNE 6TH 1944
499033

87

attended the twenty-fifth anniversary ceremonies, but was struck by how "none of this brings the event any nearer."

"Only memory speaks," he wrote.

"Can it ever really be recaptured? The biting cold of the water, the dead bobbing in the waves, the unending clamor of guns, planes, and exploding mines, the good men gone, the stench of death, the exultation when the thing was done.

"Today when you look out from Pointe du Hoc to the sea it is not the battleship *Texas* you see but only a wallowing fishing boat. Did those portly men over there once rush this position? Was this whole thing the climax of a great war effort?

"In the manicured, touristy Normandy of today it is hard to believe that something great was done here. Even when you drive down the quiet lanes in the evening and people them with men who lie in the cemeteries, the greatness of the deed is intangible.

"Only the dead, in their graves a quarter of a century now, are secure from doubt.

"A. E. Housman said it for them and for all the dead in all the wars when he wrote in *Collected Poems*:

> Here dead lie we because we did not choose
> To live and shame the land from which we sprung.
> Life, to be sure, is nothing much to lose;
> But young men think it is, and we were young."

87 *Memorial erected by the French Government: "The Allied Forces Landing on This Shore Which They Call Omaha Beach Liberate Europe—June 6th 1944."*
(National Archives)

Sources

PERSONAL RECOLLECTIONS

I'm grateful to the following people for providing remembrances of D-Day:

Ralph Goranson, Fielding Greaves, Jean Greaves, Richard Hubbard, Marvin Kornegay, Stanley Kotlarz, Ted Lapres, Jr., Leonard Lomell, Tom McClean, Richard Merrill, LeGrande Moody, Jr., Robert Murphy, Isadore Naiman, George Pappas, Edward Regan, Otis Sampson, Bob Slaughter, Albert H. Smith, Jr., Herman Stein, Bill Stivison, Wallace Strobel, Frank Wawrynovic, Alan Weston, Dick Wood, Max Zera, and Ray Zuker.

BOOKS AND MONOGRAPHS

Ambrose, Stephen E. *The Supreme Commander: The War Years of General Dwight D. Eisenhower*. Garden City, N.Y.: Doubleday, 1969.

Baldwin, Hanson W. *Battles Lost and Won: Great Campaigns of World War II*. New York: Harper & Row, 1966.

Berger, Meyer. *The Story of The New York Times, 1851–1951*. New York: Simon & Schuster, 1951.

Berra, Yogi, with Tom Horton. *Yogi: It Ain't Over . . .* New York: McGraw-Hill, 1989.

Bishop, Jim. *FDR's Last Year*. New York: William Morrow, 1974.

Bliss, Edward, Jr., editor. *In Search of Light: The Broadcasts of Edward R. Murrow, 1938–1961*. New York: Alfred A. Knopf, 1967.

Bliss, Edward, Jr. *Now the News: The Story of Broadcast Journalism*. New York: Columbia University Press, 1991.

Bradley, Omar N., and Clay Blair. *A General's Life*. New York: Simon & Schuster, 1983.

Bradley, Omar N. *A Soldier's Story*. New York: Henry Holt, 1951.

Breuer, William B. *Geronimo! American Paratroopers in World War II*. New York: St. Martin's Press, 1989.

Brown, John Mason. *Many a Watchful Night*. New York: Whittlesey House, 1944.

Burgett, Donald R. *Currahee!* Boston: Houghton Mifflin, 1967.

Butcher, Harry C. *My Three Years with Eisenhower*. New York: Simon & Schuster, 1946.

Collier, Richard. *Fighting Words: The War Correspondents of World War Two*. New York: St. Martin's Press, 1989.

Columbia Broadcasting System. *How the News of the Invasion of Normandy by the Allied Forces on June 6, 1944, Came by CBS to the American People*. New York: CBS, 1945.

Columbia Broadcasting System. Interview with 1st Division D-Day veterans, April 29, 1984.

Davis, Kenneth. *Experience of War*. Garden City, N.Y.: Doubleday, 1965.

The Diary of Anne Frank: The Critical Edition. Garden City, N.Y.: Doubleday, 1989.

Drury, Allen. *A Senate Journal, 1943–1945*. New York: McGraw-Hill, 1963.

Eisenhower, David. *Eisenhower: At War, 1943–1945*. New York: Random House, 1986.

Eisenhower, Dwight D. *Crusade in Europe*. Garden City, N.Y.: Doubleday, 1948.

Eisenhower, John S. D. *Strictly Personal*. Garden City, N.Y.: Doubleday, 1974.

Ellsberg, Edward. *The Far Shore: An American at D-Day*. New York: Dodd, Mead, 1960.

European Theater of Operations, Historical Section, Regimental Unit Studies. *The Capture of Ste.-Mère-Église: An Action by the 505th Regiment of the 82nd Airborne* and *506th Parachute Infantry Regiment in Normandy Drop*.

Hale, Edwin R. W., and John Frayn Turner. *The Yanks Are Coming*. New York: Hippocrene Books, 1983.

Harrison, Gordon A. *Cross-Channel Attack*. Washington: War Department, Historical Division, 1951.

Hastings, Max. *Overlord: D-Day & the Battle for Normandy*. New York: Simon & Schuster, 1984.

Keegan, John. *Six Armies in Normandy*. New York: The Viking Press, 1982.

Kluger, Steve. *Yank: World War II from the Guys Who Brought You Victory*. New York: St. Martin's Press, 1990.

Lash, Joseph P. *A World of Love: Eleanor Roosevelt and Her Friends, 1943–1962*. Garden City, N.Y.: Doubleday, 1984.

Lash, Joseph P. *Eleanor and Franklin*. New York: W. W. Norton, 1971.

Lewis, Nigel, *Exercise Tiger*. New York: Prentice Hall, 1990.

Longmate, Norman. *The G.I.'s: The Americans in Britain, 1942–1945*. New York: Charles Scribner's Sons, 1975.

MacVane, John. *On the Air in World War II*. New York: William Morrow, 1979.

Marshall, S.L.A. *Night Drop: The American Airborne Invasion of Normandy*. Boston: Little, Brown and Company, 1962.

Morison, Samuel Eliot. *History of United States Naval Operations in World War II: The Invasion of France and Germany, 1944–1945*. Boston: Little, Brown, 1957.

Morris, Sylvia Jukes. *Edith Kermit Roosevelt: Portrait of a First Lady*. New York: Coward, McCann and Geoghegan, 1980.

National Broadcasting Company. *H-Hour—1944*. New York: NBC, 1944.

Perret, Geoffrey. *There's a War to Be Won: The United States Army in World War II*. New York: Random House, 1991.

Persico, Joseph E. *Edward R. Murrow: An American Original*. New York: McGraw-Hill, 1988.

Pyle, Ernie. *Brave Men*. New York: Henry Holt, 1944.

Ridgway, Matthew B., as told to Harold H. Martin. *Soldier: The Memoirs of Matthew B. Ridgway*. New York: Harper & Brothers, 1956.

Ruppenthal, R. G. *Utah Beach to Cherbourg*. Washington: War Department, Historical Division, 1947.

Ryan, Cornelius. *The Longest Day*. New York: Simon & Schuster, 1959.

Sampson, Francis L. *Look Out Below!* Washington, D.C.: The Catholic University Press, 1958.

Smith, S. E., editor. *The United States Navy in World War II*. New York: William Morrow, 1966.

Spaulding, Lieutenant John. Combat interview on D-Day landing, conducted by

U.S. Army V Corps at Herve, Belgium, February 9, 1945. National Archives.

Stone, I. F. *The War Years, 1939–1945*. Boston: Little, Brown, 1988.

Tapert, Annette, editor. *Lines of Battle: Letters from American Servicemen, 1941–1945*. New York: Times Books, 1987.

Taylor, Charles H. *Omaha Beachhead*. Washington: War Department, Historical Division, 1945.

Taylor, Maxwell D. *Swords and Plowshares*. New York: W. W. Norton, 1972.

Terkel, Studs. *The Good War: An Oral History of World War Two*. New York: Pantheon Books, 1984.

Tully, Grace. *FDR: My Boss*. New York: Charles Scribner's Sons, 1949.

War Department, Historical Division. *Small Unit Actions*. [Pointe du Hoc.] Washington, 1946.

NEWSPAPERS AND MAGAZINES

The New York Times and *Time, Newsweek*, and *Life* magazines were especially helpful. I also used the *Boston Herald, Baltimore Sun, Chicago Daily News*, New York *Herald Tribune, New York Post, Philadelphia Inquirer, St. Louis Post-Dispatch, San Francisco Chronicle*, and *Washington Star*.

ARTICLES

Bryant, Nelson. "The Sorcery of War," *The New York Times Magazine*, June 3, 1984.

Cawthon, Charles. "On Omaha Beach," *American Heritage*, October/November 1983.

Eisenhower, John S. D. "The Allies Have Landed," *Life*, June 1990.

Greene, Ralph C., and Oliver E. Allen. "What Happened at Devon," *American Heritage*, February/March 1985.

Heinz, W. C., with James E. Rudder. "I Took My Son to Omaha Beach," *Collier's*, June 11, 1954.

Hemingway, Ernest. "Voyage to Victory," *Collier's*, July 22, 1944.

Marshall, S.L.A. "First Wave at Omaha Beach," *The Atlantic Monthly*, November 1960.

Mesta, Perle. "Mamie Eisenhower's Longest Day (D-Day)," *McCall's*, June 1964.

Reeder, Red. "Daybreak on D-Day Was Calm; Suddenly There Was a Roar," *The New York Times*, June 6, 1984.

Remington, Guy. "Second Man Out," *The New Yorker*, August 19, 1944.

Stone, I. F. "How Washington Took the News," *The Nation*, June 17, 1944.

Strobel, Wallace C. "What Ike Really Said," *American Heritage*, April 1990.

Wiener, Alan. "The First Wave," *American Heritage*, May/June 1987.

Wolf, Thomas H. "D-Day Remembered," *Smithsonian*, May 1984.

Index

A

Allen, Maj. Gen. Terry, 128–129
Allie, Pfc. Ambrose, 144
Angoville-au-Plain, 63
Angus, George, 32
Armies: *see* British Army; Canadian Army; German Army; United States Army
Arnold, Gen. Hap, 257
Associated Press, 30–32, 106, 108, 246
Atlanta Constitution, 232
Atlantic Charter, 37
Augeri, Sgt. Sal, 103
Avery, Sewell, 256–257

B

Bankhead, Sen. John, 256
Barr, Robert, 36
Barrett, Jay O., 27
Barton, Maj. Gen. Raymond O., 82, 129
Battle of Britain, 3
Bayeux, 227
Bernstein, Ted, 108–109
Berra, Yogi, 89, 91
Beukema, Henry, 247, 250
"Bigot" list, 24
Bingham, Maj. Sidney, 222
Bisco, Sgt. Fred, 215
Blades, Sgt. Hubert, 213
Blanchard, Ernest, 64
Block, Capt. Walter, 170
Boettiger, Anna, 258, 262
Boettiger, Maj. John, 262
Bombardons, 81
Borok, Pfc. Stanley, 185–186
Bowen, Pvt. George, 196
Bradley, Elizabeth, 247, 250
Bradley, Lieut. Gen. Omar N., 8, 10, 37, 46, 76, 78, 128–129, 152, 155, 174, 175, 179, 207, 218, 220, 222, 226, 227, 247, 251, 275
Bradley, Mary, 251
Brandenberger, Lieut. Elmer, 141–142
Brannen, Lieut. Malcolm, 71
Brault, Georges, 285
Brault, Juliette, 285
Breedin, Medic Cecil, 183, 208
Brewer, Don, 29
Brimblecombe, Glen, 26
British Army
  3rd Infantry Division, 5, 36
  6th Airborne Division, 5
  21st Army Group, 8
  50th Infantry Division, 5, 36
British House of Commons, 255
British Navy ships
  Azalea, 23, 24, 26
  Belfast, 78
  Black Prince, 78, 84, 86

British Navy ships (*cont.*)
  Curaçao, 94
  Empire Anvil, 93–95
  Enterprise, 82, 84
  Glasgow, 78
  Onslow, 23
  Ramillies, 78, 91
  Rodney, 78
  Scimitar, 23
  Talybont, 163
  Vigilant, 78
  Warspite, 78, 91
Broughton, Gov. J. Melville, 1
Brown, Corp. Bill, 71
Brown, Lieut. John Mason, 37, 39, 86–87
Bruenn, Lieut. Comm. Howard G., 258
Bryan, Wright, 55, 111–112
Bryant, Pvt. Nelson, 51–52
Burch, Robert, 36
Burgett, Pvt. Donald, 51, 63
Burt, Pvt. William, 141, 142
Butcher, Capt. Harry, 36, 245
Butcher, Ruth, 245

C

Caen, 227
Caffrey, Ambassador Jefferson, 272
Calmer, Ned, 105–107
Camien, Pvt. John, 142
Canadian Army, 227
  3rd division, 5
Canadian Parliament, 255
Canaris, Adm. Wilhelm, 35
Canham, Col. Charles, 206, 208
Capa, Robert, 199–200, 268, 270
Carnes, Cecil, 75
Carreau, Raymond, 284
Carter, Capt. Elmer, 283–284
Casey, Robert, 87, 89
Cassidy, Lieut. Col. Patrick, 141
Cherbourg Peninsula, 4, 5, 46, 58, 105, 139
Churchill, Winston, 2, 13, 37, 106, 238, 255, 257
Church of the Holy Cross, 231–232
Civil War, 1–2
Clark, Capt. A. Dayton, 81
Coates, Pvt. Roland, 103
Colleville-sur-Mer, 5, 174, 210, 212–213, 215, 226, 227, 264
Collingwood, Charles, 40
Collins, Maj. Gen. J. Lawton, 82, 179, 274
Colson, Sgt. Clarence, 215
Columbia Broadcasting System (CBS), 105–109
Colwell, Pvt. Curtis, 197
Connally, Sen. Tom, 255
Corder, Capt. Frank, 190
Corlett, Maj. Gen. Charles, 179
Costa, Sgt. Frank, 72, 74
Cota, Brig. Gen. Norman D., 9, 205–207
Coty, René, 274
Crawford, Kenneth, 135–136, 139
Crayton, Corp. H. W., 263
Crisson, Capt. Robert, 139
Cronkite, Walter, 276
Crouch, Joel, 59

Curley, Pfc. Raymond, 213
Cutler, First Lieut. Robert, Jr., 217

D

Daily Telegraph, 21–22
Daniell, Raymond, 113
Daniels, Jonathan, 258, 260
Darlington, Erwin, 105
Davis, Elmer, 104
Davis, Tech. 5 Preacher, 161
Dawe, Leonard Sidney, 22
Dawson, Capt. Joseph, 203, 210, 212–213
DeLong, Capt. Walter, 119
De Tullio, Pvt. Dominick, 121
Deyo, Rear Adm. Morton, 82, 84, 86
Dieppe, raid on, 3–4
DiGaetano, Pfc. Vincent, 196–197, 215
Dollman, Gen. Friedrich, 140
Douve River, 64
Drury, Allen, 252
Dulaney, Capt. Jack, 62, 70, 72
Dunkirk, evacuation of, 3
Dupuy, Col. R. Ernest, 109–110
Dutch sloop *Soemba,* 78

E

Editor & Publisher magazine, 261
Eisenhower, Gen. Dwight D., 6, 8, 10, 11, 13, 21, 27, 32–34, 36, 44, 46–49, 51, 85, 110–111, 179, 220, 221, 226, 243, 245, 255, 260, 270, 271, 276
Eisenhower, John, 244–248
Eisenhower, Mamie, 245–246, 248, 261
Ekman, Col. William, 120
Elder, Capt. Ned, 179, 190–191
Ellis, Joan, 31
Ewell, Lieut. Col. Julian, 144
Exercise Tiger, 23–26, 282

F

Falley, Gen. Wilhelm, 71–72
Fleeson, Doris, 30
Fortitude North, 20
Frank, Anne, 111
French, Ronald, 22
French Navy ships
  Georges Leygues, 78
  Montcalm, 78, 276
French Underground, 35, 149
Fuller, Corp. Samuel, 210
FUSAG, 20

G

Gavin, Brig. Gen. James M., 56
Gearing, Lieut. Edward, 183
George VI, King of England, 255
Gerhardt, Maj. Gen. Charles, 9
German Army
  divisions
    91st, 71, 118, 122

German Army, divisions (*cont.*)
243rd, 71
352nd, 14, 179, 203
709th, 71, 139–140
726th, 178
Fifteenth, 35
Seventh, 35, 140
1058th Grenadier Regiment, 148
Gerow, Maj. Gen. Leonard T., 218, 220, 222
Gold Beach, 5, 76
Gooseberries, 81
Goranson, Capt. Ralph, 158, 186, 187, 203–205, 265
Gordon, Chaplain R. G., 37
Grandcamp, 155, 160, 166, 170
Greaves, Fielding, 247
Greaves, Jean, 247
Greek corvette *Tompazis,* 78
Greene, Dr. Ralph, 25
Gruenther, Gen. Alfred A., 274

H

Hagen, Maj. Bill, 121
Hall, Rear Adm. John L., 78
Hangsterfer, Capt. Hank, 195
Harris, Frederick Brown, 255
Hassett, William, 112
Hawks, Capt. Berthier, 208
Hemingway, Ernest, 87
Henshall, Irene, 32
Herman, George, 105
Hicks, George, 91
Hiesville, 64, 143
Higgins landing craft, 136
Hill, Lieut. Jake, 169, 170, 279
Hill, Sgt. O. B., 70–71
Hillman, Mrs. Ronald, 55, 58, 111
Hillman, Pvt. Robert, 55, 58, 111
Hitler, Adolf, 3, 226, 255, 261, 278
Hoback, Pvt. Bedford, 263–264
Hoback, Pvt. Raymond, 263–264
Hobby, Col. Oveta Culp, 257
Hodenfield, Lieut. G. K., 161
Hoffman, Lieut. Cmndr. George, 131
Hope, Bob, 237–238
Hopkins, Harry, 30
Housman, A. E., 287
Hubbard, Pfc. Richard, 156, 159, 163–164
Huebner, Maj. Gen. Clarence, 129, 170

I

Intelligence, 14, 20–23, 34–35
International News Service, 106, 108, 110

J

Jodl, Col. Gen. Alfred, 226
Johnson, Col. Howard R. (Jumpy), 41, 42, 62
Jones, Col. Harris, 247
Jones, Melville, 22
Juno Beach, 5, 76

K

Kaltenborn, H. V., 237
Kanin, Garson, 12–13
Kansas City Star, 236
Kelly, Corp. James, 123
Kelly, Seaman 2nd Class John, 102
Kendall, Col. James, 25
Kennedy, Sgt. Bob, 188
Keseric, Maj. Nicholas, 225
Kimmel, Adm. Husband E., 256
King, Adm. Ernest J., 257
King, Mackenzie, 255
Kirk, Adm. Alan G., 37, 78
Knowlton, Lieut. Luther, 148
Kohl, Helmut, 278
Kornegay, Seaman Marvin, 75–76, 87
Kotlarz, Pfc. Stanley, 68, 122–125
Krancke, Adm. Theodor, 35
Krause, Lieut. Col. Edward (Cannonball), 42, 44, 119–121
Kuhn, Staff Sgt. Jack, 166, 168

L

La Guardia, Fiorello, 252
Lalonde, Maurice, 255
Lambert, Pvt. Ingram, 208
Lapres, Lieut. Ted, Jr., 158–159, 164, 166, 170, 171, 279
Lash, Joseph, 30, 261
Lavally, Lieut., 59
Lee, Maj. Gen. Bill, 50
Lee, Maj. Gen. John C. H., 11
Leigh-Mallory, Air Chief Marshal Trafford, 33, 46
Lemin, Sgt. Maj. Robert, 189–190
Liberty Bell, 231
Liebling, A. J., 10
Life magazine, 199, 236, 268, 270
Lillyman, Capt. Frank, 59, 61
Lincoln, Abraham, 1
Lobnitzes, 81
Lomell, 1st Sgt. Leonard, 166, 168
Lovejoy, Pvt. Thomas, 185

M

Mabry, Capt. George, 148
MacArthur, Gen. Douglas, 6
MacVane, John, 20, 21, 84–85
Marshall, Gen. George, 6, 10, 48, 104, 220, 221, 247, 257
Marshall, S. L. A., 141
Martin, Congressman Joseph, 256
Masny, Capt. Otto, 165
Maternowski, Chaplain Ignatius, 64
McAuliffe, Brig. Gen. Anthony C., 144
McBride, Mary Margaret, 251
McCanless, Pvt. Ernest, 100, 103
McClean, Lieut. Tom, 121
McCormack, Congressman John, 255
McDonald, Master Sgt. Gordon, 206, 208
McIntire, Vice Adm. Ross T., 258
McKeogh, Mickey, 32
Medal of Honor, 152, 218

Merderet River, 58, 63–64, 118
Merrill, Capt. Richard, 190, 279
Mertes, Alois, 278
Michaelman, Lieut. Isaac, 122–123
Middleton, Drew, 285, 287
Miller, Maj. Gen. Henry J., 21
Miller, Sgt. Robert, 65
Mitterand, François, 276–278
Monteith, Lieut. Jimmie W., Jr., 217–219
Montgomery, Gen. Bernard L., 3, 8, 33, 34, 85
Moody, Chaplain LeGrande, Jr., 264–267
Moody, Lieut. Bill, 188, 204, 205
Moon, Rear Adm. Don Pardee, 5, 26, 78, 85
Morgan, Lieut. Gen. Frederick, 4
Morrison, Herbert, 27
Mueller, Merrill, 36, 48
Mulberry artificial harbors, 81, 83
Mullins, Lieut. Col. Thornton, 181–182
Murphy, Col. Mike, 64–65
Murphy, Pvt. Robert, 59, 61, 275
Murrow, Edward R., 26, 92, 107, 110
Murrow, Janet, 27

N

Naiman, Sgt. Isadore, 175, 178
Nance, Lieut. Elijah, 183
Nash, Pfc. Leo, 183
National Broadcasting Company (NBC), 106–107, 109, 237, 251, 261
Neuville-au-Plain, 118, 121, 124, 275
Newsweek magazine, 135
New York Daily Mirror, 236
New York Daily News, 232
New York Post, 246
New York Stock Exchange, 232
New York Times, 28, 108–109, 112–113, 252, 285
Nickrent, Staff Sgt. Roy, 143
Niland, Sgt. Robert, 123–124
Norfleet, Tech. Sgt. Willard, 95, 99
Norweigan destroyer *Svenner,* 78, 91
Nye, Barlow, 198
Nye, Gerald, 198

O

Omaha Beach, 1, 5, 14, 33, 76, 78, 84, 93, 95–97, 99–100, 103, 127, 155, 161, 162, 168, 174–227, 236, 260, 263–269, 272, 276, 279, 283–285
Operation Mulberry, 78, 81, 83, 284
Operation Neptune, 4, 5
Osgood, Nancy, 262

P

Pappas, George, 243, 245
Paris, Lieut. Peter, 199

Pas de Calais, 4, 35, 178
Patton, Lieut. Gen. George S., Jr., 10, 20, 152
Pearl Harbor attack, 76, 89, 256
Peterson, Sgt. Kenneth, 213, 215
Petty, Sgt. Bill, 170
Phelps, Staff Sgt. Grant, 213
Phoenixes, 81
Piasecki, Sgt. Edwin, 196
Pointe de la Percée, 162, 186, 203–205, 222
Pointe du Hoc, 5, 155–173, 186, 189, 265, 274, 276, 279, 281
Polish destroyer *Krakowiak,* 78
Pouppeville, 144, 148
Pratt, Brig. Gen. Don F., 65, 66
Pravda, 278
Pressley, Sgt. Bill, 208, 210
Pyle, Ernie, 135, 199, 200, 202

R

Ramsay, Rear Adm. Bertram, 33, 34
Ramundo, Pfc. Lewis, 197
Ravenoville, 63
Reagan, Ronald, 276–280
Reed, Carol, 13
Reed, Col. Frank, 55
Reeder, Col. Russell P. (Red), 85, 130, 148–149
Regan, Pfc. Edward, 266, 268–270
Remington, Lieut. Guy, 62–63
Renaud, Alexandre, 125, 275
Renaud, Simone, 125, 275
Richards, Pvt. Jake, 161, 169
Ridgway, Maj. Gen. Matthew B., 50, 52, 55, 56, 70, 275
Roberts, Edward, 36
Roberts, Pfc. Harry, 164
Rockwell, Lieut. Dean, 179
Rommel, Field Marshal Erwin, 3, 8, 35, 175, 222, 226
Rommel, Manfred, 278
Roncoli, Jean-Paul, 284–285
Roosevelt, Eleanor, 30, 257, 261
Roosevelt, Franklin D., 3, 6, 37, 104–105, 128, 252, 256–262, 270, 272
Roosevelt, Quentin, 128, 152
Roosevelt, Capt. Quentin, 127, 128, 152
Roosevelt, President Theodore, 128, 152
Roosevelt, Brig. Gen. Theodore, Jr., 85, 127–129, 135–136, 139, 152–154
Roper, Pvt. William, 197
Rudder, Lieut. Col. James Earl, 155, 156, 158, 162, 169–171, 274–275
Rupinski, Sgt. Frank, 168

S

St.-Côme-du-Mont, 40, 72
St.-Germain-de-Varreville, 59
St. Laurent-sur-Mer, 174, 213, 226, 227, 264, 279, 285
St.-Marcouf islands, 130, 139
St.-Marcouf village, 146, 147
Ste.-Marie-du-Mont, 143, 144, 272

Ste.-Martin-de-Varreville, 130, 141, 149
Ste.-Mère-Église, 5, 44, 61, 64, 72, 116–126, 140, 152, 230, 264, 275
St. Patrick's Cathedral, 231
Salomon, Lieut. Sid, 188, 265
Sampson, Chaplain Francis L., 40, 42, 65, 68, 69
Sampson, Sgt. Otis, 124
Samuel, Mayor Bernard, 231
Sanders, Lieut. Gus, 120
Schneider, Lieut. Col. Max, 156, 189, 208, 209
Schwartz, Lieut. Stanley, 208
Sebastian, Pvt. Joseph, 123, 124
Seekings, Dorothy, 283
Shea, Lieut. Jack, 206
Sheehan, Bob, 39–40
Shefer, Pvt. Jake, 185
Sherbourne, Col. Thomas, 143
Ships: *see* British Navy ships; French Navy ships; United States Navy ships
Shirer, William L., 105
Short, Gen. Walter C., 256
Sink, Col. Robert, 72
Skelton, Red, 237
Slapton Sands, 23–26, 94, 149, 175, 282–283
Slater, Capt. Harold, 161
Slaughter, Sgt. Bob, 93–95, 97, 99–100, 103, 283
Smith, Alfred E., 128
Smith, Capt. Al, 191–192, 195, 217
Smith, Gen. Walter Bedell, 33–34, 236
Smitson, Corp. Raymond, 123, 124
Somervell, Gen. Brehon B., 11, 245
Songer, Capt. Francis, 132
Sours, Maj. John, 205
Spaulding, Lieut. John, 196, 197, 203, 213, 215, 217
Speidel, Maj. Gen. Hans, 226
Stagg, Group Capt. J. M., 33, 34
Stalin, Joseph, 3, 104, 257
Stars and Stripes newspaper, 161
Statue of Liberty, 262
Steele, Pvt. John, 116–120
Stein, Gertrude, 111
Stein, Tech. 5 Herman, 161, 165, 169, 279, 282
Stimson, Henry, 104, 112
Stivison, Staff Sgt. Bill, 160, 166
Stone, I. F., 256, 261
Stover, Pvt. Robert, 103
Streczyk, Tech. Sgt. Philip, 196–197, 215
Strobel, Lieut. Wallace, 47–49, 270–271
Strout, Richard Lee, 82, 84
Struble, Rear Adm. Arthur D., 26
Summers, Staff Sgt. Harrison, 141–143
Summersby, Kay, 47
Supplies, 11–13
Sword Beach, 5, 76

T

Talley, Col. Benjamin, 218, 220
Taylor, Col. George, 210, 211

Taylor, Maj. Gen. Maxwell D., 47, 48, 50, 55, 57, 58, 68, 70, 143–144, 148, 275
Tedder, Air Chief Marshal Arthur, 9
Thatcher, Margaret, 278
Thornton, Capt. James, 191
Thorson, Col. Truman, 155
Tidrick, Lieut. Edward, 183
Tilley, Pvt. Virgil, 197, 213
Time magazine, 8, 10
Tribolet, Col. Hervey, 130
Trinity Church, 232
Trope, Nolan, 282, 283
Trout, Robert, 107–108
Tucker, Pfc. William, 120
Tully, Grace, 258, 272
Turnbull, Lieut. Turner, 122–125, 275

U

Ultra, 14
United Press, 106–108
United States Army
  Airborne Divisions
    82nd, 5, 40, 50, 55, 59, 64, 105, 116–126, 140, 142
    101st, 5, 40, 42, 45–52, 55, 57–59, 61–65, 68–71, 105, 129, 140, 143–146, 270–271
  Battalions
    2nd Ranger, 155–156, 158–172, 186, 188–190, 203–206, 265, 279
    5th Ranger, 160, 189, 208, 209
    70th Tank, 132
    111th Field Artillery, 181–182
    112th Engineer, 175, 178
    741st Tank, 191
    743rd Tank, 179
  1st Amphibious Engineering Brigade, 23
  Infantry Divisions
    1st, 5, 93, 96, 127, 128, 170, 174, 180, 182, 190–199, 210, 212–215, 217–218, 264, 266
    4th, 4–5, 23, 82, 85, 86, 127, 129–131, 133, 135–143, 148–150, 152
    22nd, 129, 130
    29th, 2, 5, 9, 88–93, 161, 164, 170, 171, 174, 175, 178–183, 185–186, 188–191, 196, 205, 206, 223, 266, 283–284
    90th, 65
  Regiments
    8th, 129, 131, 136, 139, 148, 150
    12th, 130, 148
    16th, 96, 182, 191–197, 210, 212–215, 217–218
    26th, 128
    115th, 282
    116th, 93–100, 103, 170, 182–183, 185, 186, 188, 196, 204–206, 208, 210, 222, 264, 266
    501st, 40, 42, 62, 143–144
    502nd, 46, 47, 140–143, 270–271
    505th, 42, 59, 65, 118–124, 275

United States Army, Regiments (*cont.*)
506th, 40, 44, 51, 58, 63, 65, 72, 140, 144, 272
507th, 63–64, 72, 74
508th, 64, 65, 70–72
Squadrons
4th Cavalry, 39, 130
24th Cavalry, 130
United States Army Air Force
8th Air Force, 12, 75, 180
9th Air Force, 12, 130, 159
52nd Troop Carrier Command, 52
486th Bomb Group, 75, 181, 282
United States Coast Guard, 97, 98, 136
United States Merchant Marine, 284
United States Military Academy, 6, 21, 243–250
United States Naval Academy, 251
United States Navy ships
Ancon, 78, 91, 218
Arkansas, 76, 84, 88, 175
Augusta, 37, 76, 86, 218, 229
Bayfield, 5, 78, 82
Charles Carroll, 266
Corry, 78, 131–133, 260
Forrest, 86
Glennon, 86
Herndon, 78, 82, 85
Hobson, 86
Jeffers, 86
McCook, 78
Nevada, 76, 77, 84, 86, 89, 90
Osprey, 76
Quincy, 82, 84, 86
Satterlee, 73, 163, 205
Texas, 75–77, 84, 87, 97, 159, 162, 168, 175, 205, 222, 264, 265
Thomas Jefferson, 2
Tuscaloosa, 82, 84, 86
Unsworth, Harry, 24
Utah Beach, 4, 5, 24, 33, 46, 76, 78, 82, 84–86, 90, 93, 127, 129–152, 155, 168, 220, 227, 272, 274, 276, 284, 285

V

Vandervoort, Lieut. Col. Benjamin, 121, 123
Van Fleet, Col. James, 129
Vierville-sur-Mer, 5, 97, 160, 161, 174, 180, 183, 204, 223, 226, 227, 264, 283
Von Rundstedt, Field Marshal Gerd, 35, 203, 226

W

Wadsworth, Loring, 281
Walsh, David I., 252
Walton, William, 68
Washington, Maj. Bill, 195
Watson, Edwin (Pa), 262
Wawrynovic, Pvt. Frank, 283–284
Wertenbaker, Christian, 10
Weston, Alan, 244, 245

Whales, 81
White, Paul, 106, 107, 109
Whitehead, Don, 199
Williams, Pfc. Walfred, 103
Winant, Ambassador John, 26–27
Wintz, Lieut. Dick, 165
Wolfe, Thomas, 85–86
Wolverton, Lieut. Col. Robert, 43, 44, 63, 272
Wood, Tech. Sgt. Dick, 181
WRENS, 40
Wyman, Brig. Gen. Willard, 195

Y

Yank magazine, 185, 199, 270
York, Sgt. Alvin, 141
Young, Capt. Charles, 191

Z

Zera, Lieut. Max, 198–199
Zousmer, Jesse, 105–107
Zuker, Lieut. Ray, 75, 282